Roy Lancaster
My life
with plants

Happy Days

Roy Lancaster

Roy Lancaster

My life with plants

Royal Horticultural Society
Sharing the best in Gardening

filbert press

For my family

Published in association with the Royal Horticultural Society.

The Royal Horticultural Society is the UK's leading gardening charity dedicated to advancing horticulture and promoting good gardening. Its charitable work includes providing expert advice and information, training the next generation of gardeners, creating hands-on opportunities for children to grow plants, and conducting research into plants, pests and environmental issues affecting gardeners.

For more information, visit www.rhs.org.uk or call 020 3176 5800.

FRONTISPIECE The author in his garden with *Cordyline indivisa*, the mountain cabbage tree of New Zealand

COVER ILLUSTRATION Grahame Baker Smith

Published in 2017 by Filbert Press Ltd
filbertpress.com

ISBN 978-0-9933892-5-2

Printed in China
A catalogue record for this book is available from the British Library

Contents

Preface

Plants, people and places, three words which in a nutshell encompass the diversity of my working life and not just work but much of my leisure time too. Now in my 80th year I can look back on a journey that has taken me through some of the world's most exciting wild and garden landscapes and brought me experiences that have been enriching as well as humbling. My childhood ambition was to be an engine driver in the age of steam but fate had other things in mind and I have never once experienced regret. The world of plants, and what could be more important to life on earth than the green leaf, has brought me so much joy and sense of purpose. An optimist by nature, I have always believed that plants promote hope as well as pleasure and it is not surprising that gardeners and others involved with plants are commonly regarded as among the friendliest and most contented of people.

The seed for the present book was sown several years ago when I began writing an account of my garden and its plants. Other matters intervened however and the plan was shelved only to be re-ignited by my family and friends who urged me to do it, if only for their sakes. Having made the decision, I was further encouraged by remarks made by Chris Young and Phil Clayton, Editor and Deputy Editor respectively, of the Royal Horticultural Society's magazine *The Garden*, along with RHS Publisher Rae Spencer-Jones, who suggested I contact Anna Mumford who had just set up her own publishing company Filbert Press. I had known Anna for many years in her role as Acquisitions Editor for the American Publisher Timber Press of Portland in Oregon for whom I had provided forewords for a number of their horticultural titles.

As with all my previous books this would be very much a joint venture involving me writing the copy long hand (yes, I am a dinosaur) and Sue typing (and re-typing) the results. Unlike my previous books written on specific themes and subjects this would be very different in covering a lifetime of activities and experiences. Fortunately, dating from the 1950s I had generated a wealth of reference material, written and photographic, involving notebooks and journals, scrapbooks and correspondence plus a huge number of photographs, mostly colour transparencies and for the last seven years, digital images.

Although a good number of people I've met over the years are mentioned in the following pages, it has not been possible to include them all and express to them my gratitude. Most importantly I would like to thank my wife Sue without whom the bulk of this story would not have happened, let alone come to press. Her patience, understanding, determination, encouragement and support never fails to amaze me.

During a lifetime of gardening and travels I have enjoyed (and still do) the help and encouragement, the company, hospitality and the friendship of a great many people and their kindnesses will never be forgotten. I would also like to thank the travel companies who helped make many of my travels possible and the following individuals for helpful information or comments in writing this book – Clifford Heyes, Maureen Thompson, Julie Lamara, David Butcher (Friends of Moss Bank Park), Bob Ashcroft, James Tetlow, Frederick Hudson, Henry Oakley, Phillip Cribb, Mathew Soper, Sally Pettit, Jean Hillier, Archie Bingham, Aileen Bryce, Trevor Taylor, Arthur Taylor, Jaime Blake, Peter del Tredici and Bryony Hall.

I know from my own experience how helpful it is to have one's enthusiasm and endeavours recognised and encouraged, especially at an early age. I have never stopped believing that the full potential of knowledge is only realised by passing it on to others. I was once asked by a young would-be plant explorer why he should visit China when so many plant people had already been there. "But you haven't been there" I told him, "and whatever you have heard or read about others' experiences may help shape but not replace your own." I hope that the stories and experiences described in the following pages will help encourage others to make their own journeys and contributions to the world of plants at a time when our natural environment is threatened as never before.

CHAPTER ONE

A pinch of tobacco

It is a beautiful spring morning in April 2015 as I open my eyes to see through our bedroom window the crown of a magnolia tree, *M. cylindrica*, growing in the garden, its branches flooded with sumptuous white blooms, each tepal faintly suffused with rose-purple at its base. It dominates the blue sky beyond and the garden below. Close by is a maple, *Acer triflorum*, also in bloom, the drooping, downy clusters of small bell-shaped flowers glowing golden-green in the early sunlight, demure and dainty companions to those of the magnolia. From our neighbour's garden rises the broad-domed crown of a weeping willow, *Salix × sepulcralis* var. *chrysocoma*, its long, golden, whip-like branchlets studded with the pale green of the emerging leaves and slim yellow catkins. The magnolia was sent to me as a seed from China, the maple from Korea. In another month or more I can look forward to the Chilean fire tree (*Embothrium coccineum*), also in my neighbour Dorothy (Dot) Cooper's garden, erupting in a broad column of firecracker blooms, while a silvery-grey-leaved tea tree, *Leptospermum grandifolium*, beneath our window and originally from south-east Australia will cover its arching branches with a foam of white, bee-buzzing flowers. Every year, this slowly unfolding spectacle – and I mention only the tiniest vanguard – reminds me of my good fortune in having spent my life in the company of plants. I am also reminded that but for the love and encouragement and support of family and friends it might not have happened.

I was born and brought up in Bolton, Lancashire, spending most of my adolescent years living with my family on a council estate on the northern fringe of the town. To the north-west lay Smithills Moor, at 1390ft (427m) a western outlier of the Pennines, which offered a convenient escape route to wilder country and adventures beyond.

..

The spectacular canopy of *Magnolia cylindrica* blooming in April, viewed from our bedroom window.

'Our gang' from Cameron Street, returning with fuel for our Guy Fawkes bonfire in the late 1940s. I am the one with the axe and my sister Maureen is on the far left.

Both my parents, Charles and Norah, worked for much of this time in the cotton mills, the tall, stark chimneys dominating the town. My brother, Leonard, 10 years older than I, spent several years serving with the Royal Scots Fusiliers, latterly in India, returning home with his company's Union Jack following that country's independence. My sister Maureen, four years younger than I, completed the family.

In common with most houses on the estate, ours had a small garden fronting onto the street and a larger patch at the rear. My father enjoyed gardening as a hobby, tending a vegetable plot at the back, while his ornamental favourites included dahlias and chrysanthemums, bedding plants (especially petunias and snapdragons), herbaceous perennials

..

Laburnum × watereri 'Vossii', the golden chain, was common in our neighbourhood and my earliest memory of a garden tree.

and roses. It was to help keep his roses, hybrid tea and polyanthus, in good fettle that he had my sister and me scuttling out into the street armed with a small shovel and a bucket whenever a horse-drawn wagon or cart appeared, especially the coalman, milkman or rag and bone man. The competition from gardening neighbours to scoop up any dung deposited was fierce, for its benefits as a mulch beneath the roses, it was claimed, made all the difference between average and exceptional blooms and, when dug in, to the quality and size of vegetables. I was early aware of the competitive spirit among mill men when it came to their gardens and those in our street were no exception; the longest runner beans, the biggest onions and the most prolific sweet peas were all part of the annual sow, grow and show ritual, while the tallest lupins and delphiniums ultimately depended on one's battle with slugs.

While I was aware of all this, it is perhaps indicative of things to come that my earliest memories of plants – certainly woody plants – were of the golden chain tree (*Laburnum × watereri* 'Vossii') in our front garden and of the privet hedge (*Ligustrum ovalifolium*) which was standard planting on all council estates at the time. Without knowing their names or their origins, I was totally familiar with the fragrant yellow pea-flowered tassels of the one and the white, sickly sweet-scented flowers of the other. It brought me great pleasure many years later to see both parents of this hybrid laburnum growing wild in the mountains of Europe.

...

Bird-watching

Despite these initial contacts, my overriding interest in the natural world lay not with plants, but with birds. It was an interest which gradually developed into a passion as I spent an increasing amount of my free time, particularly at weekends, in the countryside around Bolton, especially on the moors – curlew country – where I could combine bird-watching with the equally enjoyable pastime of whimberry-picking for my mother's scrumptious pies. The best local populations of this delicious bloomy black berry, also known as bilberry or whortleberry (*Vaccinium myrtillus*), were to be found on nearby Whimberry Hill. I believe my subsequent and lifelong preference for mountain travel developed from the hours I spent slogging up those steep, bracken- and heather-clad slopes in order to explore the unknown.

Some of these adventures, which is how I regarded them, were in the company of other boys from our street, but more usually I was on my own. All this changed in September 1949 when, having left primary school, I began my next period of education at Castle Hill County Secondary School for Boys less than 2 miles (3km) from my home. The four years I attended this school, whose most famous old boy was my football hero Nat Lofthouse, the then Bolton Wanderers and England

Class 2e at Castle Hill County Secondary School for Boys, Bolton, in 1950.
I am standing second row, sixth from right, with my pal Clifford Heyes on my left.
Mr Frank Milner, the Headmaster, is in the centre of the front row.

. . .

11

centre forward, provided me with the opportunities to further my interests in birds and much else. For a start, I found myself in the same class as Clifford Heyes, a fellow bird enthusiast with whom I struck up a firm and lasting friendship which gradually saw us travelling on foot, bicycle, scooter, bus and train in search of birds.

Most of these travels were initially centred on the Bolton area. Here, despite the town's industrial heritage, we found green fields and pastures to explore as well as woodlands, rivers and streams, ponds, reservoirs and moorland. Our reward was a rich variety of birds and in many instances their nests too. In 1951 alone we recorded finding 236 nests belonging to 46 different species. Among our favourite birds were the owls, of which four or possibly five species occurred in our area. We wrote an account of them, illustrated with photographs taken by Clifford, which caused quite a stir among the teaching staff at school. It was the encouragement given to us by one man in particular, our biology teacher Mr Leslie Huffadine, which helped to increase our confidence in pursuing our interests.

Mystery plant
Up to this point, birds dominated my out-of-school activities, though train-spotting came a close second. As far as I can remember, plants, let alone gardens, had yet to occupy my thoughts – but on a warm afternoon in September 1951 something happened that was to change my life forever. Wednesday afternoons at school were devoted to special interest classes, each member of the teaching staff offering a subject close to their heart. Not all subjects on offer related to the normal curriculum and when Mr Huffadine announced that he would be doing ornithology, Clifford and I immediately signed on. His course involved both class work and, best of all, field studies when we would head off into the nearby countryside to observe birds. It was while returning from one such trip that we happened to pass some allotments. On glancing over the fence I spotted a strange plant growing as a weed in a potato patch. Why it caught my eye and registered as something special I shall never know, but I decided to climb over the fence and take a closer look.

...

Nicotiana rustica, the Mexican tobacco I found on an allotment near my school. It proved to be a new record for Lancashire.

The plant was about 3¼ft (1m) tall, with large, flannelly leaves and a terminal cluster of bell-shaped green flowers. Both stem and leaves were covered in a dense pelt of pale, soft hairs, clammy to the touch. I plucked a specimen with leaves and flowers and carried it back to school, where Mr Huffadine and I consulted the only wild flower book in the school library, *The Observer's Book of Wild Flowers*, sadly to no avail. I decided to take it to the Bolton Museum, whose curator, Mr Alfred Hazelwood, had been for some time a great help to Clifford and me with bird identifications. He compared it with dried specimens in his herbarium and with descriptions in several authoritative works, without success. Having pressed and dried it, he then sent the specimen to a friend at the Botany Department of the University of Manchester, who in turn sent it on to the British Museum (Natural History) in London.

When Mr Hazelwood informed me of this I was amazed. I had never travelled further south than the next county, Cheshire, and London was completely out of my orbit. Anyway, a week later, I received a typed letter addressed to my home from a professor in the Botany Department. It began 'Dear Mr Lancaster . . .' and went on to explain that my mystery plant was a Mexican tobacco (*Nicotiana rustica*), adding that it was new to Lancashire and only the second recorded occurrence of this

. . .

plant wild in the British Isles. I was stunned. I read it several times before showing it to Mr Huffadine, who promptly passed it on to the headmaster. The next morning at assembly I found myself having to stand on the dais with the head while he read the letter out loud to a sea of faces, most of which looked baffled, though the pupils followed his lead in applauding. Although my family and friends today find it hard to believe, I was rather shy as a boy, and this early and totally unexpected accolade had me wishing for the proverbial ground to open up beneath me. For some time afterwards I was known as the boy who found the Mexican tobacco. Many years later, I read that this tobacco probably originated in the Andes and has since been widely cultivated elsewhere, including Mexico. My discovery was a stroke of luck, but it had me thinking that if I could find such a rare plant by accident, what might I find out there if I really tried? The answer came sooner than I expected.

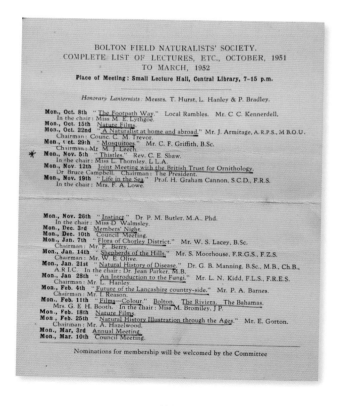

BOLTON FIELD NATURALISTS' SOCIETY.
COMPLETE LIST OF LECTURES, ETC., OCTOBER, 1951
TO MARCH, 1952
Place of Meeting : Small Lecture Hall, Central Library, 7-15 p.m.

Honorary Lanternists : Messrs. T. Hurst, L. Hanley & P. Bradley.

Mon., Oct. 8th " The Footpath Way." Local Rambles. Mr. C. C. Kennerdell.
In the chair : Miss M. E. Lythgoe.
Mon., Oct. 15th Nature Films.
Mon., Oct. 22nd " A Naturalist at home and abroad." Mr. J. Armitage, A.R.P.S., M.B.O.U.
Chairman : Counc. C. M. Trevor.
Mon., Oct. 29th " Mosquitoes." Mr. C. F. Griffith, B.Sc.
Chairman : Mr. M. J. Leech.
Mon., Nov. 5th " Thistles." Rev. C. E. Shaw.
In the chair : Miss L. Thornley, L.L.A.
Mon., Nov. 12th Joint Meeting with the British Trust for Ornithology.
Dr. Bruce Campbell. Chairman : The President.
Mon., Nov. 19th " Life in the Sea " Prof. H. Graham Cannon, S.C.D., F.R.S.
In the chair : Mrs. F. A. Lowe.

Mon., Nov. 26th " Instinct " Dr. P. M. Butler, M.A., Phd.
In the chair : Miss D. Walmsley.
Mon., Dec. 3rd Members' Night.
Mon., Dec. 10th Council Meeting.
Mon., Jan. 7th " Flora of Chorley District." Mr. W. S. Lacey, B.Sc.
Chairman : Mr. F. Berry.
Mon., Jan. 14th " Shepherds of the Hills." Mr. S. Moorhouse, F.R.G.S., F.Z.S.
Chairman : Mr. W. E. Olive.
Mon., Jan. 21st " Natural History of Disease." Dr. G. B. Manning. B.Sc., M.B., Ch.B.,
A.R.I.C. In the chair : Dr. Jean Parker. M.B.
Mon., Jan. 28th " An Introduction to the Fungi." Mr. L. N. Kidd, F.L.S., F.R.E.S.
Chairman : Mr. L. Hanley.
Mon., Feb. 4th " Future of the Lancashire country-side." Mr. P. A. Barnes.
Chairman : Mr. I. Reason.
Mon., Feb. 11th " Films—Colour." Bolton. The Riviera. The Bahamas.
Mrs. G. E. H. Booth. In the chair : Miss M. Bromiley, J.P.
Mon., Feb. 18th Nature Films.
Mon., Feb. 25th " Natural History Illustration through the Ages." Mr. E. Gorton.
Chairman : Mr. A. Hazelwood.
Mon., Mar. 3rd Annual Meeting.
Mon., Mar. 10th Council Meeting.

Nominations for membership will be welcomed by the Committee

· · ·

OPPOSITE PAGE
The winter lecture programme of the Bolton Field Naturalists' Society for 1951–52. I attended most of the lectures including the one by the Rev. Shaw on 'Thistles'.

The Rev. C.E. Shaw (Vicar Shaw), pictured here in June 1982, was my first mentor on British wildflowers and a most remarkable character and friend.

The 'Field Nats'

In November of that year, following Clifford's lead, I became a junior member of the Bolton Field Naturalists' Society, paying two shillings and sixpence for the privilege. Founded in 1907 from earlier beginnings, the 'Field Nats', as it was familiarly known, boasted an active membership of men and women, many of retired age, who shared an interest in one or more areas of natural history. It held weekly evening meetings from November to March in a room in Bolton Civic Centre, while from spring through the summer, field forays and excursions were organized in the countryside. The winter meetings attracted talks by leading naturalists, most of whom gave lantern presentations with glass-mounted slides (this was long before we had TV). Some of the speakers exhibited interesting and occasionally amusing idiosyncrasies when performing. One such, a noted amateur ornithologist who had spent many hours up a tree in a bird hide photographing herons at their nests, appeared to have acquired some of their characteristics. These included sharp, thrusting movements of his head and immediate eye contact when emphasizing a point while, hands in his jacket pockets, he would waggle his arms as if they were the wings of a hungry chick.

. . .

One of the most memorable speakers was the Reverend C. E. Shaw, or Vicar Shaw as I came to know him, whose many interests outside his professional life included fossils, draughts, amateur operatics, Lancashire dialect poetry and cars. He belonged to a long tradition of clergymen naturalists going back to the Reverend Gilbert White of Selborne fame and more recently the Reverend Johns, whose book *Flowers of the Field* I was to acquire from a secondhand bookshop. Like Johns, Vicar Shaw had a particular passion for wild flowers. The first of his talks that I can recall was devoted to reeds and sedges, followed a year later by thistles. I had never imagined that there could possibly be more than a handful of wild thistles native to Britain until that evening. He described and illustrated 6½ft (2m) giants such as the silvery-grey hairy cotton thistle (*Onopordum acanthium*), right down to the dwarf or stemless thistle (*Cirsium acaule*) whose spiny leaf rosettes, he explained, were commonly found in the short grass of those chalk downlands favoured by courting couples, hence its local name of 'lover's curse'! When I asked for his autograph at the end of the evening he told me that he was preparing his next talk on docks, and should I be interested I might like to help him find them. At the time I remember thinking this was an opportunity not to be missed.

The summer following, I joined Vicar Shaw on several of his adventures, which found us locating, among others, fiddle dock (*Rumex pulcher*) on a village green, monk's rhubarb (*R. alpinus*) naturalized by a Pennine stream and great water dock (*R. hydrolapathum*) in a river. The one dock we most wanted to see and didn't was the blood-veined dock (*R. sanguineus* var. *sanguineus*), obviously named for its red veins. Eventually he arranged for a friend in Essex to send him a specimen. I can still see him in my mind's eye, Vicar Shaw showing me the envelope from which he produced with a flourish a single green dock leaf with dark red veins, and hear him triumphantly declaring, 'Here it is, lad, the bloody dock.'

Vicar Shaw was to become my first mentor in the world of wild plants and I shall have more to relate about subsequent adventures with him, but there was another member of the 'Field Nats' whose help on native flora was especially valuable to me. I only knew him as Mr

. . .

Jackson, a Yorkshireman from Doncaster in his sixties, who led some of the Society's field forays. His knowledge of native plants was extensive and he seemed determined to teach me all he knew. He was a stocky man with a ruddy face and slightly bulging eyes and carried with him on a shoulder strap a canvas bag, possibly ex-army, in which he kept a flora (Bentham and Hooker), a notebook and pencil, a penknife, and an x10 hand lens for examining flower details, plus a tin box of sandwiches and a flask of tea. The field forays could be all-day trips with a snack recommended in case a café or tea room could not be found. I can't begin to count the number of field forays I attended, all on a Saturday, but the drill was the same for all but a few.

The group would travel by bus or car to a starting point and then begin our walk, Mr Jackson leading the way on the flower forays, stopping to point out and explain plants of interest on the route. Despite his detailed flora, he used the common names for the plants rather than their scientific names and he made sure that I was in the group gathered around him when he spoke. It wasn't just the names he shared with us but details of the plants' characteristics and habitats. He also knew a good deal about their folklore, especially their uses as medicine or food. He was a good, old-fashioned field botanist who

The blood-veined dock (*Rumex sanguineus* var. *sanguineus*) which almost eluded Vicar Shaw.

relied more on the living plant in the wild than a dried specimen in the herbarium. When the time came to stop for lunch or tea he would select a suitable place to sit, weather permitting, and while we enjoyed our sandwiches and cake he would produce from his bag fragments of some of the plants seen and discussed and ask me to name them. I found it difficult to begin with but gradually, with practice, I began to memorize their special features and I was naturally anxious to please him, given the amount of effort he was putting into my education.

Most memorable among our excursions were the Society's occasional canal trips, when we boarded a narrowboat and spent a relaxing and

...

enjoyable few hours passing through delightful countryside while Mr Jackson pointed out the various marginal and floating aquatic plants such as frogbit (*Hydrocharis morsus-ranae*), flowering rush (*Butomus umbellatus*), arrowhead (*Sagittaria sagittifolia*), sweet flag (*Acorus calamus*) and gipsywort (*Lycopus europaeus*). I particularly remember one canal trip which began from Wigan Pier and ended up in the midst of the Lancashire countryside at Rufford Old Hall. It was one of those golden summer days that belong to one's childhood and the boat made a pleasant swishing sound as it chugged through the water. We were all plant-spotting and names were thick in the air while pencils worked overtime in recording them in our notebooks. Every so often, there would be a flurry of excitement as Mr Jackson, with a weighted hook on a line, fished out a glutinous length of pondweed (*Potamogeton* species) which he returned to the canal depths once it had been identified.

Keeping a notebook

I so enjoyed those excursions and it was as a result of them that I came to appreciate the importance of writing things down in a notebook, a habit I have continued to this day. I also discovered the satisfaction of using a hand lens, especially one of x20 magnification, to see more clearly the details and beauty of small things – hairs on a leaf, the inner parts of a flower, the characteristics of a bug or seed. Two of the most treasured reminders I possess of those happy-go-lucky years and the Society whose members treated me as one of the family are a vasculum and a copy, now in fragile condition, of the *Flora of Bolton*, compiled by T. Greenlees and T. K. Holden and published in 1920. Both were given to me by the Society to encourage and further my studies of the local flora and both were in regular use to that effect. Indeed, I still prefer the vasculum, a black, oblong, metal container with a lengthwise lid secured by a sliding catch, to the now ubiquitous polythene bag in which to collect flower and plant samples.

At one time no self-respecting field botanist would feel properly equipped without a vasculum in which to keep plant specimens cool and fresh. I felt honoured and as pleased as punch to have my own, which I carried with me on most of my forays into the wild. On one

...

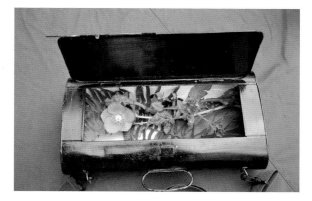

Arrowhead (*Sagittaria sagittifolia*), one of many aquatics seen on the Bolton Field Naturalists' Society's canal trips.

ABOVE The vasculum presented to me by the Bolton Field Naturalists' Society, which I still use occasionally when collecting plant specimens.

BELOW My now battered and weathered copy of *The Flora of Bolton*, published in 1929. My numerous additions and notes were made in the 1950s.

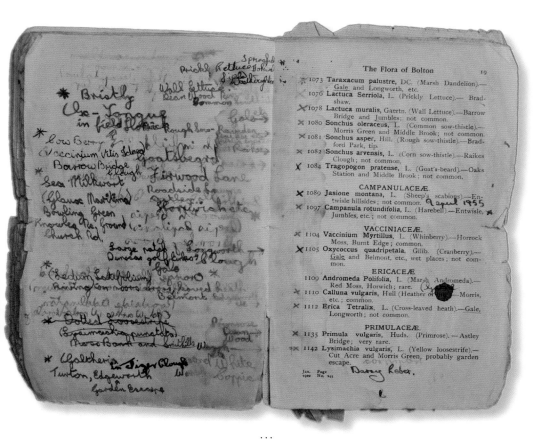

occasion, while I was walking along a country road, a passing police car stopped and the driver wound down his window to ask me what I had in the black box. I obliged by opening the lid to reveal a vetch, two ferns and a collection of grasses. Why was I collecting weeds, he wanted to know. I was tempted to answer that they were for my pet rabbit but afraid he might not appreciate my sense of humour, I told him the truth.

As for the *Flora of Bolton*, it proved a godsend in reminding me which plant species still grew or had once been recorded in the Bolton area, some 500 in total. Examining it today, I am reminded of my endeavours throughout the 1950s to see for myself all those plants then recorded, ticking them off as religiously as I did the steam engines in another treasured booklet. It was not, however, merely a spotting exercise. To me, the *Flora* was a fascinating directory of curious plants and equally curious locations. Even today, having in the meantime travelled worldwide, place names such as Anglezarke, Jumbles, Chequerbent, Rocky Brook and Tockholes, to mention but a few, conjure up vivid memories of early plant explorations and first discoveries.

To begin with, the scientific or botanical names, principally of Latin or Greek origin, meant nothing to me and I concentrated on the more easily remembered English names. These, too, sometimes had me scratching my head as to their meaning. Names like water blinks (*Montia fontana*), gold of pleasure (*Camelina sativa*), Solomon's seal (*Polygonatum multiflorum*) and moschatel (*Adoxa moschatellina*) particularly come to mind, especially the last, which was also known locally as townhall clock, describing the pill-sized head of five tiny green flowers, four of which face outwards while the fifth, in the centre, faces upwards. To my mind the *Flora* represented an exciting world ripe for exploration and adventures waiting to happen. In the event, I never did find all of the plants listed in the *Flora*, and some, like my Mexican tobacco, had been once-only occurrences, or casuals, as they are known. I did, however, discover many new plants along the way: crimson and hare's-foot clover (*Trifolium incarnatum* and *T. arvense* respectively), evergreen alkanet (*Pentaglottis sempervirens*), lesser broomrape (*Orobanche minor*) and yellow vetch (*Vicia lutea*), to name but a few, none of which had previously been recorded in the Bolton area.

. . .

Leaves of coltsfoot (*Tussilago farfara*), when dried, were smoked by my paternal grandfather as a herbal tobacco to relieve coughs and colds.

Before I move on, I feel I should mention my paternal grandfather, William Edward Lancaster, whom I only really got to know in the late 1940s and early 1950s, when he was in his seventies. At this time he lived not far from my home and on one of my visits I found him pegging leaves to dry on a line he had fixed beneath the kitchen ceiling. He explained that he was drying them for use as a herbal tobacco which he smoked in his pipe to help as a relief for coughs. The leaves were those of coltsfoot (*Tussilago farfara*), a common native perennial and a relative of the dandelion. It is also known as 'baccy plant' or 'poor man's baccy' (tobacco) and was also once used in pectoral beers (a cough medicine) as well as in jellies and wine, though I have no personal experience of such. I do, however, remember enjoying fluted sticks of coltsfoot rock, a pale brown confectionery sold by chemists as a cough remedy even when real sweets were rationed during the war.

It turned out that my grandfather had been something of an amateur herbalist in his day and a favourite story of his recalled a collecting trip to a local beauty spot known as Jumbles, from which he returned to Bolton on the upper deck of a tram. He became aware of something tugging at his jacket and on turning he found it was a small terrier. Grandfather was not at all surprised, for his pocket contained a bundle of shoots and seeds he had gathered of the wild anise, or sweet cicely (*Myrrhis odorata*), a pleasantly aromatic herb of the carrot family. Many years later, I was astonished to learn that my grandfather had been a founder member of the Bolton Field Naturalists' Society who, according to an old photograph of 1908, appeared to enjoy country rambles dressed in their Sunday best!

...

By now my passion for plants and birds was occupying much of my free time. This is not to say that I neglected all else. Like most of my schoolmates I was a railway enthusiast, or rather a trainspotter, and would occasionally join fellow enthusiasts crowding an iron bridge spanning the main lines into Bolton's Trinity Street Station. We could hear the loud speakers on the station platforms announcing the arrivals and departures from and to distant destinations and one in particular roused my imagination. Leaving Bolton, the train would head north to Preston, Lancaster, Carnforth, Silverdale and Arnside before crossing the estuary of the River Kent to Grange-over-Sands, Ulverston (birth place of Stan Laurel of Laurel and Hardy fame) and Barrow-in-Furness. Of all these, Silverdale most attracted my curiosity, though I had to wait another year or two before fulfilling my desire to go there.

The main line from Bolton to the Pennine cotton towns of Blackburn, Burnley, Nelson and Colne headed north past our school and it always intrigued me how the train drivers, as often as not with cap on head, pipe in mouth and elbow resting on the window frame, could also manage a smile and a wave while driving their engines. I visited innumerable stations and engine sheds across the north in pursuit of my quarries, especially those engines with name plates, and was determined that one

. . .

One of the few images
I have of my father,
here with my mother,
sister and me on
holiday in Blackpool
in the 1940s.

day I would be in charge of one of these magnificent, rushing, hissing, smoking and steaming machines. Maybe I would drive one to Silverdale.

Of other pastimes, I was a regular attender at the Saturday afternoon children's matinées at our local cinema, The Belle, where its owner, a large man named Mr Prendergast, once exhorted us to persuade our parents to vote for him in his bid to become an MP in return for which, should he succeed, we would receive free ice creams. On one occasion the seat on which he was standing gave way under his weight and he disappeared from view mid-sentence. Sadly for him and us, his bid for fame failed. Of the many films we watched, my favourites, apart from Laurel and Hardy and the Three Stooges, were Flash Gordon (starring Buster Crabbe), Nyoka the Jungle Girl and Tarzan of the Apes starring Johnny Weissmuller. On many occasions in summer, after having watched our rope-swinging hero, a group of friends and I would head for a local river where the huge leaves of butterbur (*Petasites hybridus*) formed dense colonies and a thicket of bamboo from an abandoned garden provided our own jungle in which to act out our own adventures. The bamboo canes also provided us with an unlimited supply of 'Zulu spears'.

In May 1952, my last year at Castle Hill School, my father died aged 46 after a short illness. Looking back to my childhood now, I realize

. . .

how little I remember about him. A man of quiet disposition, no doubt due to longterm deafness in one ear, he worked long and hard in providing for his family. Away from work, he enjoyed his gardening and was a member of a concertina band which played at local venues and events. For a time, the band's instruments, including a piano accordion, were stored in their cases beneath my bed. His overwhelming passion, however, was for his violin, which was his most prized possession. His choice of music was light classical and his favourite violinist/composer, Fritz Kreisler, though he also appreciated the virtuoso skills of Jascha Heifetz, Yehudi Menuhin and Alfredo Campoli among others whenever their performances were broadcast on the wireless. He had a large collection of sheet music which he added to at every opportunity and practised regularly in the evenings and at weekends alone in an upstairs bedroom. On many occasions I would sit on the stairs listening to him, which I believe is how I came to develop a love for the music of the classical orchestras and soloists which I still enjoy, though my musical tastes are now more catholic. Not surprisingly, I regret that he did not live to enjoy at least the beginning of my career, which I think would have pleased and comforted him as it did my mother.

First job

I left school at the end of the Christmas term in December 1952, having reached my 15th birthday on the fifth of the month. Some weeks earlier, I had called to see Mr Hazelwood at the museum with a batch of plant specimens I had been pressing, as usual, between sheets of newspaper under our living room carpet. My mother had by now grown to accept this occasional if unusual practice so long as I tidied things up afterwards. Mr Hazelwood and I were discussing the specimens when he casually enquired as to when I would be leaving school and whether I had a job to go to. I told him of my plan to drive a steam engine, to which he replied, 'Have you looked into it?' Unfortunately, I had not. Gently he explained that I would probably have to spend several years as an apprentice in the engine sheds cleaning out boilers and doing similar dirty and oily but necessary jobs before getting a sniff of the footplate, let alone drive an engine, which persuaded me not to take the idea any further.

. . .

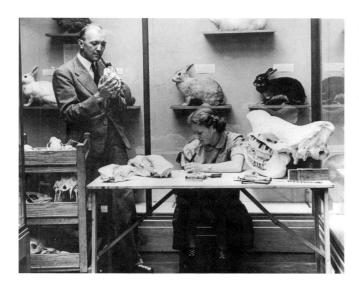

Alfred Hazelwood, Curator at the Bolton Museum, who persuaded me to become a gardener rather than an engine driver.

'Could I work here in the museum?' I ventured to ask. In answer to that he took me through a corridor lined with cabinets containing shallow drawers housing stuffed birds, bats and rodents, which failed to excite me. After I had been shown a goodly selection we returned to his office, where we discussed other possibilities. He suggested to me that my mother might perhaps be hoping for me to get a job sooner rather than later to help pay the bills. He also pointed out that as I so obviously loved the outdoor life and plants maybe that might be my best option. I was considering this when he suddenly asked me, 'Have you ever thought of being a gardener?' The short answer was 'No', but before I could say any more he picked up his telephone and dialled a number, explaining to me that he knew someone on the local parks department who might help. There followed a short exchange of words before he replaced the receiver and confirmed that he had arranged for me to go for an interview.

. . .

CHAPTER TWO
Are you the nipper who wants a job?

I had never attended an interview, formal or otherwise, and it was with some trepidation that on a cold morning in December 1952 I caught a bus into town and then another to reach Heaton Cemetery, inside the entrance gates of which lay the Bolton Parks Department Head Office. I had arrived earlier than necessary, so I decided to have a wander around before reporting in. There had been an overnight frost and the gravestones were still coated with rime, in sharp contrast to the dark cypresses and hollies around the office. Little did I know then the part that this cemetery and the world of conifers in particular would come to play in my life.

On announcing my arrival at reception, I was told to wait in an adjoining room where someone would be coming to see me. The room was bare except for a table and two chairs and I had only been seated for a few minutes when the door opened slightly to reveal a man's head with white hair, ruddy cheeks and a pipe clasped firmly in his teeth. 'Are you the nipper who wants a job?' he asked. I quickly rose to my feet, replying, 'Yes, sir.' The man then stepped briefly into the room, saying, 'I'm Jack Fishwick, park keeper at Moss Bank, do you know it?' I nodded that I did, and he continued, 'You'll be starting with me on Monday morning at 8 o'clock sharp.' He then made to leave before turning to add, 'And bring your own dinner.' That was the briefest of only three job interviews I have ever had, yet it was to set me off on a voyage of discovery that has continued to this day.

When I returned home and told my mother that I had got a job as an apprentice gardener she gave me a lovely smile, saying, 'Well luv, if it makes you happy then I'm happy,' and so it proved. Mind you, when some of my old schoolmates intent on a career as a mechanic, a footballer or a job in an office heard of my choice they almost pitied me. 'Why choose a job digging soil all your life?' one boy asked me. The answer to

. . .

BELOW Jack Fishwick, park keeper at Bolton's Moss Bank Park and my first boss, in June 1952.

RIGHT Barrow Bridge Chimney seen from Moss Bank Park in September 1991.

that, I have to say, is I didn't rightly know, but it was a job with a weekly wage and it was outside rather than inside and that was all that mattered.

Moss Bank Park, together with the nearby fold (hamlet) of Barrow Bridge, was a popular venue for Bolton families, especially at Easter and bank holidays, and ours was no exception. It is situated on the north-west fringe of the town, within easy walking distance of my home. So it was on the morning of my first working day that I set out in my clogs (iron shod), wearing long trousers, a warm jerkin and a woollen scarf and balaclava knitted by my mother. She had reasoned that there had to be an oven available where I could heat up the pie she had made for me of mincemeat, onions and potatoes in a deep dish for my lunch. This I carried by hand, wrapped in a large cloth.

Walk to work

My route took me out of the estate, west through fields to Smithills Wood, known locally as Bluebell Wood, scene of many boyhood adventures and escapades. Skirting the wood, mostly beech and oak, I followed a lane past the half-timbered part 14th-century Smithills Hall, on into a small clough (valley) where a tall brick-built chimney rose above a former bleach works. When first built in 1863 it was, at 306ft (93m), the tallest in Lancashire, since when it had twice been reduced

...

and then for a third time in 1995 by that redoubtable Boltonian the late Fred Dibner. For some reason this chimney, a local landmark, has long been known as Barrow Bridge Chimney, referring to the hamlet upstream which once boasted a chimney, of lesser stature, of its own.

From the chimney, a short uphill and cobbled road brought me to the eastern boundary of Moss Bank Park. It was formerly a private estate owned by successive members of a local family of cotton barons, the Ainsworths, who had bleachworks in the area. The green pastures around the family home, Moss Bank House, were once used to lay out the bleached cotton sheets. It was Peter Ainsworth (1737–1807), known as the 'opulent bleacher', who in 1786 commenced the building of the house for his son Richard and his family, and Richard continued adding to the structure. On Richard's death in 1833 his youngest son, John Horrocks Ainsworth (1800–64), inherited the estate and he it was who showed a particular interest in the gardens, especially the large brick-walled kitchen garden. Following his death the family let the house in 1870 and a period of neglect ensued. In 1928 the house and 72 acres (29 hectares) of land were acquired by Bolton Corporation for use as a municipal park. Moss Bank House, having lain empty for some years, was finally demolished in the winter of 1950–1, not long before my arrival, though I remembered it from visits when a boy.

I had been told to report to the staff quarters, or cabin as it was called, which was situated in the brick-built former stables. I had arrived in good time and Mr Fishwick, on spotting me, introduced me to members of his staff including Doug Rugman and Dennis Newton, foremen respectively in charge of the Rock Garden and the Old English Garden. Mr Fishwick then took me into the staff room, which had a well-worn concrete floor and a large table with a mixture of chairs. Against the walls were sundry shelves and cupboards for personal things. Metal hooks screwed to wooden battens fixed to the wall provided support for outer clothes, especially wet weather gear, while on the floor beneath, a collection of wellingtons and rubber boots had been assembled in line.

The room had a single window looking out onto playing fields and was dominated by a large black iron range with fireplace and flanking

. . .

ovens. A coke fire had just been lit and above it on a stout hook hung a large, heavy-duty iron kettle supplied with a small tap near its base to release the boiling water. As the nipper (boy) I would be responsible for daily 'housekeeping' duties which began immediately on arrival each morning with preparing and lighting the fire before filling the kettle from an outside tap. The water had to be on the boil and ready in time for the morning break around 10 o'clock when the staff (all men at the time) came in to make their own tea. Each had his own mug, mostly a pint pot, and these I had to wash after use ready for the dinner (lunch) break at half-past twelve. It was the same routine after lunch in preparation for the afternoon break at 3 o'clock.

Other morning jobs included sweeping out the cabin floor with a large stiff brush and chopping wood to provide kindling for the fire. I was quite good at the latter task, having previously worked Saturday mornings doing the same for a woodman who sold his bundles of kindling from a pony-drawn cart in the streets around my home. Garden and grass-cutting machinery was kept in a locked room adjoining the cabin, as were the tools – spades, forks, hoes, rakes, and so forth. These were hung from hooks in a wall and every man was responsible for keeping his tools clean and oiled when not in use.

The Old English Garden at Moss Bank Park where I first began work as a garden apprentice, shown here in July 1981.

...

Galtonia candicans, a bulbous perennial from South Africa that was planted with Russell lupins in a border in the Old English Garden.

Moss Bank gardens

In between these daily chores I was employed on gardening and general park duties, which were far more interesting and instructive. On day one I was told by Mr Fishwick to go with Doug Rugman and Dennis Newton to see the two gardens under their charge. First we viewed the Old English Garden, formerly the kitchen garden to the old house, which had been redesigned and planted by Mr Fishwick to include rose beds, perennial borders and beds for summer-flowering bedding displays, plus a variety of shrubs and trees. There was one long border used for Russell lupins interspersed with the bulbous South African *Galtonia candicans*, with its spires of drooping white bell-shaped flowers. Another border would be planted with myriad coloured dahlias for late summer and autumn displays, and yet another with large-flowered gladiolus hybrids.

Some of the beds and borders were edged with low-growing perennials such as London pride (*Saxifraga × urbium*), which preferred the shade, while *Saponaria ocymoides*, border pinks, lavender and catmint enjoyed the sun. Seasonal displays popular with the public included wallflowers and Brompton stocks, whose fragrance filled the garden and still re-awaken happy memories whenever and wherever I smell them today. Against the walls were climbing and rambler roses, honeysuckles, summer-flowering jasmine (*Jasminum officinale*) and large-flowered clematis, all well grown and expertly trained on wires to give of their best. But my memory races ahead. On that cold, crisp winter morning the garden looked decidedly bare but for the evergreen ivies, green and variegated, clinging to the walls, the tumbling green stems and yellow flowers of winter-flowering jasmine (*Jasminum nudiflorum*) and the low beetroot-coloured mounds of *Bergenia* foliage.

...

The Rock Garden, meanwhile, was constructed of Westmorland carboniferous limestone on a slope, curving like a horseshoe to embrace a central pool with grass surround. Here were intricate paths through which a tumbling stream with a string of small pools threaded its way down to the main pool. I noted Japanese maples now bare, dwarf rhododendrons and a variety of dwarf and slow-growing conifers including pines, spruce, firs, cypress in a range of shapes and colours. What I could not see nor even imagine then was the amazing transformation which would take place in both these gardens once spring got underway.

Learning plant names

Both foremen assured me that I would be given ample time to work in these gardens and the opportunity to get to know and grow the many plants in their charge. Dennis then pointed out the fact that although I already recognized many plants, they were British natives and I knew only their common names. 'If you want to get on in your career,' he told me, 'you will need to get to know these garden plants and learn their proper names.' With that he pointed at one of the many wooden labels in the ground inscribed with words that I couldn't even pronounce let alone understand. We had never experienced Latin or Greek at school, so how was I going to remember them? 'We will make a deal with you,' Doug said. 'We will teach you three new names a day, and not only the names but what they mean. In return, you must make a real effort to remember them.' It seemed a formidable task but I agreed to give it a try.

A modern cultivar of *Buddleja davidii* a name commemorating both the English cleric and botanist the Rev. Adam Buddle (1660-1715) and the French missionary and naturalist Abbé Armand David (1826-1900) who first made this Chinese species known to science in 1869.

. . .

They recommended that I write each new name in a notebook together with a brief comment about its appearance, especially an important characteristic easily seen. Dennis also gave me a spare copy he had of *Plant Names Simplified* by A.T. Johnson and H.A. Smith, a slim book in green covers that was a glossary of some of the more commonly cultivated plants in alphabetical order using their botanical names. A brief explanation as to the meaning of each name was given, plus a helpful guide to its correct pronunciation, using phonetic spelling. This book became my plant 'bible' and as I turn its pages today it provides a pleasurable memory of my early progression in the study of plant nomenclature. The more I referred to it the more I came to understand that each name was a key to further knowledge, a key which opened a door to a seemingly never-ending world of adventure and discovery.

My notebooks soon began to fill as I listed names and their meanings in categories, for example colours (*viridis*=green, *caerulea*=blue, *rubra*=red) and habitats (*sylvatica*=of woods and *rupestris*=growing on rocks). Even more interesting were those names commemorating places and people and I particularly remember *Buddleja davidii*, the first (generic) name recalling the Rev. Adam Buddle and the second name (specific epithet) after the Abbé David, a French missionary naturalist of the 19th century who first made known to science many Chinese plants including this one, as well as animals, fish and insects. Many years later I bought another edition of the guide, revised and enlarged by Professor William Stearn and published under the title *A Gardener's Dictionary of Plant Names*, which is well thumbed and a valuable reference to which I continue to refer.

After mathematics, history and geography had been my weakest subjects at school, but thanks to my burgeoning interest in the scientific names of plants, both people and faraway places became subjects of special interest to me – and one person and place in particular, E.H. Wilson, whose exploits in China in the early 20th century made him my first plant-explorer hero. At Moss Bank Park I encountered several plants first introduced to Western cultivation by Wilson, including the prickly-stemmed, red-berried *Berberis wilsoniae* (named for his wife) and *Senecio tanguticus* (now *Sinacalia tangutica*), a bold herbaceous perennial with

. . .

My first garden hero, the English plant-hunter E.H. Wilson, here on an expedition to Korea in 1915.

deeply lobed leaves and dense terminal plumes of yellow flowers, a large colony of which occupied a damp corner of the Old English Garden. Indeed, one of my first jobs with spade and fork was to reduce the advance of this plant and that was before I had seen it in leaf or flower. Little did I know then that many years later I would see it in the wild occupying riversides and lake margins in China's Sichuan province.

By the end of my first year, encouraged by the foremen and helped by a little game I invented to help me recognize plants at a distance, I had become familiar with a wide range of plants and their scientific names. The road outside the park was lined with private houses with front gardens I could look into as I passed. The game involved my identifying and speaking out loud the names of plants growing in the gardens. I set my own rules as follows: I wasn't allowed to stop or even hesitate and initially I could only list one or two before I was looking into the next garden. As time went on, I began to increase my speed and my attempts to identify and name plants became more hectic. It was not uncommon to see people staring through their windows doubtlessly wondering what on earth I was up to.

. . .

A trio of names I will never forget were the three A's *Alyssum*, *Arabis* and *Aubrieta* often growing in the same garden, draping low stone walls or rockeries. I memorized the flower colours, yellow for *Alyssum saxatile* (now *Aurinia saxatilis*), white for *Arabis albida* (now *A. alpina* subsp. *caucasica*) and blue or purple for *Aubrieta deltoidea*. For most of that year, except when helping on general park duties, I worked in the Old English Garden and was taught by my foreman Dennis Newton a wide variety of garden skills and practices, from soil preparation and planting through to more specialist operations such as pruning, tying and training. I loved the seasonal changes which brought daffodils, tulips and a wealth of bulb displays in spring, together with the pink, orange and red flowers of the 'japonicas' (*Chaenomeles* cultivars) against the red brick walls.

In summer the Russell lupins dominated and visitors flocked to see their dense, tapered spikes in both richly coloured and pastel shades. I have tried several times to replicate these displays on a small scale in the clay soil of my present garden but snails and slugs have defeated me time and again. Pyramids of sweet peas and rustic arches smothered with climbing and rambling roses and large-flowered clematis entwined are just two of the many memories I have of this time, and I must not

RIGHT Aged 15 working in the herb border in the Old English Garden, Moss Bank Park, in the summer of 1953.

FAR RIGHT On the right is Doug Rugman, foreman in the Rock Garden who became a long-time friend and mentor.

. . .

forget Mr Fishwick's favourites, the beds of German or flag iris with their exotic colours – though many visitors came in summer simply to enjoy the rose beds where hybrid tea and polyantha roses provided a wealth of colour and scent.

By contrast, I remember the herb border as much for its dominance of green or grey foliage as for its distinct aromas. Fennel (*Foeniculum vulgare*), lovage (*Levisticum officinale*), sage (*Salvia officinalis*), marsh mallow (*Althaea officinalis*), good King Henry (*Chenopodium bonus-henricus*), liquorice (*Glycyrrhiza glabra*), elecampane (*Inula helenium*), and sweet cicely (*Myrrhis odorata*) were just a few of those grown. I particularly remember the liquorice plant whose dried, yellow-stained roots known as liquorice sticks we used to buy to chew when children from a corner sweet shop near our primary school.

Early mentors

My foreman Dennis Newton's knowledge of plants and their cultivation had been gained and honed as a gardener working on various private estates in the area. As was the case of so many of his kind, the aftermath of the Second World War found him seeking employment in public parks whose quality and professional care improved considerably as a result. By contrast, Doug Rugman had trained and worked in the commercial plant world. A Gloucestershire man by birth, he had worked for a time at Merriot's Nursery near Thornbury, where his many skills included rose budding. He once told me he could identify hundreds of roses simply by their wood. which really impressed me. Having married a Bolton girl and moved north, he found employment with Bolton Parks and ended up in charge of the Rock Garden which had first been opened to the public in 1932. His knowledge of plants in general and alpines and rock plants in particular was formidable and when I eventually began working with him on a daily basis my interest in these plants increased as a result.

Doug encouraged me to join the local group of the Alpine Garden Society and to construct a small rock feature in my home garden which I planted with a variety of saxifrages, sedums, bellflowers and other easily grown subjects. I was even allowed to grow a range of alpines in

. . .

My first success in show
business with a little help
from Doug Rugman.

pots in a frame at work, some of which I entered in the Alpine Garden
Society's local shows. Our relationship had not begun well. He was
generally of a quiet nature yet had a sharp tongue when annoyed.
Though I did not know it at the time, he was virtually blind in one eye,
the result of a botched operation when a boy. I was initially unnerved
by his seemingly stern gaze, so much so that I went out of my way not
to upset him.

On one occasion, however, I had taken orders from the staff for food
to be bought from shops on a road in the area. Orders varied from day
to day but on this occasion they included sandwiches and fruit tarts as
well as fish and chips and meat and potato pies. This was one of my
duties as 'nipper' and I duly set off on my bicycle with a deep wicker
basket hanging from the handle bar. The plan was to cycle out of the
park to a busy road where several shops sold food hot and cold. It was
imperative that I make my purchases and return in sufficient time to
place the hot food in the heated oven before the staff arrived for lunch.
Unfortunately, everything went horribly wrong when, racing back
down the road towards the park entrance, I had to brake suddenly when
the upcoming traffic lights changed to red. This caused the basket to
swing wildly, depositing most of its contents ahead of me onto the road
where, unable to stop in time, I ran over the pies. Panicking, I hurriedly
scooped up the food, all of which was wrapped in individual paper
bags, and refilled the basket before rushing on to the staff cabin.
Assessing the damage on my arrival and fearing the wrath of Doug

. . .

should he be presented with a damaged pie, I selected the only reasonably intact sample for him before preparing myself to face his not so lucky colleagues with my amazing story of a close call.

Things between us had long since improved by the time I began work on the Rock Garden but even then I almost caused a relapse when, having been instructed by him to fork through and clean up the shrub borders which embraced the Garden, I cut to the ground several tall, stout, prickle-clad stems which to my untutored eye in their winter nakedness looked decidedly dead. The next morning, after examining my handiwork, he said that the stems belonged to the deciduous Japanese angelica tree (*Aralia elata*) and far from being dead were very much alive. Luckily for me, he explained, the removal of these stems would simply encourage new ones to develop from the underground rootstock, which is what happened. Chastened by this experience, I resolved to double check any plant I was inclined to prune or remove, and from then on my year in the Rock Garden was a time of continual discovery and pleasure.

Primulas

Doug's passion for the Rock Garden and its plants ensured a regular supply of new and unusual species covering a wide selection of genera, among which *Primula* and *Gentiana* were his special favourites. It is here that I first encountered candelabra primulas with their bold leaf rosettes topped by sturdy, erect stems sporting tiers (whorls) of flowers in a galaxy of colours. I particularly remember the robust *P. pulverulenta*, an E.H. Wilson introduction from China's south-western Sichuan province with white, mealy stems up to 3 ¼ft (1m) tall and flowers of a rich carmine-red. Equally striking were *P. bulleyana*, an introduction from the mountains of north-west Yunnan by the Scottish plant explorer George Forrest which has golden to pale orange flowers, and *P. japonica*, another robust grower with flowers vary-

A candelabra primula *P. pulverulenta* first introduced from W. China by E.H. Wilson.

. . .

Called by some the red-hot poker primula, *P. vialii* proved a popular attraction with the public.

ing in colour from a deep red through purple to pink or white. Unlike the previous two, this species, as its name implies, is native to Japan, from where it was first successfully introduced in 1870. All three planted by the pond and streamside provided a breathtaking display in May and early June, while a fourth species, *P. florindae*, representing a different section, carried its pendant, bell-shaped, sulphur-yellow fragrant flowers in terminal heads on strong, cream-mealy stems up to 3¼ft (1m) or more from late June through to August. The last named was first introduced to cultivation from south-east Tibet by yet another great plant explorer, Frank Kingdon-Ward, in 1924 and it has long remained a favourite of mine. I love the story that likens the tall stems and drooping yellow flowers to the long-legged and blonde Florinda, his first wife after whom it is named.

The most popular *Primula* species, with visitors certainly, was the so-called 'drumstick' (*P. denticulata*). It was widely grown, especially in northern Pennine gardens, and we had several groups of it in the Rock Garden which required regular division to keep them in good heart. I recall having to lift older clumps to separate the individual crowns for replanting elsewhere. At the same time I was instructed to search for and feed to a friendly robin the plump white grubs of vine weevil which was and still is a common pest of primulas and other perennials. Many years later I was fortunate enough to see this species growing by the thousands in the damp turf of our camp site in the mountains of Bhutan. However, the strikingly bicoloured *P. vialii* from north-west Yunnan and south-west Sichuan was by far the most eye-catching species we grew and it never failed to attract visitor attention.

In addition to the moisture-loving kinds, the rock garden proved an excellent home for many of those primulas such as *P. marginata* which required planting in well-drained sites, including rock crevices. So enamoured of primulas did I become that I vowed to make them my specialist subject, that is, until a flood of other fascinating plants came

...

into my life. Having since seen many species in the wild, *Primula* remains one of my favourite genera.

Of the several gentians that Doug had planted out, all of them beautiful, I liked best the European willow gentian (*Gentiana asclepiadea*) for its robust clumps of elegantly arching stems, its narrow willow-like leaves in pairs and its rich blue flowers in early autumn. Then there was *G. sino-ornata*, a Chinese species from alpine meadows for whose special needs Doug had prepared a large pocket of lime-free soil where its trailing shoots and glorious blue trumpet flowers in autumn held visitors spellbound. We even boasted *G. saxosa*, a coastal species from the South Island of New Zealand which I remember for its neat, low, tufted habit to 6in (15cm) and its small white flowers.

Among the commonly grown shrubs that were growing in the flanking borders Doug pointed out to me a curious bigeneric hybrid named × *Mahoberberis neubertii*. It was the result of a cross between *Mahonia aquifolium* from west coast North America and the European *Berberis vulgaris*. Both parents grew in the park but this plant had arisen in German cultivation around 1850. It was an evergreen bush, semi-evergreen in cold winters, which according to Doug had never flowered, being grown more for its curiosity value. How many public parks today, I wonder, would give space to such plants?

The Rock Garden was home to a goodly collection of conifers, mostly the so-called dwarf or slow-growing selections of Scot's pine (*Pinus sylvestris*) and *P. mugo*; spruce, especially *Picea glauca* var. *albertiana* 'Conica' and *P. abies* 'Nidiformis', plus attractive selections of *Chamaecyparis obtusa*, *Thuja occidentalis* and *Cryptomeria japonica*. One famous conifer, the dawn redwood (*Metasequoia glyptostroboides*), although available from at least one nursery at that time, was not planted in the park until some years following my departure – more's the pity, as I should love to have studied it at first hand.

In between my work in the gardens I was given experience working in other areas of the park including Jack Fishwick's pride and joy, the crown bowling greens. According to his daughter Marion in a letter to me following his death in 1956, he worked for Bolton Parks all his life and following his service in the trenches during the Great War he

. . .

returned to a job as greenkeeper at Queen's Park, Bolton's flagship park. In 1930 he was promoted and sent to Moss Bank Park as park keeper with special responsibility for replanting the Old English Garden and the construction of a second bowling green. These greens were maintained in excellent condition, not a weed to be seen, and were much admired by visiting players. However, it was another bowling green not far from these which provided a different story.

It belonged to a sports and recreation ground, maintained for the use of a local cotton mill's staff by a man called Jack Barber, who was about to play an important role in my horticultural training. Jack had obtained a degree in botany from Manchester University but instead of following an academic career had taken on a groundsman's position to help support his wife's burgeoning career at a local hospital. Both were highly qualified and talented with it and the arrangement was seen as a benefit to them and later their family. The ground's facilities included a bowling green which the previous year had been relaid with seawashed turf from Westmorland. The summer following, Jack contacted me about some weeds that had emerged in the new green. On visiting I was shown a number of plants which I was able to identify as buckshorn plantain (*Plantago coronopus*), Danish scurvy-grass (*Cochlearia danica*) and the sea milkwort (*Glaux maritima*). All three were native to coastal districts and all represented new records for the Bolton Flora. I was thrilled, Jack too I am pleased to say, but we both knew that they would have to go. Little did I know then that the tiny annual scurvy grass which belongs to the same family of plants, Cruciferae, as the radish and the water cress, would one day occur by the billion, forming drifts along miles of central reservations on some of Britain's highways in spring.

Plant evenings at Tognarelli's

Jack Barber used his knowledge and experience as a part-time teacher at the local technical college, where night school courses in practical horticulture and botany were popular during the winter terms. As an apprentice I was encouraged to attend these, held on a weekly basis. Jack was an inspirational teacher and I looked forward to these evenings

. . .

Jack Barber became my friend and mentor in all things horticultural and botanical.

especially when, at their conclusion, we retired to Tognarelli's, an Italian ice cream parlour in town. Here, over a hot chocolate or a banana split, discussions would continue and questions would be asked until the time came for us to say our goodnights and head for home and bed. One result of these Tognarelli discussions was an offer from Jack to organize and accompany visits to gardens and plant collections beyond Bolton. Given Jack's botanical expertise and friendly manner these trips, usually on a Saturday, proved popular and helped to broaden my understanding of the plant kingdom considerably.

One of the more interesting places we visited was a derelict garden on a hillside above the village of Rivington, near Horwich, north of Bolton. I knew Horwich best for its locomotive works in which an early steam engine, 'Coppernob', was preserved. Rivington Pike, a hill of 1187ft (362m) rising above the village, was a popular venue for walkers and picnickers, especially on Easter and bank holidays. On its rounded summit and visible from miles around was a squat, stone tower built as a hunting lodge in 1733 on the site of an ancient beacon first mentioned during the reign of Elizabeth I. This was one of a chain established countrywide to give warning of impending invasion by the Spanish Armada. On a clear day breathtaking views can be had from the Pike, especially to the west; if you know where to look, Blackpool Tower can be identified on the Lancashire coast. With a telescope, so can the

...

yellow azaleas, we found *Pieris japonica* and *P. floribunda* with their terminal heads of white pitcher-shaped flowers and drifts of Japanese evergreen azaleas with flowers in several colours and shades.

Quite new to me was *Chamaedaphne calyculata* or leatherleaf, a small wiry-stemmed evergreen shrub of the heather family (Ericaceae) with small leaves and arching sprays of white flowers. New to me also was *Halesia carolina*, the Carolina snowdrop tree from the south-eastern USA. Its slender branches were draped with nodding, white, bell-shaped flowers which later produced small green pear-shaped, four-winged fruits. Growing with the *Halesia* in a wood not far from the gardens was a large widespreading multi-stemmed specimen of the Japanese witch hazel (*Hamamelis japonica*). I remember returning to this shrub in winter so as to examine the curious spidery yellow flower clusters decorating the naked twigs.

On another occasion, I collected samples of some of the conifers planted in the gardens and sent them to the Royal Botanic Garden Kew for naming. In a reply, they were confirmed as giant fir (*Abies grandis*); noble fir (*A. procera*); Bhutan pine (*Pinus wallichiana*); Austrian pine (*P. nigra*) and mountain pine (*P. mugo*). The last two had proved to be the best suited to the exposed site.

. . .

OPPOSITE PAGE The Carolina snowdrop tree (*Halesia carolina*) flowering in April at Rivington near Bolton.

RIGHT A page of colour plates from Benjamin Maund's *The Botanic Garden*, published between 1826 and 1832.

Jack Barber was a true friend and the most generous of mentors. We shared many outings to study plants both wild and cultivated and he would often pop into Moss Bank Park to see what special plants I had to show him. He was one of those friends I always thought of when seeing a new or special plant and I still do now, long after his death. He had an excellent private collection of gardening and plant books which he consulted when I brought an unknown plant specimen to him for naming. A surprise was the contents of a cardboard box he presented me with on visiting him following my return from Malaya in 1958. It contained a quantity of loose parts covering four volumes of *The Botanic Garden* by Benjamin Maund, published in London between 1826 and 1832. The high-quality hand-coloured engraved plant portraits it contains in blocks of four are accompanied by informative descriptions and comments relating to each plant, its cultivation, origin, date of introduction and much else. I eventually had them professionally

. . .

bound into two volumes and they remain one of my most precious possessions, a joy to behold. Some years after his death his family presented me with his much-annotated, four-volume copy of the Royal Horticultural Society's *Dictionary of Gardening* and browsing through its pages it pleased me to read the frequent pencilled marginal comments he had made against plants we had seen together.

I shall never forget the first Christmas I experienced at Moss Bank Park. I had only been there a couple of weeks and was surprised and delighted when informed by Mr Fishwick that at the Park's Christmas party, the staff would be having a whip round to give me a Christmas bonus. There was a catch, however; to earn it I would have to sing a song. As Christmas Eve approached I began to dread the moment, but I needed the bonus and reluctantly began considering a suitable song, listening to the wireless at home for inspiration. At 3 o'clock on Christmas Eve the party began and my legs were like jelly. The staff were in a merry mood, having finished work, cleaned their tools and settled in the cabin, warmed by the fire, which had been fortified with logs. The table was laden with food – pork pies, sausage rolls and sandwiches plus assorted cakes, mixed nuts and the inevitable mince tarts. Beer was available and for those who wanted their regular mug of tea there was a drop of rum or whisky to strengthen it.

Just when I was hoping they had forgotten the entertainment, the call came for me to fulfil my promise and I was obliged to stand on a chair and deliver. The most popular song of Christmas 1952 was 'I saw Mommy kissing Santa Claus' recorded by 13-year-old Tommy Boyd, and that's what I had chosen. I felt conspicuous, nervous and embarrassed, but somehow I saw it through, my last words being greeted by cheers and applause. Only then was I handed my bonus sealed in a brown envelope, and on examining its contents later I discovered it was more than my week's wage.

Exploring limestone and chalk
Thumbing through the pages of my notebook for 1953, I find references to my having visited several noted plant locations including Colt Park Wood in Yorkshire, described by Edward (Ted) Lousley in his book

. . .

Wild Flowers of Chalk and Limestone as 'one of the most remarkable and uncanny woods in Britain' and 'the best example in Britain of an aboriginal scar limestone ashwood'. The trees occupy an extensive area of carboniferous limestone paving which is raised several feet in places and in the deep crevices (grikes) can be found, among other plants, baneberry (*Actaea spicata*, syn. *A. nigra*), lily-of-the-valley (*Convallaria majalis*), angular Solomon's seal (*Polygonatum odoratum*) and the magnificent giant bellflower (*Campanula latifolia*). On the surface of the great rock slabs (clints), I noted a perennial form of *Viola tricolor*, once known as *Viola lepida*, and mossy saxifrage (*Saxifraga hypnoides*), hybrids of which grew on the Rock Garden at Moss Bank Park; in damp places around were colonies of one of my favourite native thistles, *Cirsium heterophyllum*, the melancholy thistle, named presumably for its initially nodding flowerheads and white hairy stems and leaf undersides. Appropriately, my companion on this trip was Vicar Shaw, whose lecture on thistles I had attended in Bolton in November 1951. Not surprisingly, limestone areas became a favourite destination of mine and none more so than the area around Silverdale and Arnside either side of the Lancashire-Westmorland border.

To my mind there was a ring to the name Silverdale akin to that of the Elvin kingdom of Lothlorien in Tolkien's *Lord of the Rings*. Several visits over several years did nothing to dispel this and for a time I regarded it as the place I would one day like to live and yes, to end my days. My first visit, in May 1953, was made by train on a Special Sunday Excursion ticket from Bolton's Trinity Street Station costing the princely sum of six shillings and sixpence return. For me, it was the start of an adventure, something I had long dreamt of, not unlike a trip today might be for Harry Potter fans on the Hogwart Express. The train steamed out of the station and soon all vestiges of the town were left behind us as we sped north, stopping briefly at Preston, Lancaster and Carnforth, beyond which the landscape became more rugged, dominated by the limestone massive of Warton Crag (590ft/180m) on our right.

The village of Silverdale lies just inland from the sea at the north-east corner of Morecambe Bay. To keen gardeners it was well known for its nursery, which specialized in alpine and rock plants and hardy ferns. Its

...

Polystichum setiferum
Plumosodivilisibum
Group, one of
Reginald Kaye's
'tongue twister' ferns.

Alchemilla alpina,
the true alpine lady's
mantle, with leaflets
divided to the base.

proprietor, Reginald Kaye, was a near-legendary figure who lived for his plants and knew their likes and dislikes intimately. He was a popular and well-travelled speaker, generous with his advice. I later attended one of his lectures on the subject of hardy garden ferns, which are notorious for their tortuous nomenclature, *Polystichum setiferum* Plumosodivilisibum Group being an example. Referring to this problem, Reg assured his audience that 'if you grow them and get to know them you'll find that their names will trip off your tongue'. He, of course, spoke their names fluently, emphasizing each word of the name as if it was a member of his family which, in a way, it was.

...

Silverdale station lies east of the village and on alighting I followed what would become over the years a familiar route, crossing the bridge over the line and down the lane to the first stop, Leighton Moss, now a well-run RSPB reserve, where I walked the reed-fringed meres and the marshy marginal ground on the look-out for birds and plants. I once had a brief view of an otter here and on another occasion heard a bittern booming in the reed beds, which had me wishing even more that I lived near enough to visit regularly.

Reviewing my list of plants seen that day, I have special memories of herb Paris (*Paris quadrifolia*) and green hellebore (*Helleborus viridis* subsp. *occidentalis*) growing with lily-of-the-valley in the oak and ash woods and of a disused limestone quarry in Middlebarrow Wood where I saw my first wild small-leaved lime (*Tilia cordata*), columbine (*Aquilegia vulgaris*) and, on a later visit in June, dark red helleborine (*Epipactis atrorubens)* growing from crevices in the rock. There is another memory I cherish of a small tarn, Hawes Water, where in June I was thrilled to find the delicate pink bird's-eye primrose (*Primula farinosa*) growing with grass of Parnassus (*Parnassia palustris*) in the boggy marginal ground. The former is a close ally of the Bulgarian endemic species *Primula frondosa* which we grew on the Rock Garden at Moss Bank Park.

Highlights of 1954 included a summer holiday with my friend Clifford to the Farne Isles off the Northumbrian coast, where we were able to indulge our passion for birds and plants, a theme we repeated in May–June the following year when we spent a week in the Highlands of Scotland cycling and rambling in the mountains and woods. The many special moments on this trip included our discovery of a dotterel's nest on the moors above Dalwhinnie and crested tits nesting in the pine woods around Aviemore, while alpine lady's mantle (*Alchemilla alpina*), purple saxifrage (*Saxifraga oppositifolia*) and no fewer than three club mosses (*Lycopodium* species) were just a handful of the many plants new to me. The *Alchemilla* was the real thing with smaller leaves and separate leaflets, not the plant so often sold under this name, *A. conjuncta* from the Alps, which has larger leaves and the apparent leaflets joined towards their base.

. . .

Just one of the myriad forms of the Croton (*Codiaeum variegatum* var. *pictum*) a tropical evergreen once popular as an indoor display plant on civic occasions.

Tropical plants

In 1954 Bolton Parks Department was given the go-ahead to establish a new nursery with a range of glasshouses in which to grow decorative plants, in particular those needing heat in winter including a stove house for tropical plants. Such plants would be used for foliage and floral displays on special civic occasions including the Mayor's Ball, the annual highlight. I was offered the chance to be part of the new venture which I found an exciting prospect, given that I would be handling and growing a whole new range of plants. Both Doug Rugman and Jack Barber advised me to make the most of the opportunity and I needed no persuading.

Having started my career growing and getting to know hardy plants, I now turned my attention to dealing with a new and equally interesting nomenclature, together with a wealth of stories of countries and habitats outside my normal territory. From Michaelmas daisies, clematis, rhododendrons and dwarf conifers and the like, I now found myself rubbing shoulders with plants such as crotons (*Codiaeum variegatum* var. *pictum*), evergreen shrubs from South East Asia, ubiquitous in gardens and parks of the tropics where they are sometimes grown as hedges. The range of shape, size and colour exhibited by their bold evergreen leaves I found astonishing. *Coleus* (now *Solenostemon*), although unrelated botanically, provided another huge variety of

. . .

coloured foliage subjects and between them these two were the backbone of civic indoor displays which might also feature palms in variety – *Dracaena*, especially the many variegated cultivars of the tropical West African *D. deremensis* – *Alocacia*, *Peperomia* and *Schefflera arboricola*.

Flowering plants grown in the nursery included *Bougainvillea* in several colours; *Acalypha*; *Justicia brandegeeana*, the shrimp plant; *Strelitzia* and *Clivia*; *Streptosolen jamesonii*, the so-called marmalade bush from the colour of the flowers; the powder-blue-flowered *Plumbago capensis* (now *P. auriculata*); *Plectranthus*, *Achimenes*, *Saintpaulia*, *Gloxinia* and *Streptocarpus*; and begonias, especially the *B. rex* cultivars for their beautiful leaves, the large-flowered tuberous hybrids and the pink-flowered 'Gloire de Lorraine'. Ever-present in all displays were the tender evergreen ferns, especially the ubiquitous Boston fern (*Nephrolepis exaltata* 'Bostoniensis') and the many forms of *Pteris cretica*, while on very special occasions large prized specimens of the bird's-nest fern (*Asplenium nidus*) with dark-stalked polished green, strap-shaped fronds would be given a prominent position. I would be seeing this magnificent fern three years later growing wild in Malaya but that is a story for the next chapter.

On one occasion, we staged a group of incense plants, *Humea* (now *Calomeria*) *amaranthoides*, an aromatic biennial or perennial native to South East Australia whose tiny pink to reddish-brown flower heads are carried in huge arching terminal heads (panicles). It was highly effective and much commented upon. When required for display purposes, all our plants would be carefully selected, securely packed and driven to the venue in a closed van or truck. Once we had finished the display we returned to the nursery, but on one occasion I was required to go and make a last-minute check to make sure that nothing had been disturbed and that no plants needed watering. I concluded my inspection just in time to see the first guests arriving, gentlemen in black ties and ladies in their evening gowns.

Another big occasion requiring our input was the annual Autumn Chrysanthemum Show, attended by exhibitors and visitors from all over the country. Like the Mayor's Ball, it was held in the Albert Hall in the Civic Centre and the Parks Department was expected to put on a good display of cut-flower and pot-grown chrysanthemums, which

· · ·

we did in style. Watching the commercial growers staging their large exhibits and the amateur entrants in the competitive classes arranging their best cut specimens in vases was for me a new and exciting experience. I have never forgotten the ranks of blooms of all sizes and forms, the colours and of course the unforgettable aroma of foliage which remained in the air long after the show was over.

Some years later I became a regular weekly visitor to the Albert Hall on those Sunday evenings when classical recitals by famous soloists were staged. It was here that I first heard the great pianists Yonty Solomon and Benno Moiseiwitsch perform. Around this time too I began collecting records of classical music. Many of my favourites are on the old 78rpm shellac discs bought at a closing-down sale in Manchester and include one featuring the legendary Italian tenor Enrico Caruso singing 'The Lost Chord'.

In the autumn of 1955, to further my training, I was transferred to Heaton Nursery, the Parks Department's older establishment in Bolton where, in a series of long greenhouses and rows of cold frames, thousands of bedding plants were grown to satisfy the needs of the borough in its public spaces, parks and town centre displays. Prime plants in this huge operation were geraniums (zonal pelargoniums), especially the then overwhelmingly popular 'Paul Crampel' with its dazzling scarlet single flowers. These were grown each year from cuttings taken from stock plants and from display beds elsewhere. Cuttings were taken in late summer and placed 5–6 in a pot of compost and thence in rows on long raised benches where they would remain until spring when, having rooted, they were potted individually, ready for planting once all danger of frost had receded. I cannot begin to imagine the number of cuttings I prepared and potted-on during the weeks or even months we spent on this task, nor the number of used clay pots I was given to wash and clean with a scrubbing brush and cold water in a large metal tub (dandy). It was like a penance!

But that was nothing compared to my least favourite job – helping to fill and empty a large oblong and lidded metal tank used to sterilize soil previously stacked, turf down, in a corner of the nursery. First it had to be cut with a spade then broken down or shredded then wheeled to the sterilizer. This worked by means of a fire in a box beneath the tank which heated a water container above, the steam produced rising through holes in lengths of metal pipe along the bottom of the tank to pass through the soil, apparently killing any lurking pests and diseases. Filling this tank was back-breaking work but emptying it was worse because we had to stand in the tank, in our boots, in hot, sticky, smelly, steaming soil to spade it out again. Eventually, when cold, in accordance with the famous John Innes formula it had to be mixed with peat and sand with the required nutrients added for use as compost.

Grave duties

The following summer I was part of a team delegated to plant geraniums on the graves of those buried in the cemetery next door whose family had paid to have this carried out by the council. I recall driving a small tractor and truck full of plants to these graves and setting out the agreed number. The standard planting was three or four geraniums down the centre of the plot plus a line of white alyssum and blue lobelia alternating along the edges. It was boring work but I viewed it as an experience and certainly more satisfying than my next stint in the same cemetery the following winter. Due to the cold, wet conditions, several of the gravediggers had signed off work with colds or flu and in order to fill the vacancies three or four of the nursery staff including me were drafted in to help out. Gravediggers worked in pairs, one doing the digging while his mate stood at the edge of the grave stacking on a wooden board the soil excavated by the digger. Fortunately, I was not expected to do the digging, only the stacking. Even then I was concerned one day when the digger I was helping, having dug down to the required depth, suddenly shouted an expletive and drew my attention to what he had found. Having already heard some gruesome grave-digging stories I was fearful of what I might see as I gingerly peered into the grave, only to find the gravedigger pulling from the soil a long, dark thong which on closer examination turned out to be the root of the field horsetail (*Equisetum arvense*), a common weed especially in cultivation. It must have been 6½ft (2m) or more down, which drew from the gravedigger a comment that given time, they would travel all the way to Australia!

· · ·

It was certainly a consideration, but any thought I might have had of investigating the theory evaporated when, after a week in the cemetery and with the return of the professionals, I was back in the nursery putting my mind to yet another batch of dirty pots.

Towards the end of the year I was presented with a new challenge in helping to plant a Garden of Remembrance around a newly built crematorium, which had me worrying that my future was heading in an unwanted direction. In the event, it proved an enjoyable experience as I found myself working with hardy plants again and was expected to use my experience and imagination in their placing. A highlight of the year for me was a letter from the Royal Horticultural Society signed by D. Bowes Lyon, President, informing me of my success in passing the RHS General Certificate in Horticulture for Juniors.

National Service

The summer following I received news of a totally different nature, notifying me that I was due to be called up for National Service and must report to register at a recruitment centre in nearby Manchester. One of my colleagues had recently returned to Heaton Nursery having served his two years, he claimed, at a military base in Wales where he was put to work as the gardener, a job which included the garden and vegetable plot of the commanding officer. He urged me to tell the recruiting officer of my calling and maybe I too would land a similar post, a 'cushy number' as he termed it. On the day, I attended the centre and joined a queue. When my turn came, the recruiting officer, looking up from the form on his desk, asked me a series of questions, one of which was what I did for a living. 'I'm a gardener,' I replied. I could not help but notice him writing in the appropriate space a single word, Infantry. Then followed a medical check-up that I passed, after which I left the centre and caught the bus back to Bolton and Heaton Nursery. It was a week or two later that I received a brown envelope containing official notification of my call up in August. I would be joining The Loyal Regiment (North Lancashire) whose Colonel-in-Chief was Her Majesty the Queen and I was required to report for 12 weeks basic training at the Regimental Headquarters, Fulwood Barracks

...

in Preston. So much for being a gardener, I thought. On the bright side, Preston was the home of the football club Preston North End, where the great Tom Finney played, so it might not be a bad thing after all.

Cycle tour of Somerset

Shortly after this I was moved from Heaton Nursery to Queens Park, Bolton's flagship park, where I remained until my call up. There were still a couple of months or so before that happened and I decided to make the most of the time I had left. I had never travelled in the southern half of England, so I took a week off at the end of June and early July to go on a bicycle tour in Somerset. My first bicycle had been a Phillips Kingfisher and my present one was a Merlin, which accompanied me on the train to Bristol Temple Meads. I then headed to the local youth hostel, where I booked in for bed and breakfast before continuing to the nearby limestone cliffs of Clifton Gorge to look at the native flora for which this location is famous. I ended up with a long list of discoveries, among which the round-headed leek (*Allium sphaerocephalum*) with tall stems and dense terminal heads of deep red-purple flowers and the blue-flowered *Veronica spicata* were particularly special, though I had previously seen the latter on Great Orme's Head in North Wales and on Humphrey Head in north Lancashire. I was also thrilled to see the broad-leaved limes (*Tilia platyphyllos*) in the woods. This noble tree I knew well enough in cultivation and as a parent of the common lime (*T.* × *europaea*), formerly widely planted as an avenue.

Before leaving the city the next morning, I spent an hour or so in the University of Bristol Botanic Garden enjoying and listing all those plants new to me. I remember how well-labelled the collection was. My next destination was Bath, where I was hoping to find the so-called Bath asparagus (*Ornithogalum pyrenaicum*) which I eventually did, in a meadow and in roadside hedges. Its tall tapering racemes of milky-white flowers were easily spotted from my bicycle. I recorded many other interesting wild plants over the next two days, including greater dodder (*Cuscuta europaea*), its dense coils of reddish leafless stems embracing a patch of nettles on which it is a root parasite.

. . .

Cheddar Gorge had long been known to me as a location for Cheddar pink *Dianthus caesius* (now known as *D. gratianopolitanus*, a cumbersome name). We grew it on the Rock Garden at Moss Bank Park, but I could not miss the opportunity of seeing it in the wild and again Lady Luck was with me; when cycling through the gorge I spotted high on the limestone cliffs several hummocks and mats of this lovely pink which I was able to study more closely through my binoculars.

Sadly, Lady Luck chose not to accompany me when I rode off in search of another special plant known as purple gromwell (*Lithospermum purpurocaeruleum*, now *Buglossoides purpurocaerulea*, the last word referring to the purplish-blue flowers). I had been told by a botanist friend that it could be found in some quantity in a hedge bottom somewhere west of Cheddar. I was given a location near a Shipham Farm and I believed I was on to a winner, but after riding up and down several narrow lanes I had found neither the gromwell nor even the farm so I decided to call in at a local pub to make enquiries. Entering the snug, I found it was full of regulars sitting with their pints and enjoying a good yarn. I walked straight to the bar, where the landlord asked what I would be having. I asked him what he would recommend, in answer to which he described several local ales before adding 'or you can try our rough', which was the local cider. Though my back was turned to them I could sense that the locals had taken an interest in my request and there was a pregnant silence. Foolishly, as it turned out, I rose to the challenge and nodded my agreement. I was used to northern ales, after all – what could possibly go wrong from drinking the juice of apples?

With pint in hand and following an initial sip, I turned to ask the assembled throng if they knew where I might find Shipham Farm. Their blank faces indicated they did not, so, taking another, larger sip, I found myself telling them that I was looking for the purple gromwell. From the look on their faces I might as well have been Captain Ahab asking them if they had seen a white whale. It was clear to me that I would get no further in my enquiries here so, gulping down the remains of my drink, I thanked them and left. Once outside, I decided to continue down the lane and head for my final destination, Brean Down, on the coast above Weston-super-Mare. I hadn't travelled far, however, when I felt my head

. . .

Cheddar Gorge in Somerset, home of the Cheddar pink and other special plants.

swimming, my legs rubbery and the wheels of my cycle heading into the grassy verge before offloading me into a ditch. I would love this story to have ended with me lying there before noticing the purple gromwell peeping at me from the hedge bottom, but no. I simply walked my bicycle further along the lane to where an inviting bank, screened from passing traffic, allowed me to have a brief but comfortable nap.

At least this saga had a happy ending. Having found the white rock-rose (*Helianthemum apenninum*), the ivy broomrape (*Orobanche hederae*) and the rare Somerset hair grass (*Koeleria vallesiana*) on the limestone down, I could head for home with a feeling of accomplishment. On returning to Bolton I was considerably cheered to read in my book Grasses by C.E. Hubbard that the above species had first been discovered in England on Brean Down in 1726 by Johann Jacob Dillenius (1684–1747), a German botanist who became Professor of Botany at Oxford, during a tour of the west of England and Wales in search of plants. Following his discovery this grass remained unknown until 1904 when rediscovered by Dr G.C. Druce. It gave me a thrill to think that I had trodden in the footsteps of such legendary botanists.

I enjoyed other trips locally and to Norfolk with my friend Clifford before that fateful day in August when I packed my necessary belongings, gave my mother and sister a kiss and a hug and headed for Preston and an uncertain future.

...

CHAPTER THREE

On Her Majesty's Service

L ooking back on my two years of National Service, the early
months seem to have passed quickly compared with what
followed. This was mainly due to the intensity of training and
concentration required in preparing raw recruits for active service; there
was so much to learn and not just drilling, physical training and the use
of firearms. Discipline was paramount in moulding a diverse group of
individuals into a close-knit unit. We were left in no doubt that our
ability to work together as a team might one day help to save our lives.
This didn't happen overnight and barrack-room rivalries and incidents
were inevitable, especially in the early weeks.

Most of my fellow recruits were drawn from the Bolton and Preston
areas, others from Manchester and Liverpool, and I shall never forget
one particularly bullish individual who, having bragged about his
fighting prowess, threatened our training corporal and ignored several
official warnings, was invited one night to settle the matter outside.
Naturally, we were encouraged to accompany the two as witnesses to the
action which in the event was short and sharp, leaving the bully with a
bruised ego while his attitude towards the rest of us was considerably
improved. He later earned the plaudits of his company as a boxer.

We had been informed that on completing our 12 weeks basic
training we would be heading for Barnard Castle in Durham, there to
join the 1st Battalion which was soon to travel to Malaya to share with
units already there the continuing fight to rid the jungle of Communist
terrorists (CTs). This conflict, known as the Malayan Campaign, had
begun in 1948 and was to continue until 1960, as was National Service.
Prior to our passing-out parade I was informed one day by our senior
training corporal that as one of two current recruits who had excelled in
physical training, I was being offered the opportunity of remaining at
Fulwood Barracks and becoming a physical training instructor. Not

...

The Lancashire Lad – Journal of The Loyal Regiment (North Lancashire)

having regarded myself as a likely candidate for such a role, I was quite taken aback. It was a tough decision, but having made several friends in my platoon and with the exciting prospect of the Malayan jungle with its rich tropical flora and fauna, I declined the offer. The corporal was astounded and asked me to think again, pointing out that should I accept, it would mean instant promotion to lance corporal and regular weekend leave to be with family and friends plus other benefits – a cushy number compared with slogging in the jungle with its snakes, spiders, scorpions and bloodsucking leeches and mosquitoes, not to mention the CTs out to kill you and always the heat and humidity. It was a compelling argument, but his very mention of the jungle fauna and the climate that would produce the exotic vegetation made me even more determined to experience it for myself.

Accordingly, in late October, when my colleagues reported to the 1st Battalion Headquarters at Barnard Castle, I was happy to be with them.

. . .

Most of us were assigned to C Company and with winter fast approaching we undertook a period of further training which, given our destination, included 'jungle' warfare. In the absence of tropical rainforest we spent our time in local woods learning to construct bivouacs with our ponchos and brushwood and following trails, moving as quietly as mice in single file and totally alert. This afforded me plenty of opportunities to observe the local flora and fauna. In my journal I made several lists of plants I saw, among which were two large cushions of houseleek (*Sempervivum tectorum*) growing on the slate roof of an outhouse by the Brown Jug Inn. I noted these while on a route march on 21 November and the following month while on guard duty I saw a female hen harrier, my first, flying along the Tees valley. Its slow wingbeats, long narrow wings and the characteristic white rump were unmistakable.

Jungle training

Our platoon sergeant, 'Tip' O'Reardon, whose bulging eyes and ruddy complexion reminded me of the film actor Robert Newton who played Bill Sykes in the film Oliver Twist, was a stickler for detail. When, on one of his weekly barrack room kit inspections, he found dust on the top of my bedside locker, he placed me on Company Commander's Orders, for which I received three days jankers (punishment). This required me to deliver my locker, in effect a tall metal wardrobe, to the guard room by the camp's main gate, there to be inspected by the duty officer. For three nights I made the journey with the help of a friendly colleague, a fellow Boltonian, Walter (Wally) Chamberlain, who felt sorry for me.

Our jungle training was proceeding apace when suddenly the battalion's well-laid plans were thrown into doubt by the Suez crisis following the decision of Egypt's President Nasser to nationalize the famous canal before blocking it to shipping. British and French troops were being flown in to help secure the situation and our battalion, as part of a rapid reaction brigade, was put on standby to join them. Our jungle greens were to be replaced by khaki drill or 'desert sands' and our training was likewise adapted to a very different mode of warfare, with Sergeant O'Reardon taking us to the rifle ranges for bayonet as well as normal rifle practice. Thoughts of seeing my first wild tropical orchids

. . .

and jungle flora had begun to recede when just as suddenly, with the cessation of hostilities, we were informed that Egypt was out and we would be heading for Malaya as planned with a new date of departure – 22 January 1957.

The next few weeks seemed a blur and then it was Christmas with a spell of embarkation leave and a chance to say our farewells to family and friends. I remember one day in January, accompanied by my friend Clifford, visiting Doug Rugman, now tree and shrub foreman at Bolton Park's nursery in a walled garden near Smithills Hall, followed by a trip to Moss Bank Park and lastly my other mentor, Jack Barber. I promised both Doug and Jack that I would keep them informed of plants seen in Malaya and this I did.

To Malaya

The Regimental Band was assembled on the quayside at Southampton Docks to provide a fitting send off as the 1st Battalion boarded the troop ship SS *Empire Orwell*. We had travelled overnight by train from Barnard Castle and having stood or sat in the corridor for the entire journey I was feeling somewhat frayed. How anyone can sleep while standing as one of my companions did I do not know, but I was considerably relieved and reinvigorated when dawn broke and I could see through the carriage windows green meadows and woods emerging from the gloom. To loud cheers and vigorous waving from the assembled

The troop ship SS *Empire Orwell* departing Southampton with the 1st Battalion The Loyal Regiment (North Lancashire).

...

dignitaries and others on the quayside and with the band playing the regimental march 'The Red, Red Rose', our ship cast off into Southampton Water and headed for the Solent and the open sea. On the way we passed by the Isle of Wight which I had long wished to see ever since, as a boy growing up in Cameron Street, I had been impressed by a friend's stories of his family holidays there. Blessed with my fertile imagination, the very mention of the Isle of Wight suggested to me some sun-soaked tropical paradise a million miles away from my family's regular holiday destination, Blackpool.

Due to the closure of the Suez Canal, our voyage to Malaya would be taking the long route south around the Cape of Good Hope then north-east through the Indian Ocean to Ceylon, now Sri Lanka, and finally east for the Straits of Malacca and to Singapore. It was expected to take six weeks. Despite the army's efforts to keep us all occupied, which included regular physical and weapon training and competitive deck games, there were days when some of my colleagues suffered periods of boredom which not even the on-board evening entertainment, talent and film shows could disperse. For my part, I had decided to keep a journal of all things living seen from the ship which in the early days included a pod of dolphins with gannets in attendance in a feeding frenzy. The arrival of warmer climes, however, brought more interesting sightings of petrels, shearwaters, black-browed albatross, flying fish and a whale.

Having crossed the Bay of Biscay on a particularly rough day which saw many soldiers lying prone on the outside decks feeling unwell, we reached our first port of call, Las Palmas on Grand Canaria. For someone who had never previously visited the Isle of Man, let alone the Canary Islands, this was a magical moment. I had awoken before dawn on the 27th to see the lights of the town through a porthole, twinkling in the gloom, and continued watching as the sun gradually rose to reveal craggy, volcanic mountains, their peaks wrapped in cloud. We were allowed off the ship at 10am and Wally (Walter Chamberlain) and I lost no time in hurrying along a very long causeway into the dock area. We saw many houses with cool entrance halls where selections of pot plants flourished, large-flowered *Hibiscus rosa-sinensis* hybrids, pelargoniums

...

and powder-blue *Plumbago auriculata* among them. It was now quite hot and the pale walls reflected the blinding light, except where they were covered with red and pink rambler roses and blue-trumpeted morning glory (*Ipomoea purpurea*).

Several times in the narrow streets we heard caged canaries singing their hearts out and everywhere children pestered us for cigarettes. It took ages for us to reach the main promenade and a tempting stretch of beach, only to turn around and head back to the ship in time for a mid-afternoon departure. Having explored the extraordinary Canary Island flora in recent years and seen wild canaries (*Serinus canaria*) there, it is probably as well that I was ignorant of what I might have seen then had there been the time and opportunity.

The next few days brought further sightings of birds, sharks and two species of flying fish, of which there are said to be 64. One of these was smaller than the other, around 6–8in (15–20cm) long, pale blue above and white beneath, with almost transparent pectoral fins held horizontally like wings and with their tails down-curved. On leaping out of the sea they then glided just above the water surface, sometimes for 328ft (100m) or more before, fins folded over their back, they achieved re-entry with a splash. The larger species, up to 12in (30cm) long or more, was a dark brown colour above. We continued to see both kinds gliding across or into the wind, sometimes in shoals of 20–30.

Equator

At 10 am on 2 February we crossed the Equator, the sun directly above us as we all took part in the traditional crossing of the line ceremony with duckings in the pool, watched over by a green-bearded King Neptune. Six days later we arrived at Cape Town for what we had been promised would be a special day ashore and so it proved. We were all assembled on the upper decks to see the famous Table Mountain, its long, level summit obscured by a layer of fleecy white cloud, the 'tablecloth', and having had an early breakfast we were raring to go and make the most of our seven-hour shore leave. The city's mayor had arranged a free 75 mile (120km) tour by bus and together with Wally and another friend I signed on for this.

. . .

LEFT For most of us it was a first crossing of the Equator, with a certificate to prove it.

ABOVE *Erica cerinthoides* growing on a hillside below Table Mountain, Cape Town, S. Africa.

On leaving the quayside, our bus drove out of the city through residential areas where gardens were overflowing with colourful plants, many of which were quite new to me. Familiar plants such as sunflowers, nasturtiums (*Tropaeolum majus*) and large bushy pelargoniums grew with *Tagetes*, *Nicotiana* and multi-coloured *Canna* hybrids to create brilliant tapestries, while sky-blue morning glory (*Ipomoea purpurea*) was as common here as our native hedge bindweed (*Calystegia sepium*) back home. Both belong to the same family, Convolvulaceae, and I have often wondered whether British gardeners would regard the bindweed with such loathing if its flowers were blue rather than white.

At one point on the tour, in a wild mountainous landscape, we were invited to disembark for 10 minutes. It was just the opportunity I was hoping for and while the others took in the view I quickly headed for a nearby slope to look at the native flora. To my surprise and joy it contained several plants I knew well enough from British gardens, such as *Kniphofia uvaria* (red hot poker), *Agapanthus africanus* and *Lobelia erinus*, the ubiquitous blue lobelia, untold numbers of which I recalled

. . .

having planted on graves in Bolton's Heaton Cemetery as well as in bedding displays, hanging baskets and window boxes. To see such familiar garden plants in the wild where they choose to grow, as against where we as gardeners want them to grow, was for me a salutary and exciting experience. These were the first non-British natives I had ever seen growing in their country of origin. I was equally thrilled to find the red-flowered *Erica cerinthoides* and bushy, pink-flowered *Pelargonium capitatum*, neither of which I had seen before. I could have lingered here for the rest of the day but when called for the third time I reluctantly returned to the bus and yes, I was the last to board. Our tour ended with an amazing barbecue in the grounds of a large estate.

Two days later we were steaming into Durban, where the temperature and humidity were even higher than in Cape Town. We had gathered on the upper deck to watch our arrival when we noticed a woman dressed all in white with a broad-brimmed red hat standing at the end of a long jetty known locally as The Point. As we came within earshot we could hear her singing patriotic and sentimental songs using a megaphone. 'Rule Britannia', 'Jerusalem' and 'There'll Always Be an England' were just three such in her repertoire. We were informed by the ship's captain that she was Mrs Perla Siedle Gibson, a native of Durban, who used to sing troopships in and out of the harbour during and after the Second World War. She was fondly remembered by thousands of older servicemen as the 'Lady in White' and she had been determined to welcome us as in the old days. Ours, apparently, was the first troopship to visit in a very long time.

Due to a spell as ship's guard duty on the officer's gangplank, I was left with only half our allotted time of 7½ hours shore leave and as soon as I was relieved I lost no time in catching a bus to the Durban Botanic Gardens. Once inside I then devised a plan of action. There were exotic plants new to me in every direction, plus Indian mynah birds, cattle egrets and a fiscal shrike with black and white plumage, a long tail and a harsh jay-like call. As time was limited I decided to move briskly around the garden, stopping for a closer look only when some unusual or spectacular plants caught my eye. I made several stops, including one at the garden office where a member of the staff kindly located for me

. . .

an old garden catalogue, the last one, for which I thanked him before hurrying away to locate and visit the Durban Museum. Here, I spent some time in the bird galleries checking out those species I had seen at sea over the past week or so. I then asked an attendant if I might speak to the curator and that is how I came to meet Mr P.A. Clancey, the director, who on hearing that I came from Bolton asked if I knew Alfred Hazelwood, my old mentor and curator at the Bolton Museum.

Alfred Hazelwood, in Clancey's estimation, was one of the best in the business. He told me how, some years previously, he too had first visited the Durban Museum as a National Service man and also again later as a member of an expedition from the British Museum. Never in his wildest dreams had he thought that one day he would be its Director. We continued talking and examining bird skins for some time until, realizing the lateness of the day, I thanked him for his help and advice before excusing myself. Before I left he gave me a copy of *A Preliminary List of the Birds of Natal and Zululand*, which he had prepared for publication in 1953.

The Lady in White, as expected, was again in her customary position at the end of the jetty as we left the harbour, delivering a heart-rending farewell with a stirring rendition of 'Land of Hope and Glory'. The following day, 15 February, we passed the volcanic island of Réunion, her highest mountain being the Piton des Neiges at 10,070ft (3071m). The following evening, in the darkness on our starboard side we could just make out the lights of Port Louis on the island of Mauritius, once the home of the now extinct dodo.

We reached Colombo on the island of Sri Lanka on 21 February and here we spent just a few hours ashore, taking in the exotic sights and activities including snake-charmers and the fakirs on their beds of nails. If I had then but known about it and had both the time and the means I would have headed for the mountains in the hope of finding the striking crimson-flowered *Rhododendron arboreum* subsp. *zeylanicum*, a localized endemic tree. I was reminded of this occasion 46 years later in 2002, when I eventually saw a magnificent example of this rhododendron growing in the gardens at Arduaine on Scotland's west coast. It was well worth the wait.

...

Arrival in Singapore

On 24 February the *Empire Orwell* rounded the northern tip of the island of Sumatra and headed south through the Straits of Malacca. We passed many smaller islands, most of which were jungle-clad and quite hilly. At one point the ship moved through large scattered populations of jellyfish and later, a party of 20 frigate birds with their characteristic long tails came skimming over the water, occasionally congregating in a quarrelsome cluster before moving on. Their dark head and upperparts contrasted most strikingly with their white belly and lower breast. Towards the end of the day we reached our final destination, Singapore, where a Gurkha pipe band on the quayside provided a welcoming sight and sound while a brahminy kite with its unmistakable white head and breast and contrasting rich chestnut lower body provided an exciting new bird for me, my first in Malaya. It had been a long but for me an exciting voyage of discovery, far preferable in many ways to today's faster, more direct travel by air. Whatever else awaited us in the coming months, I was determined to take every opportunity to observe and record the natural history of the rainforest – plants, birds, mammals, insects and, yes, snakes, spiders and leeches too.

Before being assigned to our operational area, our battalion was to undergo a six-week period of jungle training, this time in real jungle, or correctly tropical rainforest. Our base during this time was Nyassa Camp, across the causeway from Singapore Island in Malaya's southernmost state of Johor. Having crossed the causeway in trucks, we stopped at a military depot where we were issued with 303 Lee Enfield rifles and ammunition before continuing our journey. The jungle training school at Nyassa Camp near Kota Tinga was situated on sloping ground above a sluggish stream. We were accommodated in corrugated tin huts which had been erected in terraced rows, known to some of us as Silver City.

Once settled into C Company lines, I was a member of 7 Platoon, we were familiarized with what would become our daily routine: Reveille (wake-up call on a bugle at 7am) followed later by a second bugle call to breakfast. We then had a period to prepare ourselves for whatever training programme had been arranged for the day. This was

. . .

preceded by another bugle sounding 'paludrine parade', when we all had to line up outside our huts to receive the anti-malarial tablet paludrine, placed on our tongue by a corporal overseen by a sergeant. The tablet did not taste very nice and the temptation to dispose of it was such that we had to be seen to have swallowed it. Should we not take the medicine regularly the consequence was the possibility of suffering one of the world's most common and debilitating diseases. I had vivid memories of seeing, when I was a boy, my brother, recently returned from service in India, sweating and shivering uncontrollably with a high temperature and fever during several nights he spent at home with us. There is no way I would not swallow that tablet and yet, there came a day when I actually missed a paludrine parade.

From our camp on the hillside I could see the jungle edge on the other side of the stream and I found myself pondering what strange flora and wildlife it might contain. I had observed Gurkha soldiers from a nearby camp catching catfish up to 12in (30cm) long by hand in its muddy waters and I eventually worked out a plan of action which, if I skipped breakfast, would give me sufficient time to descend the slope to explore at least the nearest area of jungle before returning in time for the all-important paludrine parade. On the day, having informed some of my mates of my intention, I slipped away and hurried down to the stream, crossing to the other side by a plank bridge. The jungle here was not of a primary nature but secondary growth resulting from the old forest having been cleared. It was still jungle, however, with scattered trees of medium size and a wealth of dense mixed scrub and tropical creepers.

Sunbirds and flowerpeckers
I soon began collecting unfamiliar plants and then, observing that most bird activity appeared to be in the canopy above, I placed my bundle of plants at the base of the nearest tree, climbed its trunk to a convenient branch and settled myself to see what might come my way. I didn't have long to wait before a most colourful little bird arrived. It was olive green above, yellow beneath, with a dark metallic blue throat and a slender curved beak. With the aid of an illustrated book I

. . .

subsequently acquired, I identified it later as a yellow-bellied sunbird. This was only the beginning and soon after my tree was visited by a crimson-breasted flowerpecker, a yellow-vented bulbul with a song similar to that of a song thrush and a long-tailed tailorbird whose nest is a pouch made by 'stitching' one or more large leaves together. I was really beginning to enjoy myself when I had a sudden thought. Was that a bugle call I heard a while ago? I looked at my watch and realized I had missed paludrine parade.

Sliding down the tree and grabbing my plant specimens, now somewhat wilted, I raced back to the camp and C Company lines, where I was informed by my mates that Company Sergeant-Major Walsh wanted to see me. Known as 'Gripper' Walsh, he was a tough professional of the old school and was feared as much as admired by the new recruits. Fearing the worst, I immediately headed for the Company Office to face the music. I was placed on Company Commander's Orders and my punishment (jankers) devised by Gripper, once he had listened to the reasons for my absence, was to clean out the deep monsoon ditches through C Company lines which during the monsoon season channelled the raging water down the hillside to the stream. During the dry season, however, these ditches became choked with weeds harbouring bugs and beetles and sometimes snakes or worse. 'Given your interest in wildlife,' Gripper declared, 'this should be right up your street.' It was fair comment and his smile (or was it a sneer?) as he said it told me that I was already seen as a bit of an oddball. In the event it took several hours of my free time clearing the ditches and the only interesting thing I discovered was a green stick insect! If this incident taught me anything it was to keep a sharp ear open to the various bugle calls and their messages. Like many an old soldier, I still remember them today and, for that matter, my army number – 23330054.

Not long after our arrival at Nyassa camp we were assigned our personal firearms which would be our responsibility for the duration of our active service in Malaya. Our platoon paraded outside the hut while our sergeant read out the names and the weapons we had been assigned. Most of my colleagues were issued with the recently delivered Belgian

...

On patrol with my Bren gun in an area of cultivated ground which included bananas.

FN rifles and I expected the same. To my complete surprise, when my name was called I had been assigned a Bren gun or LMG (light machine gun). This was a heavier weapon which was normally fired from a lying position, the body of the gun supported on a pair of sturdy metal legs which could be folded beneath the gun when in transit. Not only that, it came with large, bulkier, curved magazines which, when filled with ammunition, added considerably to the total weight. Two other Bren guns were issued, both to taller, sturdier individuals while I was of slighter build, which puzzled the rest of my colleagues. There must have been a mistake, I thought, but when I looked quizzically at the sergeant he just shrugged!

Gradually I became used to carrying the Bren gun on patrols, though on more protracted operations, especially in primary forest in mountainous or swampy terrain, it could make life a little more difficult. Crawling under or over fallen trees or pushing through spine-clad palms or bamboos, not to mention twining vines and creepers, had a cumulative effect on energy, especially in hot, humid conditions. Had it not been for the wealth of wildlife and plants I saw on the trails the days would have seemed even longer. As it was, I always looked forward to the night's camp when I could relieve myself of the weight for several hours. However, carrying a Bren gun did have one bonus apart from its potential for rapid fire when needed: I was provided with two large ammunition pouches to carry the curved magazines.

...

These would normally be clipped on to my belt but from early on I found that by carrying the magazines in my large trouser pockets, one on each leg, I could free up the pouches for specimens of plants, bugs and even snakes collected on the trail.

Jungle patrols

Over the next few weeks we spent an increasing amount of time in the jungle, which we soldiers referred to as the 'ulu', either on one-day patrols or for longer periods with overnight camps. It was on one of these patrols that I found my first wild pitcher plant, *Nepenthes gracilis* – several specimens with long, sprawling stems covering a steep slope in shade. I had seen these carnivorous plants in greenhouse cultivation back home, but it gave me a special pleasure to see them in their native habitat. Some of the leaf appendages were supplied with typical green, red-streaked, funnel-shaped 'pitchers', in one of which I discovered a tiny red crab spider plus the debris of tiny, partly digested insects including an ant. A day or two later I encountered another species, *N. ampullaria*, whose tubby green, occasionally red-tinted, basal pitchers formed dense clusters at ground level.

Of the new birds I was encountering on a daily basis, one which particularly pleased me was a red jungle fowl, the evolutionary ancestor of all domestic poultry. A single cock bird resplendent in its iridescent black and flame-coloured plumage appeared to us unexpectedly one day while we were enjoying a quiet break on a jungle trail. It was accompanied by several hens.

Before continuing with this account I should remind the reader of the conditions in which jungle or evergreen tropical rainforest flourishes, at least in Malaya (now known as Peninsular Malaysia), which

Nepenthes gracilis, my first wild pitcher plant. The bladders are specialized appendages to the leaf tips and a temptation to inquisitive insects.

Drawing and describing *Nepenthes gracilis* in my journal in Nyassa camp.

. . .

ABOVE My journal entries covered everything from plants, insects and beetles to birds, snakes and mammals.

BELOW LEFT *Platycerium coronarium*, a stag's horn fern shown here in the Singapore Botanic Garden, was common in jungle and rubber plantations in the crotches of trees.

BELOW RIGHT *Asplenium nidus* (bird's nest fern) often shared the same trees as stag's horn fern, both eventually capable of making magnificent clumps.

. . .

lies between latitudes 1° and 7° North. The climate boasts a high rainfall with frequent heavy showers. Average humidity is high and daily temperatures in the lowlands are 82–95°F (28–35°C) while in the highlands the average is around 18°F (10°C) lower.

It wasn't long before the wildlife described to me by my training corporal in Preston as a good reason not to be in the jungle began to reveal itself, much to my delight. To my fellow soldiers, any insect that crawled was an 'urby-clurby' and anything that flew an 'eeby-jeeby'. For them it was a precise, simple nomenclature covering creatures that they perceived as potentially annoying if not dangerous. Observing me collecting bugs, not to mention plants, as I did most days in the jungle never failed to amaze them. Lest it be thought that my mind and attention was totally engaged in these 'distractions', be assured that I was never at any time negligent of my duties nor my priorities as a member of my platoon and my activities were never questioned by my superiors who, it later emerged, were more than tolerant and not a little amused by them. On one occasion my platoon commander asked if he could have loan of one of my journals in order to share the information I had gleaned with his fellow officers. It was returned shortly afterwards with an encouraging request to keep it up; it seemed they were rather pleased to have such a character in their midst.

Singapore Botanical Gardens

In March, a weekend leave in Singapore gave me the opportunity to visit the famous Botanical Gardens, which had been developed from an experimental spice plot established in 1819 by Singapore's founder, Sir Thomas Stamford Raffles. On this occasion I had time only for a brief reconnaissance of the trees, especially the palm collection, but was so impressed that I determined to return as soon as possible. I also visited the Raffles Museum, to which I had already sent a package of dried plant specimens collected in the vicinity of Nyassa Camp. On making enquiries, I was told that as the Museum had no botany department the specimens had been forwarded to the Botanic Gardens. On my return to Nyassa Camp I found a letter awaiting me from the Singapore Botanic Gardens containing a list of names of these specimens. It was

...

an extensive list which included *Melastoma malabathricum*, a common shrub with attractive mauve-pink flowers known as the Straits rhododendron, though it is in no way related to the rhododendrons grown in British gardens.

A small specimen of a large fern I sent to them together with a sketch and description was identified as stag's horn fern (*Platycerium coronarium*), a common epiphytic fern of jungle habitats where it forms magnificent eye-catching clumps in the crotches of a variety of trees. Seeing it in its native habitat and in Singapore gardens, I was reminded of those I had first seen and tended to in the Stove House (hot house) in the Central Nursery at Moss Bank Park. Another epiphytic tropical fern, equally striking in its size and aspect, was *Asplenium nidus*, the bird's nest fern, so called for the nest-like centre to the rosettes of deep, shining green, strap-shaped fronds. I saw it wild on many occasions, sometimes in old rubber plantations, and occasionally associated with the stag's horn fern, whose pendulous branching grey or silvery-powdered fronds provided a striking contrast.

I shall never forget my first overnight camp in the jungle. Actually, it was for three nights. Our platoon had risen before dawn for an early breakfast then, shouldering our packs containing clothes and rations and carrying our weapons, we had boarded 3-ton Bedford army trucks to take us to the jungle edge in a hilly region some distance from camp. On arrival we lost no time in heading single file into the trees which was like walking into a black hole, so dense was the vegetation. Once inside we became aware of many strange sounds, mostly those made by cicadas and other insects. One in particular reminded me of the honking of an old-fashioned bus, while another sounded like a referee's whistle. We travelled without talking, following our leading scout and guide. Although I could see little to begin with, we were following what appeared to be a well-worn track on relatively level ground before heading uphill towards a ridge. It was a new and exciting experience travelling at an easy pace while little by little the morning light began to filter through the canopy above, revealing increasing details of tree and leaf. Later, as the sun gained height it pierced the high canopy in places with a display of needled brilliance.

. . .

Jungle camp

Eventually, towards the end of the morning, we descended into a valley where a suitable site for our base camp was chosen on a slope close to a fresh water source, in this case a small but swift running river. Once it was confirmed by our platoon officer, standing in what would be the centre of the camp, the rest of the platoon moved forward to form a circle around him. The first task was to construct a perimeter vine as a handrail around our position, using lengths of woody climbers (lianas) which are readily available in the jungle. The perimeter vine needed to be securely fixed as it defined our territory which, though obvious enough in daylight, would be virtually invisible at night. Our next job was to construct our basha (bivouac) using our ponchos as roof and groundsheet, plus leafy brushwood and vines to provide both shelter and camouflage. We worked in pairs, each pair responsible for their shared basha and their section of the perimeter vine.

Two other vine lines were fixed, one leading down to the fresh water source and the other to the latrine, which was a hole dug in the jungle floor. During the day, both these positions were assigned a sentry in case of danger from CTs or wild animals, including pythons, one of which was seen close to another, later camp. At night a single guard took up his position in the centre of the camp close to the platoon officer's basha. We all took our turn in providing the two-hour guard shift and on completing your shift it was your responsibility to alert the next guard in turn as quickly and as quietly as possible. It was then that we came to understand the importance of the perimeter vine as in the inky darkness, its reassuring touch was your only connection with your basha. Only once, on a later training camp, did a broken section of vine cause a problem when a night guard returning to his basha walked out of the camp into the jungle. The next man on guard duty luckily was lying awake and waiting to be given the okay. Once he discovered that the man he was to replace was missing, the platoon officer was informed. They examined the perimeter vine, discovered the broken section and realized what had happened. They could neither see nor hear any sign of activity and as they dared not call out for fear of alerting unwelcome visitors we spent an anxious few hours waiting

...

A beautiful orchid, *Vanda hookeriana* (now *Papilionanthe hookeriana*) we saw from our train growing in swamps around Batu Gajah in Perak.

for daylight when, calm as you please, the missing guard strolled into camp none the worse for his experience. Following training instructions, once he had realized his predicament he simply settled down until he could see to retrace his steps.

It was in this camp, while on sentry duty at our water point, that I observed a most fascinating battle between two species of ants. One of them, which I took to be the resident species, had a golden-brown abdomen and they appeared to be busy foraging in the leaf litter when a party of much larger black ants with a brick-red abdomen appeared on the scene. They quickly became engaged in a fierce struggle. At one point I noticed that some individuals of the former species, positioned on leaves overlooking the battle scene, were tapping the leaf surface rapidly with their abdomens, making a clearly audible sound. I did not see the outcome of the struggle as my replacement arrived at the height of the conflict.

Ants of many species were everywhere, especially in the jungle, but the ones we came to fear most were the tailor ants whose nests were made by 'stitching' together two or more large leaves of a bush or tree to make a protective green cocoon. It was easy to brush by one of these nests by accident, especially, as I once found to my cost, in the dark when moving into an ambush position. In this instance an added distraction was that we were moving calf-deep in a swamp. I realized what I had done when the ants began pouring out of their nest on to my arm and neck, their bite was almost as painful as a bee sting.

It was in or around that first camp that I also met with my first fireflies, scorpions, orchids and giant centipedes, one of which crawled across a colleague's exposed chest at night leaving an angry red mark. Curious too were the larvae of a kind of beetle known as trilobite larvae

. . .

from their slight resemblance to those extinct crustaceans. I sent a specimen of this to Mr M.W. Tweedie, director of the Raffles Museum, who replied 'These larvae appear to be females which probably never complete their life-cycle and must breed in the larval form. The males (presumably normal beetles) appear to be unknown.'

Towards the end of April, our jungle training course was completed, though we would be continuing to learn from new experiences for the rest of our time in Malaya. The 1st Battalion now transferred by train to its operational area in the state of Perak in the northwest, where all bar two companies settled into their new headquarters at Colombo Camp in Ipoh, the state capital, while the A and C companies were hived off to Siputeh Camp near the village of that name some 12 miles (19km) from Ipoh. During the train journey north, I had observed the landscape changing and becoming more mountainous as we approached Perak. A four-hour stop at Kuala Lumpur, the country's capital, had allowed us a tour around the city, including the amazing Raj-style architecture of the railway station where I spotted my first Java sparrows in the rafters.

Just before we arrived in Ipoh, at Batu Gajah, the railway had passed through swamp country where a tall orchid with conspicuous purple and mauve flowers caught my eye. It seemed quite common on both sides of the track and I later saw it again elsewhere in the Ipoh area, enabling me to identify it as *Vanda hookeriana*, the so-called Kinta weed, referring to its common occurrence in the Kinta valley area of Perak. This species, native to Malaysia and North Sumatra, along with *V. teres* from Thailand, Burma and the Himalayan foothills, is a parent of Singapore's national flower, *Vanda* 'Miss Joaquim', a natural hybrid which appeared in the Singapore garden of Miss Agnes Joaquim in 1893 and was subsequently grown extensively for cut flowers, especially in Hawaii. Both of these species and their hybrid are now classified in the genus *Papilionanthe*.

Deep jungle

When I first saw it, Siputeh Camp reminded me of one of the German concentration camps I had seen in Second World War films. It was surrounded by a high wire perimeter fence, while our accommodation

...

consisted of brick-based wooden huts with sloping corrugated tin roofs. The jungle here had long since been cleared and the camp sat in a relatively open landscape of rubber plantations, tin mine workings (tailings) and a scattering of cultivated crops which made it difficult to approach, certainly in daylight, without being spotted by those on sentry duty. Once we had settled in, however, the camp's austere appearance and sense of isolation were soon forgotten and life for us continued as before, except that we were now fully engaged in the serious business of finding and dealing with the CTs. Over the following months much of our time was spent on local patrols, occasional ambushes and more extended operations in deep jungle. To assist us in our efforts, we were now joined by a unit of Iban tribesmen from the Sarawak Rangers. To say they proved helpful in the success of our activities would be putting it mildly. Native to the Bornean jungles, they were natural trackers and hunters and their jungle awareness in terms of sight, hearing and sense of smell and taste were second to none. I marvelled at their ability to determine, from the careful examination of a jungle track and its surrounds, whether a person or persons had recently passed that way and if so approximately when and whether or not they had been travelling light or carrying heavy packs.

My platoon had two Ibans, Naga and Achan, assigned to it and on those jungle operations in which I was involved one of them would follow close behind the lead scout, who would be armed with a shotgun. Next in line would be the patrol leader followed by the Bren gunner (me), which allowed me to observe and hopefully learn from the Ibans' jungle skills. On one occasion when following a jungle trail our lead scout halted, holding his hand up to signal caution. He had seen, heard or sensed a potential problem or threat. The rest of us crouched and remained quiet and alert, ready to act. Meanwhile, Naga began peeling the loose bark from the stem of a dead tree close to the trail, revealing a scurrying mass of black beetles which he proceeded to scoop up and eat, offering to share them with me, which I declined.

On another occasion while following a trail we heard the sound of something or someone crashing through the jungle close by and then a large lizard, a water monitor (*Varanus salvator*), emerged onto the track

. . .

LEFT Ibans of the Sarawak Rangers at Siputeh Camp including (centre) Sebat and Jimun, the two Chief Ibans of all Borneo.

BELOW 7 Platoon C. Company assembled in Siputeh Camp, October 1957. I am in the back row fifth from right. Our two Iban trackers are Achan (front row far left) and Naga (far right) of the Sarawak Rangers.

ahead and set off with a waddling gait, only to be pursued by Naga, who brought it down with one swipe of his parang (long-bladed knife). It all happened so quickly that the rest of us could only stare in amazement. That evening the monitor, which measured 5ft 9in (175cm) from nose to tail tip, was prepared and cooked for supper by the Ibans, who saw it as an unexpected and welcome addition to their usual fare. Its meat was not unlike that of a chicken.

We saw several different lizards while in Malaya, but the one that most intrigued and entertained us was the so-called flying dragon (*Draco volans*), which by means of the loose folds of skin between the front and back legs and supported by elongated ribs becomes taut on

...

take-off, allowing it to glide for some distance from a high point on a tree trunk to the base of another, scampering upwards, especially when pursued, to a new position ready to do the same again. More familiar and widespread was the house gecko, or 'chit-chat' as we called it, which was to be seen in dwellings in town and country clinging to walls, ceilings and other surfaces by means of the sucker pads on its toes. These creatures could move quickly in pursuit of a prey, usually a fly or moth, or when protecting their territory and were tolerated and even welcomed in our huts, where they helped to control insect pests as well as amusing us by their antics.

It was in the Malayan jungles that I first encountered leeches and they were just one of the many disagreeable creatures that we had to deal with. I was particularly impressed by their doggedness in pursuing a prey, me and my blood in one case. I had discovered one on my hand while our section was taking a brief respite. I managed to flick it off and it landed in the leaf litter about 2ft (60cm) away. It immediately recovered and set off in looping movements in my direction and at a surprising speed. When it reached my boot it reared up, seeking to attach itself. I then coaxed it onto a leaf which I tossed a good 4ft (1.2m) away. Again it recovered and stretched itself upward then froze for a second or two before moving its body back and forth as if trying to locate a movement or scent. Failing in this, it then moved away and was gone. In wet weather it was impossible to keep leeches at bay and they had the uncanny knack of exploiting the tiniest of gaps in boots or jungle greens to reach your flesh.

Orchids and pitcher plants

In June 1957 I was allowed a week's leave and together with several others from our camp including my friend Wally, who had now become a medical orderly and lance corporal, I found myself heading for the island of Penang in the north-west of the country off the coast of Kedah state, of which the northern territory, like that of Perak, borders with Thailand. Reached by train from Ipoh and then by ferry to its capital Georgetown, Penang offered soldiers a relatively quiet and safe location in which to relax and recover from jungle activities and the Sandycroft

...

Leave Centre where we stayed, although plain and simple, was a pleasant change from Siputeh Camp.

Most of my colleagues were only too happy to spend their days swimming or sun-bathing on the sandy beach, but as soon as the opportunity arose I headed for the local Botanic Gardens, also known as the Waterfall Gardens, situated some 5 miles (8km) out of Georgetown. There I made the acquaintance of the staff, who were most welcoming and helpful. The Gardens were established in 1884 and their first superintendent was Charles Curtis, who had previously been employed as a plant collector for the famous nursery firm James Veitch & Sons of Chelsea. It was Curtis who laid out the Botanic Gardens and, given his background and his sharp eye for an ornamental plant, especially an orchid, he would have been aware of Penang's own special lady's-slipper orchid, *Paphiopedilum barbatum*, which adorns the front cover of a Guide to

A 1947 copy of the Penang Botanic Gardens Guide, depicting the once locally common lady's-slipper orchid (*Paphiopedilum barbatum*) on its cover.

the gardens published in 1947, a copy of which was given me on my visit. First found on Gunong Ledang (Mt Ophir) in Johor in 1838 by Hugh Cumming, who was then employed by another famous English nursery, Messrs Loddiges of Hackney, the lady's-slipper orchid (*P. barbatum*) has a wide though scattered distribution through Peninsular Malaysia including Penang and in North Sumatra.

I was determined to see this orchid for myself, so I took a bus tour around the island the next day, stopping off briefly to visit the Snake Temple, not for the faint-hearted as its central space is writhing with snakes, mostly Wagler's pit vipers. Later, in the mountains, we were allowed an hour's interlude to wander around and enjoy the view. Forsaking this, I quickly headed towards a large stream tumbling down a rocky gully. I had descended only a short way when to my pleasure and surprise I found the slipper orchid flowering in scattered clumps among the damp, mossy rocks in light shade. Naturally, I was elated, but more was to come. In grassy places there grew a second orchid, *Arundina graminifolia*, the so-called bamboo orchid, with its long,

...

TOP I saw
*Paphiopedilum
barbatum* wild in the
mountains, including
Penang Hill.

ABOVE On Penang
Hill and elsewhere I
found *Nepenthes
albomarginata* with its
characteristic white
band below the mouth
of the pitcher.

grass-like leaves and tall spikes of large mauve and magenta blooms. The bit was now firmly between my teeth and leaving the gully I wandered towards the edge of a rubber plantation where, perched in the crotch of an older tree, I spied a large clump of a third orchid, *Cymbidium finlaysonianum*. To round off this dream come true, I saw on a wet roadside embankment the sprawling growth of a large pitcher plant, *Nepenthes albomarginata*, its funnel-shaped, dark reddish-purple upper pitchers sporting a characteristic white band around the outside of the mouth. It was a very happy man who eventually returned to the Sandycroft Leave Centre and that night I celebrated my day of good fortune in the bar with cold Tiger beers all round.

The next day I took the funicular railway up Penang Hill, a height of 735m (2,411ft), which allowed me the luxury of botanizing without however being able to photograph the individual plants I observed in the jungle on either side. I did however see more lady's slipper orchids as well as the beautiful pitcher plant *Nepenthes albomarginata* seen the previous day. On the summit I found many other plants including *Tridax procumbens* with long-stalked daisy flowers, the dark green *Eryngium foetidum* and a most delicately attractive fern, *Sphenomeris chinensis*.

On our final day in Penang I again visited the Botanic Gardens, where a member of staff gave me a tour of the plant collections which I thoroughly enjoyed. The one plant I shall always remember, however, is the giant epiphytic orchid with an equally imposing name, *Grammatophyllum speciosum* a huge plant which was growing in the low crotch of a large, spreading rain tree (*Samanea saman*). It is native to Malaysia and undisturbed specimens can

...

live to a ripe old age with fleshy stems (pseudobulbs) up to 8ft (2.5m) or more long almost pendant under the weight of foliage; in season, flowering stems up to 10ft (3m) long sport yellow blooms with orange-brown spots. I later saw another large specimen of this orchid in the Singapore Botanic Gardens.

That evening, Wally and I and some of our colleagues from C Company took a last walk along the shore below the Leave Centre where we were amused to see an abundance of small sand crabs racing across the beach at a remarkable speed, quickly disappearing down holes in the wet sand whenever we approached too closely. More remarkable by far were the stranded bodies of horseshoe crabs (*Tachypleus gigas*) whose impressive helmeted carapace and rapier-like projecting tail reminded us of some extinct sea creature. All were lying on their backs and the few that we righted soon turned onto their backs again.

Grammatophyllum speciosum, the giant Malayan orchid, growing in the crotch of a rain tree in the Botanic Gardens.

The flowers of *Grammatophyllum speciosum* are borne in massive inflorescences as much as 10ft (3m) long on mature plants.

. . .

Collecting plant specimens

On returning to Siputeh Camp I found a package from Mr H.M. Burkhill, director of the Singapore Botanic Gardens, returning a batch of dried plant specimens I had sent them. All had been named. During a second trip to Singapore as a member of a special guard unit I had taken the opportunity to visit the Botanic Gardens, where I had made myself known to Mr Burkhill. He was intrigued by a serving soldier taking the trouble to collect specimens and he encouraged me to continue doing so. He was especially interested in plants collected in the more remote deep jungle locations I sometimes travelled in. Having established contact and good relations with both the Botanic Gardens and the Raffles Museum, plus plant specimens sent via Vicar Shaw to Kew and the British Museum (Natural History), my passion for plants and natural history would be fuelled for the rest of my time in Malaya.

But what did my fellow soldiers think of this? To begin with, my regular pressing of plant specimens between sheets of newspaper placed on a firm base beneath my mattress was a source of puzzlement and amazement. Men don't do that, do they, especially soldiers? Gradually their attitude changed and having noted that I sent the dried plants and dead insects, spiders, snakes and so forth to scientific institutions they concluded that I was being paid for my trouble. Eventually, they came to accept that I simply enjoyed doing it. It was plain to see my excitement when opening the letters I received in reply and in a way they found it a welcome distraction from the continuing business in the jungle. Word spread and it was not long before I had lots of helpers bringing me items of interest. An Indian cobra run over by a truck, an angry buzzing hornet in a cigarette tin and a bird-eating spider were just three of the specials that were given me and the donors were just as interested in the identities and stories of their collections as I was.

One Sunday in October that year something happened which set me on an unexpected path. We had recently returned from an extended period in the jungle and were enjoying a relaxing day off. I was busy writing my journal when I heard the sound of boots marching purposefully through our barrack room, stopping at the foot of my bed. On looking up I saw newly promoted Company Sergeant Major Tetlow

. . .

and he was looking expectantly at me. I rose to my feet in anticipation of bad news and he addressed me thus:

'Lancaster, you know that our Company Clerk Private Hindle has just returned home on demob?'

'Yes, Sergeant Major,' I replied, 'I went to his demob party last week.'

'Right,' he continued, 'then what does that tell you?' I thought for a moment before replying 'That we need a replacement?'

'Good thinking,' he said. There was a short pause before he announced, 'You are his replacement.'

I swallowed hard as the implications of this sank in before protesting, 'But I have never worked in an office in my life.'

'That may be,' he replied 'but you write, don't you? You keep journals and notes and you send letters to Singapore.'

'Yes,' I weakly replied.

'Then you are our new Company Clerk and you will report for duty at 8 o'clock in the morning.'

Thus began yet another new chapter in my life. I had a desk in the Company Office, filing cabinets and a typewriter which I learned to use with two fingers. In time I settled into the office routine, which had certain advantages in that I could now type my letters to Singapore and

Company Sergeant Major Tetlow of C Company, who recruited me as Company Secretary.

Kew and I became a dab-hand at lists. As for further collecting, I would no longer be going on patrols, especially in the jungle, but any worries I might have had about being starved of specimens soon faded as word having got around, my mates and not just those in my platoon redoubled their efforts in collecting things they thought might interest me. These included such strange items as a rhinoceros beetle, assorted scorpions and an Atlas moth with a wing span of 9in (23cm). As a result, letters and packages to Singapore and elsewhere continued unabated.

. . .

Cameron Highlands

I had filled my journals with lists and descriptions of plants collected and pressed and notes on insects, reptiles, amphibians and birds seen on patrols through cultivated areas, rubber estates and tin mine spoil heaps (tailings), and on jungle operations. There were also more distant locations I was lucky enough to visit, such as the Cameron Highlands, a range of mountains straddling the borders of north-west Pahang with Perak and south-west Kelantan. Best known for the hill station at Tanah Rata some 56 miles (90km) distance by road from Ipoh, these mountains visible from our camp were mostly covered in prime forest, enjoying a tropical highland climate with a mean temperature of 64°F (18°C) and an annual rainfall of around 106in (2700mm). They were also famed for their rich flora and fauna, which is why I longed for the opportunity to see it for myself.

The village of Tanah Rata had a single main street, while nearby was a Royal Army Signals Company base and hospital facilities for those convalescing from injuries or illness who benefited from the cooler climate and the cleaner air. Our battalion padre, the Reverend T.M. Quigley, was required to visit the military base every so often to conduct church services and I was surprised when, aware of my interest in natural history, he asked if I would like to accompany him for a weekend, along with my pal Wally. Accordingly, at the end of November 1957 we three were driven to the small town of Tapah from where a narrow road wound its way in snake-like coils into the mountains and eventually to Tanah Rata, where we were accommodated for two nights in the RASC base. Our journey along the winding road was the most exciting and exhausting I had ever experienced due to the wealth of vegetation and the changes in its composition the higher we climbed. There were changes, too, in the temperature and we donned light sweaters to combat the unfamiliar cool air we met with. That day we had left a hot, humid land of swamps and mosquitoes and were now rising beneath a high dark canopy of forest trees clothed with climbers and creepers and in places on the steep roadside embankments, especially in disturbed places, a scrambling pitcher plant *Nepenthes sanguinea* with distinctive pitchers varying in colour from green to red.

. . .

This species is endemic to the central mountains of Peninsular Malaysia.

Our driver pointed out to us an occasional thatched (atap) roofed village of the Sakai aborigines now known as the Orang Asli (original people), some of whom we occasionally met with on the road stalking monkeys and other arboreal creatures with their blow pipes, of which more later. Tanah Rata lies on a plateau surrounded by mountains at around 4600ft (1403m). There were several tea plantations in nearby valleys, including the Blue Valley, whose packaged tea 'Cameronian' I took a liking to. Years later I was delighted to find it available from a tea shop near Lincoln Cathedral.

On our first full day Wally, the padre and I climbed a nearby mountain, Gunong Jasar (5564ft/1696m), following a narrow track, steep in parts, through forest which near the summit became increasingly dwarfed, the track leading us, bent double, through low tunnels of contorted stems and branches richly clothed with mosses, lichens, ferns and orchids. It was my first experience of 'cloud forest'. Suddenly we emerged onto the summit and all was bright and clear. There we found a small wooden shelter with a notched log poking through a hole in the corrugated tin roof. Up the log we climbed, emerging to an excellent view of the country around and an unexpected bonus; scrambling through and over the cloud forest canopy was a beautiful pitcher plant with slender tubular upper pitchers up to 6in (15cm) long in a striking creamy-white. I made no collection of this plant but I was later reliably informed that it was the pale form of *Nepenthes macfarlanei* which is confined to the 'moss' (cloud) forests of Peninsular Malaysia.

Nepenthes sanguinea was frequent on steep embankments on the road up to the Cameron Highlands.

Nepenthes macfarlanei with its pale upper pitchers was an exciting find on Gunong Jasar in the Cameron Highlands.

. . .

First wild rhododendron

Another highlight of our weekend, from a plant point of view, was the three species of *Rhododendron* we found growing in the vicinity of Tanah Rata, my very first wild rhododendrons and a far cry from the widely planted and naturalized *Rhododendron ponticum*, now regarded as a hybrid *R. × superponticum*, which I remembered seeing rampant in Smithills Wood near my home as a boy. The Tanah Rata plants belonged to a section of *Rhododendron* known as Vireya which contains some 300 species native to tropical regions of South East Asia, especially New Guinea and Borneo. The first to catch my eye was *Rhododendron robinsonii*, a large shrub with long narrow leaves and 1 in (2.5cm) long orange, bell-shaped flowers. It was growing in the jungle near Robinson Falls, a local beauty spot. *R. jasminiflorum* var. *punctatum* was more compact in habit, with small leaves in a rosette and substantial trusses of pink, long-tubed flowers. It was common on the jungle edge above a road. Different again was *R. malayanum*, low-growing with small leaves and loose clusters of bell-shaped, scarlet flowers. Unlike the other two, this grew on the exposed summit of Gunong Jasar, where it was common.

I collected specimens of all three rhododendrons plus several other plants of the family Ericaceae and having pressed and dried them under my mattress, sent them to Dr Herman Sleumer at the Rijksherbarium in Leiden, Holland, who was then revising the account of this family for a new Flora of Malaysia. He was extremely helpful with names, even encouraging me to collect seed to send to Kew Gardens. The then director of Kew, Dr George Taylor, in his reply to a letter I had sent him about my collecting was equally encouraging, pointing out that 'there is still much to be learnt about the flora of Malaya' and enclosing a copy of Kew's 'Notes on Plant Collecting' to give me an idea of what they required, adding that 'if packages of specimens are addressed to the Director, Royal Botanic Gardens, Kew there will be no difficulties with the customs'. I took him at his word and thus began my lifelong connection with Kew.

One amusing incident arising from being Company Clerk was that my mates regarded me as the platoon scribe and as such I was asked by

...

one of them for my help in persuading pen pals, girls preferably, to write to them. I couldn't say no and so the next day I penned a letter to a then well-known British tabloid describing how my mates longed to have people writing to them from home to give them something to look forward to on coming back from long, dangerous operations in the jungle. I sent the letter together with a photograph of a group of them crowding over a recently received copy of the newspaper in question. It worked better than I could have imagined. For several weeks following the letter's publication, I received piles of letters from girls across Britain anxious to secure a pen friend. Having written the original letter I reserved the right to be the first to read the replies before passing them on! Amazingly, a few of the friendships then made continued after the soldiers returned home including, I believe, one involving a lighthouse keeper's daughter who had sent a photograph of herself playing a guitar in Elvis mode with the lighthouse towering above.

Christmas at Siputeh Camp was in many ways a strange experience. For most of us it was our first spent far away from home, family and friends. Of course the army did its best to help us celebrate the occasion with food including festive fare, cigarettes and beer – maybe too much of the latter in some cases. I will never forget waking up on Boxing Day to find that a whole line of healthy banana plants outside our barrack room had been decapitated in the night by someone letting off steam with a parang. The New Year brought further upheaval when all personnel at Siputeh Camp were transferred to Colombo Camp in Ipoh, bringing the battalion together in one place.

High in the mountains

A second visit to the Cameron Highlands at the beginning of March 1958 provided me with an opportunity to collect more plant specimens for Dr Sleumer, all of which he identified for me. On this occasion the padre arranged for Wally and me to be driven to the summit of Gunong Brinchang, at 6667ft (2032m) the Cameron Highlands' second highest mountain, which proved to be a paradise for plants, especially rhododendrons and other ericaceous plants. Among the specimens I collected that day I was particularly excited by *Ilex epiphytica*, a small

. . .

LEFT A village of the local Orang Asli with characteristic atap (thatched) roofed dwellings in the Cameron Highlands.

BELOW A member of the Orang Asli with his blowpipe, used in hunting mammals and birds.

shrubby holly with leathery evergreen leaves and terminal and axillary clusters of white flowers, growing on a mossy log; *Gaultheria malayana*, another small evergreen shrub, this time with thickly clustered spikes of pink bell-shaped flowers; *Vaccinium parakense* (now *V. viscifolium*) and several orchids among which the most striking was *Dendrobium longipes*, a truly lovely species with creamy-white flowers borne on a long stem forming dense clumps on the branches of dead trees. All the orchids grew epiphytically on moss-covered branches at the mountain's summit. Along with the more exotic plants I also noticed *Vicia hirsuta*, the hairy tare, growing on a rubbish heap. This little vetch, which I first saw as a boy in Bolton, proved to be a new record for Malaya. I even spotted our British native gorse *Ulex europaeus* growing on the summit and elsewhere, no doubt planted by an ex-patriot as a reminder of home.

As we left Tanah Rata for Ipoh on our final day, the padre suggested we take a look at one of the villages of the Orang Asli which we had passed on our way up two days before. Pulling off the road, we left the jeep to follow a narrow track which led us up and over a hill into a settlement of thatch-roofed huts raised above the ground on wooden

...

posts. It seemed deserted except for a small child, who immediately ran into one of the huts and informed his mother who informed everyone else and within five minutes we were faced by a large group, the men in front, the women and children behind. One of the men was carrying a blowpipe and on my pointing to it he came forward allowing me a closer look.

Approximately 6½ft (2m) long, it was made from bamboo, delicately carved in some sections and well polished. Noting my interest, he asked for the matchbox our driver was holding and placed it on the ground at a distance of about 30ft (9m). He then returned and, taking the blowpipe from me, handed it to one of his colleagues, an older man who, having inserted a slender dart into the mouthpiece, took up a semi-squatting position. Placing the end of the pipe to his lips while maintaining it in a steady horizontal position with both hands clasped, he gave a sudden sharp puff. We could not follow the flight of the dart but we could see the matchbox falling over with the dart firmly lodged. Both Wally and I tried to do the same but our two-handed grip was not strong enough to prevent the blowpipe from wavering and we had to admit defeat. On examining the dart we found it to be a needle-like sliver of bamboo with a small head of pith acting as a flight at one end. When used for hunting the tip is dipped in a poison before being fired. The poison, apparently, is prepared from the sap of a jungle tree, known as the Ipoh tree (*Antiaris toxicaria*), a member of the mulberry family, Moraceae.

Wally and I could not thank the Reverend Quigley enough for giving us the opportunities to visit the Cameron Highlands and see their special flora and fauna. He had one more surprise in store, however, when he invited us to join him for a 10-day expedition to the King George V National Park, which lies in the state of Pahang and neighbouring parts of Terengganu and Kelantan. Now known as Taman Negara National Park, it is situated some 125 miles (200km) north-west of Kuala Lumpur and was originally established in 1925 as a game park, being redesignated as a National Park in 1938. At the time of our visit it covered an area of 1677sq miles (4343sq km) of what is now claimed by some experts to be among the world's oldest tropical rainforest. Wally and I were definitely up for it, but would the military

. . .

authorities approve? We left the potentially tricky question to the padre and were over the moon to hear later that permission had been granted. This was no ordinary leave destination like Penang or Singapore, so we considered ourselves extremely fortunate to be heading yet once again into a flora and fauna 'hot spot'.

On 24 March 1958, with our rucksacks and baggage packed, we set off by train from Ipoh heading down country to Kuala Lumpur and thence to Gemas, where we spent the night in a small railway station waiting room. Early next morning we were heading north-east on the so-called 'Jungle' train with carriages that looked as if they had originated in the pioneer days of the American West. It was a long journey spent looking through the carriage windows at unending jungle, like a thick green quilt covering hill and valley. It wasn't, however, the same green, more like 50 shades or more, forever changing as early morning mists shifted and dissipated in the heat of the rising sun. We left the train at a place called Tembeling Halt, which was not so much a station as a request stop on the line. Here we were met by an old red and white bus. This was already filled with villagers of all ages carrying a rich assortment of baskets and bags containing fruit and vegetables, pigs, ducks and chickens. As we boarded with our baggage it was clear from their expressions that we were seen as an unexpected source of entertainment.

River passage

Sadly for them, fortunately for us, we did not fulfil their expectations as after a short bone-shaking drive we reached Kuala Tembeling, a collection of tin-roofed dwellings, where we alighted. From here, a dusty road led us to a viewpoint above a large river, the Sungai Tembeling, where a steep flight of steps led down to a jetty. Here three long, narrow boats equipped with outboard engines and with tin roofs to protect passengers from the sun and rain were moored. Following a brief wait during which time I was excited to see a black-naped oriole on the jungle edge, we were instructed to board one of the boats which we found loaded with a cargo of coconuts still in their bulky husks. Joining us were several locals who, like us, were heading upriver to the village of Kuala Tahan, gateway to the National Park.

. . .

Our journey lasted approximately 2½ hours, with plenty of activity to observe along both banks, especially in the vicinity of settlements. For much of the way the jungle crowded the river banks and there was plenty of wildlife to keep us alert. We all had binoculars, though we did not require them to admire a colony of blue-throated bee-eaters whose nesting holes peppered a large sandbank. At one point they were gliding overhead like large excitable exotic swallows, blue and green with a chocolate-brown cap and upper back. Soon after, our binoculars were quickly in use when a pair of southern pied hornbills flapped across the river from the tree canopy ahead. We were beginning to feel a little drowsy when, rounding yet another bend, we had our first sight of the park headquarters at Kuala Tahan, our home for the next seven days. It was situated on a raised site on the point where a tributary, the Sungai Tahan, joins the main river.

On landing we were welcomed by Mr Chan, the assistant superintendent, who showed us to our accommodation, a large wooden bungalow with a veranda looking out onto the jungle. The padre, meanwhile, went to see the park superintendent, Major Charles Ogilvie, who lived with his Malay wife in a most attractive lodge nearby. After we enjoyed an excellent night's sleep followed by breakfast on the veranda and a bathing trip downriver, Mr Chan arrived to discuss with us a plan for the next day. He suggested we might like to spend a night or two in a high hide in the jungle above a salt lick near Kuala Trenggan, a few miles up the Sungai Tembeling, to which we agreed. After lunch we packed our rucksacks with two changes of clothes, our cameras and binoculars and sufficient food for the duration before heading upriver on a small boat. To reach our destination we encountered no fewer than seven sets of rapids that required us to step into the shallows and drag our boat into deeper waters.

On reaching Kuala Trenggan we found a small lodge overlooking the river which was to be our base and met the man who was to be our local guide. He was so pleased to meet us that he insisted on introducing us to his wife and five children. As it was now late in the day and the high hide a good 40-minute walk away in the jungle we agreed to have an early supper so that Wally and I might then head off with our guide,

. . .

Our boat awaits us at Kuala Tahan to take us up the Sungai Tembeling to Kuala Trenggan in the King George V National Park.

Our local Malay guide and his family outside their home at Kuala Trenggan.

leaving the padre in the lodge. Meal over and rucksacks packed, Wally and I set off in the gathering gloom, following our guides along a narrow trail through the trees. The high hide was a square wooden cabin raised on a stout wooden superstructure some 20ft (6m) above ground level. Its interior housed two double bunks and a wooden bench on which to sit while observing wildlife through a long viewing slit. It overlooked a clearing containing two springs of salty water (salt licks) which we were assured attracted a variety of wildlife. Once settled in the hide, our guides having quietly departed, Wally and I sat on the bench to begin our watch. Every 30 minutes one of us switched on a powerful torch we had been provided with and swept the clearing, while the other scanned the area illuminated through the binoculars.

...

For the first few hours of darkness we saw nothing and then gradually we both nodded off, waking with a start at dawn in time to see two large male Sambar deer drinking at the salt lick. They were very wary, constantly lifting their impressively antlered heads, ears twitching, sniffing the air, eventually wandering off into the jungle. We were ready and packed when our two guides arrived with the padre and after a quick breakfast we all set off at a fast pace on a 6 mile (9.6km) trek to explore a limestone hill deep in the jungle. The conditions were warm and humid and leeches were out in force on the ground, rocks, leaves and twigs awaiting their breakfast. The padre in particular suffered. They were commonly on the track attaching themselves to our jungle boots and I was constantly knocking them off with a swipe of my hat. In just under two hours we reached the limestone hill and, leaving the padre with the guides, Wally and I climbed a barely discernible track to the top, from where we had views all round of a vast undulating ocean of green through which other limestone hills protruded. The flora here was particularly interesting and I made collections of several plants growing on the limestone, especially in crevices, one of them, *Paraboea bettiana*, a member of the *Saintpaulia* and *Streptocarpus* family (Gesneriaceae).

On descending the hill we joined the others in exploring several caverns and overhangs, one of which, according to our guides, had been occupied by the Orang Asli. From the evidence of hoof-prints and droppings, another had recently been used by seladang, a species of wild ox, or gaur, which, we were told, are only found in deep remote jungle. On our return hike I stopped on several occasions to examine and collect plant specimens including two wild gingers. The first of these, *Zingiber spectabile*, the black ginger, had stems up to 6½ft (2m) tall bearing two rows of leaves while the short-lived pale yellow flowers protruded from a stalked cone-like head of pink, fleshy, overlapping scales which turn a dark red with age. Far more striking, however, was

In the jungle on my way to the limestone hill and the cave of the seladang.

. . .

We saw many other new birds and other creatures as we continued to explore the jungle around Kuala Tahan. It was here that I saw my first Asian fairy bluebird with its red eyes and brilliant blue and black plumage and a party of yellow-eared spider hunters flitting through the jungle canopy. Even the thick-billed green pigeons we saw were multi-coloured and had me wishing we could swap them for the drab grey pigeons of British cities and towns. It really was a paradise for wildlife.

Meanwhile, we had several times visited the superintendent, Major Charles Ogilvy, to be welcomed with a cold beer or a fragrant cup of China tea. He told us he had served with an Indian regiment during the war and at its conclusion had chosen to live in Malaya rather than return to Britain. He was an elderly man who wanted nothing more than to be with his 'friends', the birds and wild creatures of the jungle. Though his knowledge and experience of the jungle and its inhabitants appeared to us extensive, he professed to know very little. Sitting in his rattan chair in the evenings, he enjoyed watching the antics of chit-chats (house geckos) on the ceiling, pointing out to us their individual characteristics – one had three tails. In his compound he cared for injured or sick animals and birds, including a family of flying squirrels and a Malayan bearcat, or binturong. On our last night he had us all to supper and gave me several back numbers of British Birds for which he had no further use, as he did not intend to return to Britain. I still wonder what eventually happened to him.

Early next morning we set off on our return to Ipoh, the villagers and park staff gathering above the landing stage to wave goodbye. Our journey down river was pleasant yet relatively uneventful except for the sight of an extraordinary large kingfisher with greenish-blue wings and back, greyish-brown head, orange underparts and collar and sporting a massive red beak. It was flying upriver and passed quite close to our boat, offering us a superb view. Checking our bird book, there was no doubt we had seen a stork-billed kingfisher which can reach 15in (38cm) in length and has a larger beak than any other species. We eventually returned to Colombo Camp physically exhausted but mentally exhilarated by all we had seen.

. . .

Towards the end of June, with demob approaching, I began to write letters of thanks to all those botanists, entomologists, ornithologists and zoologists who had helped me in dealing with the many packages of specimens I had sent them. Checking my notes, I reckoned I had collected more than 400 wild plants (though I had seen a great many more) and observed 74 species of birds and a great number of insects and other creatures. Seven of the plants collected were new records for Malaya but all were introduced weeds I was familiar with back home.

Of the many birds I had come to know in the vicinity of Colombo Camp, the strikingly marked white-breasted kingfisher perching on a favourite post and the brainfever bird are the two I am most unlikely ever to forget. The last named, a cuckoo relative whose tuneless and monotonous notes in a descending scale offered the only clue as to its presence in the top of a leafy tree, cost me many hours of sleep.

The night before I left the camp I was treated to a great send-off in the NAAFI from which, it is claimed, I had to be carried back to my quarters. The following day, 23 June, I said my goodbyes to the office staff including Company Sergeant Major Tetlow who, in a little speech, thanked me for all that I had done, before requesting if he might retain the pickled green whip snake and the large Malayan scorpion in their jars alongside C Company's trophies for boxing and football. I had brought the whip snake back from the jungle in my ammunition pouch. As I climbed aboard the 3-ton Bedford army truck to join others heading for home, including my friend Wally, Sergeant Major Tetlow had one last thing to say to me: 'We are going to miss you, Lancaster.'

My Malayan adventure ended right there in Colombo Camp and the journey from Ipoh to Singapore, where we boarded the troop ship SS *Nevasa*, passed without incident. Unlike the German-built *Empire Orwell*, the Nevasa was British built on the River Clyde in 1955, the first troopship to be built since the end of the Second World War. Compared with our outward journey, this was to prove a much shorter passage, principally because the Suez Canal was now reopened to shipping. We crossed the Bay of Bengal and the Indian Ocean, where tropicbirds and flying fish kept me occupied on deck with my binoculars. Following a short stop in Aden – 'hot, dry and dusty' was my journal entry – we

. . .

Cap badge and General Service Medal with Malaya campaign clasp.

sailed through the Gulf of Aden, where for a while I watched a school of hammer-headed sharks passing back and forth beneath our ship. The Red Sea followed, where we were entertained by barracudas leaping out of the water, and so on through the Canal into the Mediterranean where, before our final leg in the Atlantic, we spent half a day in Gibraltar. I could hardly wait to get onto dry land and explore the famous Rock to make my last few herbarium collections, which included the grey downy *Helichrysum rupestre*, the upright succulent *Sedum altissimum* and the white or sweet alison (*Lobularia maritima*), companion of the blue lobelia as an edging plant in public park and town centre bedding schemes. Seen but not collected was mainland Europe's only native palm, *Chamaerops humilis*, the dwarf fan palm. These and others were determined by Dr Melderis of the British Museum (Natural History) in a letter I received in November that year.

On our return to Southampton towards the end of July we were welcomed by another military band before boarding a train to the promised land, Lancashire. When I eventually arrived at my family home in Bolton I felt as if I had been away for a lifetime. Despite the long, interesting journey via the Middle East, my mind remained filled with images and sounds of the Malayan jungle and the many experiences I had had there. This, together with the protective nature and organized routine of army life, seemed a world away from Cameron Street and the passage from one life to another left me in a sort of daze. Gradually, the old familiar ways returned, helped by my family and friends, and another chapter in my life unfolded.

·····

CHAPTER FOUR

From aliens to academia

It was three weeks following my return from Malaya that I was required to hand in my kit and receive my official discharge from the army. In the intervening time, while on paid leave, I enjoyed the freedom and time to catch up with friends, particularly those in the Parks Department who were keen to hear of my experiences in the jungle. It was especially satisfying to visit the Park's glasshouses and touch base with those plants I had seen in the wild state, and not just tropical plants. To this day I cannot pass a hanging basket or window box dripping with blue lobelia without thinking of my experience in the hills above Cape Town where I first found it in its native state.

My old foreman Doug Rugman was now in charge of a nursery in a walled garden near Smithills Hall. It was run by the Parks Department as a source of trees, shrubs and other plants, while a couple of brick-based greenhouses heated by a coke-fired boiler provided perfect conditions for propagating and growing less hardy plants. I visited him as soon as I was able and I liked what I saw. Among the shrubs grown were *Berberis prattii*, *Pieris formosa* var. *forrestii* and *Cotoneaster conspicuus*, the last-named described in the wild by its collector Frank Kingdon Ward as 'a bubbling red cauldron of berries'. A dense, domed shrub up to 5ft (1.5m), it is equally attractive when in flower and a ready source of nectar for bees and hoverflies. Doug asked what my future plans were and not for the first time I was unable to give an immediate answer. I had been led to understand by the Parks Department that as my apprenticeship had been interrupted by National Service I would be entitled to continue it on my return.

I also went to see my old mentor Jack Barber who, when I began describing the variety of plants I had seen and noted in my journals, fetched his set of the *RHS Dictionary of Gardening* and laid the books on the table, saying, 'Now let's start from the beginning.' Another

.....

friend I was anxious to meet was my old pal Clifford, who was keen to hear about the birds I had seen. He was able to confirm, and in some instances identify, those I had described in my journals. Vicar Shaw, who together with Doug Rugman, Jack Barber and Alfred Hazelwood had played a key role in encouraging my early interest in the natural world, especially in plants, I would meet with frequently in the following years but Walter (Wally) Chamberlain, my best pal during my time in Malaya, I only met once or twice following our return. As a medical orderly at Siputeh Camp and later Colombo Camp in Ipoh, he provided me with jars and spirit in which to preserve some of the natural history specimens I collected, including the green whip snake and giant Malayan scorpion I had left with the C Company trophies on returning home. He was also responsible for introducing me to the world of classical fiction and poetry, feeding me with a succession of novels including English translations of French classics, some of which I still have. I also have on my shelf a 'complete and unexpurgated' edition of D.H. Lawrence's *Lady Chatterley's Lover* published by Heinemann in 1956, which I purchased in a bookshop in Ipoh in February the following year.

British natives
For 18 months my head had been filled with the names and images of exotic and tropical plants, but I now began to renew my acquaintance with British natives. I began in September with a visit to an old haunt, the sand dunes of Ainsdale on the south Lancashire coast, and then it was the turn of Silverdale, my favourite place, which brought my first sighting of common bladderwort (*Utricularia vulgaris*) at Haweswater, where it grew with *Sparganium natans*, the least bur-reed, a delicate floating relative of the more widespread and robust branched bur-reed (*S. erectum*). My day was made complete on finding *Carex pseudocyperus*, the hop sedge, in an overgrown pond near the village. One of our less common native species, this bold but loosely clumping perennial to 4ft (1.2m) tall is easily recognized, especially when in fruit, the dense spikes of tiny green, ripening to brown, beaked nuts hanging on long slender arching stalks from the axils of leaf-like bracts.

.....

By this time, I had made up my mind to accept the Bolton Parks Department's invitation to continue my horticultural training with them. The key attraction was that I would be rejoining my old foreman Doug Rugman at the Smithills Nursery. Given his interest in plants and birds, I reasoned that the experience would be both enjoyable and productive, and so it proved. Apart from the practical gardening skills he taught me, we hatched a plan to compile an account of the plants and birds native to the area. We agreed to restrict our survey to within a 1 mile (1.6km) radius of the nursery. This would still cover a wide variety of habitats and terrain from the southern edge of the Pennines on Smithills Moor south through pastures and areas of cultivation to Raveden Wood, also known as Smithills Wood. Our target area contained streams, ponds, boggy areas, roadsides and hedgerows. We also included the nursery for its occasional weeds and likewise

The Flora of Raveden, a brief survey of the flowering plants and ferns occurring in the area of Smithills Nursery, Bolton.

the gardens of Smithills Hall. Most of our recording was done during our lunch-breaks over the five working days, although as I lived within 2 miles (3km) of the nursery it was easy for me to make extra visits, especially on summer evenings and occasional weekends.

We started the project in June 1959 under the title *The Flora of Raveden*, being a list of plants found growing wild or naturalized in the Raveden area of Smithills, Bolton. The list was arranged as per the then recently published *List of British Vascular Plants* (1958) by Mr J.E. Dandy of the British Museum (Natural History), giving families, genera, species, subspecies and varieties. Each plant name was accompanied by the name of its author, mostly in abbreviated form, for example Mill. for Miller and Sibth. for Sibthorp. Looking through the

.....

list today, I am interested to note how many names are accompanied by L. for Linnaeus, whose seminal work *Species Plantarum*, published in 1753, is regarded as the starting point for modern botanical nomenclature. For each entry we also provided a brief comment on its status and location.

We continued listing the plants until the end of the year, having at the last moment agreed to include grasses, sedges, rushes, horsetails and ferns. At the end of our project, we had recorded a total of 301 plants, several of them new records for the Bolton area. Doug continued adding to the list long after I moved on to pastures new. Most of the plants we recorded were fairly common nationally but we did discover a few surprises, one of which, *Lopezia coronata*, a curious red-flowered Mexican annual, we found as a casual weed in the nursery, growing in a patch of groundsel. It proved to be a new record for the Bolton area. Another curious plant we were thrilled to find, this one a true native, was the adder's-tongue fern (*Ophioglossum vulgatum*) which occurred in all the pastures around the nursery, though it was easily overlooked in the long grass.

Interestingly, the English elm (*Ulmus procera*) we recorded as 'common throughout the area'. Dutch elm disease was yet to come. Two introduced and naturalized plants now regarded by gardeners and environmentalists as 'public enemies', Japanese knotweed (*Fallopia japonica*) and *Rhododendron ponticum*, were already well established. The last named, as represented by a free-seeding, self-layering and invasive evergreen in many parts of Britain, especially in the west, is now regarded as a complex hybrid swarm under the name *R. × superponticum* resulting from deliberate and perhaps subsequent natural hybridization between the true *R. ponticum* from the Caucasus, north-east Turkey and Portugal and the North American species *R. maximum* and or *R. catawbiense*. In Raveden Wood, as in many similar sites nationally, it had originally been planted both as a game cover and an ornamental.

Our list of Raveden birds was a modest 43, including a single sighting of a pied flycatcher, my first. In perusing the list recently I noted that both skylark and cuckoo, now scarcer than formerly in some areas of Britain, I recorded as common.

.....

So involved was I at this time in my plants, wild and cultivated, that some people believed I thought of nothing else. I remember that on one occasion, I had eaten my lunch of sandwiches, or butties, as we called them in Lancashire, drunk my tea and was waiting for Doug to finish talking to a friend of his who had happened by. The stranger, looking at me, asked 'Are you keen on wild flowers then, young 'un?' Before I could reply, Doug said 'Is he keen? I tell you, Roy would take a girl into the woods to collect wild flowers'– pause, nod and a wink – 'and he'd collect wildflowers!' At this the stranger guffawed and Doug beamed before following my quick exit.

Vicar Shaw

For much of 1959 I was spending my weekends and holiday periods in search of plants and to a lesser extent, birds. Vicar Shaw had for a long time been extending his botanical activities to include alien plants, most of which he found on tips, rubbish dumps and in waste places generally. So successful was he that he was referred to by one of Britain's most admired and respected amateur botanists J.E. (Ted) Lousley as 'The Weed King of the North', a title that tickled the Vicar's fancy. I found myself accompanying Vicar Shaw on many of his alien hunts which, given his idiosyncracies, were always enjoyable and sometimes amusing. By now he and his wife were living at Waterhead near Oldham where he was vicar at Holy Trinity Church, eventually becoming, aged 80, Britain's longest-serving Church of England vicar. He was delighted to see me returned from Malaya and anxious to continue, as he put it, my botanical education. He enjoyed introducing me to friends and strangers alike as his 'star pupil' and there is no question that he taught me a great deal.

His spare-time interests other than plants included fossils, Lancashire dialect, football (he was a lifelong Bury supporter), draughts (a Lancashire champion) and amateur operatics. He would frequently burst into song on discovering a new or rare plant. He also had an infectious, if slightly manic laugh, reputedly the result of shell shock from a bomb exploding in a Salford street when he was visiting parishioners during the Second World War. He claimed never to have

.....

105

paid more than £10 for a 'new' second-hand car and though they were usually in poor condition, his mechanical and DIY skills were such that he could deal with most common car problems without the need for professional help. He even had an inspection pit in his garage. The car seats were often torn and faded but they were covered with genuine leather and you could smell the quality.

On our travels I would generally sit in the front passenger seat with instructions to shout 'Stop!' should I spot a new or unusual plant on my side of the road. He, meanwhile, was keeping watch on his side. On one occasion I was in the rear seat holding a bucket of water for cut plant material when I noticed a sizeable hole in the car floor through which I could see the cat's eyes in the road. When I pointed this out, the vicar answered with gusto, 'Aye, I know, I love fresh air'!

Many of the rubbish dumps we visited were situated on the outskirts of Pennine towns along the Lancashire-Yorkshire border. Vicar Shaw had discovered from experience that the easiest way of locating these dumps, mostly council owned, was to keep an eye open for any rubbish trucks and to follow them when they went to offload. One day when we had visited several border tips, all of them productive, the light was starting to fade so the Vicar called it a day. He set off to drive me home, stopping only at one last tip, where he had recently found a single plant of cockspur grass or barnyard millet (*Echinochloa crus-galli*), a species native to warm temperate and tropical regions. By the time we reached the tip it was dark and the metal security gate was closed and padlocked. Not to be denied, the Vicar fetched a torch from the car's glove compartment and having scaled the gate we set off, picking our way in the torch's wavering beam. Suddenly, there it was, bathed in the spotlight, an innocuous-looking green spiked grass which he proceeded to tell me about. Having examined it, we set off back towards the gate only to be caught ourselves in the much brighter headlights of an approaching squad car. Halting briefly and turning his back to the light, Vicar Shaw produced a dog collar from his jacket pocket, clipping it in place around his neck before turning and continuing to the gate. By this time one of the officers had got out of the car and on observing us in the full glare of the headlights said, 'Good evening, Vicar,

.....

everything all right?' to which the Vicar replied, 'Aye, it is, I've just been showing young 'un here barnyard millet, all the way from America, do you want to see it?' Not surprisingly, the officer declined. Vicar Shaw then asked him to leave the car headlights on while we climbed back over the gate as it would save on his torch battery. To my surprise, the officer obliged before wishing us good night and departing.

Rubbish tip flora

All the council tips we visited in summer would have their quota of tomato plants, potatoes, sunflowers (*Helianthus annuus*) and the like, plus invasive perennials, especially golden rod (*Solidago canadensis*), monbretia (*Crocosmia* × *crocosmiiflora*) and hybrids of Michaelmas daisies (*Aster novi-belgii* and *A. novae-angliae*), as well as other garden cast-offs which arrived via the dustbin. Some tips, however, would surprise us with the odd rarity, annuals often, which had arrived by other means. Such a site was the Crown Wallpaper tip above the Lancashire town of Darwen near Bolton. Vicar Shaw had received a tip-off that the nearby Crown Wallpaper works had been dumping waste in a small valley in the moors just off the Bolton Road. It turned out that rags imported by the company from the Middle East, possibly Egypt, were being processed as a source of wallpaper. Apparently the rags were placed in vats of acid to dissolve the fibres, leaving any impurities contained as a film of scum on the surface. It was this that was being skimmed off and dumped on the tip. I never did fully understand the process but what is certain is that a part at least of the impurities consisted of seeds, especially those with hard, sticky or hooked coats which presumably had latched on to the clothes of people as they went about their daily business. Those which survived the acid, their tough coats weakened, were germinating on the tip, helped by rainfall.

A sunflower (*Helianthus annuus*) brightens a rubbish dump near Manchester.

I was one of a small group of keen botanists led by Vicar Shaw who first visited the tip in June 1959

.....

when, to our astonishment, we found quantities of germinating date palms (*Phoenix dactylifera*). They were accompanied by the equally unexpected ice plant (*Mesembryanthemum crystallinum*) from South Africa whose large rosettes of thick, fleshy, glistening-green leaves with wavy margins we found in several places. Neither of these, I should add, survived the first frosts of the following winter. Subsequent visits produced a whole catalogue of unusual alien plants, especially umbels, grasses, crucifers and members of the pea family (Papilionaceae) while in successive years 1959 and 1960 two Mediterranean henbanes, *Hyoscyamus muticus* and *H. albus*, appeared. Like most tips, once dumping ceased, the Crown Wallpaper tip was gradually taken over by the more dominant, mostly native perennials and that was the end of that.

I shall mention just one more example of the countless alien plants I encountered during the late 1950s and 1960s. A photograph appeared in an edition of the *Bolton Evening News* showing two men standing on a local tip, between them, a stout leafy plant around 3¼ft (1m) tall with a luridly blotched stem and a large, sinister-looking, dark purple hooded flower. It had been given a protective chicken-wire fence and one of the figures, the workman who found it, was pointing a finger at it while his companion, a policeman, was busy making a note. The caption was headed 'Alien from Outer Space?' and went on to report how the plant had been a chance discovery and no one knew what it was or where it had come from. I recognized it as the dragon arum (*Dracunculus vulgaris*), an exotic relative of our native cuckoo pint or lords and ladies (*Arum maculatum*), which had undoubtedly originated from cultivation via the dustbin. Some years later another appearance of this species, this time on a tip in Yorkshire, was reported in a Sunday newspaper as the 'Monster Mystery Plant of Barnsley'. Dragon arum, or voodoo lily as it is sometimes called, is native to southern Europe and the Mediterranean region and its tubers were, and still are, sometimes advertised for sale as a curiosity in garden magazines and national newspapers. What the adverts fail to say is that the flower emits a strong smell of carrion to attract pollinating flies, especially bluebottles, which was usually the cause of its banishment from the parlour to the dustbin. The variety of plants, especially exotics, which ended up on tips as cast offs never

.....

failed to amaze me. Few but the hardiest survived their first winter.

In case I have given the impression that all my plant exploration at this time was done on rubbish dumps, sewerage farms and other unsavoury sites, let me confirm that most of it was devoted to truly wild areas which in June 1959 included a trip, my second, with Clifford to the forests and mountains of Scotland. There, lesser twayblade (*Listera cordata*, now *Neottia cordata*), mountain azalea (*Loiseleuria procumbens*) and creeping lady's tresses (*Goodyera repens*) were just three plants I saw for the first time. Perhaps the most unlikely star of this trip, however, was *Agropyron donianum* (now *Elymus caninus* var. *donianus*). Its English name, Don's twitch, suggests a rare medical condition but this rare grass is no more than a cousin once removed of that gardener's curse, couch grass (*Elytrigia repens*), differing most obviously in its dense, clump-forming habit. The name commemorates George Don (1764–1814), a Scottish botanist and gardener who first discovered this grass on Ben Lawers in 1810. It is native only to the mountains of central and northern Scotland, where it grows on rock ledges and crevices, and that is where we eventually found it on Ben More.

On an April morning in 1960 I was weeding a border in the Smithills Nursery when I received notification from the Parks Head Office that as a continuation of my professional training I was being transferred to the Landscape and Planning Office, where I would receive instruction in the preparation of planting schemes and plans, garden design, tree planting in urban areas and, last but not least, surveying. There followed several months when I was based in an office in Heaton Cemetery where

Dragon arum (*Dracunculus vulgaris*) makes an occasional appearance on rubbish dumps in Britain via the dustbin.

Finding Don's twitch (*Elymus caninus* var. *donianus*) on a rock ledge on Ben More, Scotland, in June 1959.

Peter Hesketh and Bob Ashcroft, my two apprentices when replanting the garden at Hall i' th' Wood Museum, Bolton in 1960.

I had first arrived as a boy for an interview eight years previously. I was sorry to leave Smithills Nursery with its hands-on plant propagation and cultivation experience under the tutelage of Doug Rugman, who had become a firm friend. However, my new boss, Mr Perkins, a young man in his late twenties or early thirties, while lacking the experience of Doug was thoroughly versed in planning and design and as time proved possessed a good knowledge of plants and their uses in the garden and wider landscape. Thanks to him I was given an interesting range of projects on which to cut my teeth and he constantly encouraged me to use my imagination. Most of all, I enjoyed those days on site putting into practice what I had created on the drawing board.

My recent experience in the jungles of Malaya more than once helped me in adding an exotic touch to a summer border. Floral clocks, a carpet-bedding tribute to the Girl Guides Association, a new planting scheme for the Garden of Remembrance at Bolton Crematorium and innumerable tree planting schemes for council estates passed through my hands under the watchful eye of Mr Perkins. This might not sound very exciting compared with what many of today's professionals are engaged in, but to me then it was a new and enjoyable challenge. The most interesting project I dealt with at this time was a new planting

.....

scheme for the garden of 'Hall i' th' Wood Museum', an old manor house with a half-timbered east wing that dated to 1483. Its lasting fame, however, rests on the fact that in the second half of the 18th century part of the house was occupied by the Crompton family, whose son Samuel in 1779 invented the Mule, a machine which revolutionized the cotton spinning industry. To help with the planting I was assigned two young apprentices, one of whom, Bob Ashcroft (who now lives in Silverdale), I am still in touch with. Over a couple of weeks we prepared the ground and planted beds and borders with a variety of hardy, especially woody plants, some of which, *Parrotia persica*, *Aesculus parviflora*, *Arbutus unedo* and *Magnolia sieboldii* among them, were new to or rarely grown in Bolton at that time.

In compiling planting lists for new schemes I would trawl through the nursery catalogues held in the office in search of the unusual with a view to spicing up our local garden flora. One day, Mr Perkins handed me a green-backed catalogue which he had brought from home called

'Trees and Shrubs comprising a descriptive list of those plants which should find a place in every well stocked garden, including Climbers, Conifers, Bamboos and Grasses' offered for sale by Hillier & Sons of Winchester. Given that the company had been around since 1864 I was surprised that I had not heard of them, but I was delighted that I now had a seemingly endless choice of woody plants from which to choose. Little did I realize how important a role this nursery and its catalogues would one day play in my career and my life.

My first sight of a *Hillier's catalogue of Trees and Shrubs* while working in the Planning Office at Bolton Parks in 1960.

Student days

It was the gradual realization of the wealth of plants grown in gardens and collections beyond Bolton's parks, especially in the southern half of England, that had me thinking once more about my future progress. I was then aged 22. It was while I was day-dreaming about what might be that Mr Perkins,

.....

sensing my mood, raised the subject of further experience and from our ensuing conversation the idea of leaving Bolton for pastures new began to take shape. Mr Perkins suggested I might consider trying for a studentship course at the Royal Botanic Gardens Kew or else the RHS Garden at Wisley. Our then deputy superintendent had trained at Kew and before that at the Cambridge University Botanic Garden. On seeking his advice he was of the opinion that the latter might best suit me and that I should write to them immediately. He also offered to write a letter of support, which helped make up my mind.

In response to my letter, I received on 21 July an invitation to attend for an interview at the Botanic Garden on 2 August at 4.40pm regarding a place on the next two-year student gardeners' course, beginning in September. The invitation was signed by the Garden's director, Mr J.S.L. Gilmour, who urged me to reply as soon as possible, which I did. Before I left for the interview my deputy superintendent gave me one final piece of advice: 'If they ask you whether or not you play cricket and they almost certainly will, say yes.' I thought it an odd consideration but following my interview, as I stood up to leave the room, Mr Gilmour said, 'Just one more thing, do you play cricket?' 'Yes, I do,' I replied and I was not telling a fib, having played at school and more recently in the nursery at Heaton in the summer of 1956.

I had enjoyed myself at Bolton Parks, which at that time was certainly one of the best parks departments in the north of England. I could not have had a more thorough introduction to horticulture as a career and I have never stopped thanking my lucky stars for that. Now the time had come to expand my experience and it encouraged me a great deal that the Parks' staff and my friends and mentors thought so too.

A few days after my interview I received a letter from Mr Gilmour offering me a place on the next course. I was to report to the Garden on 12 September. A memorandum of conditions of employment accompanying the letter informed me I would be paid wages of £7.11s.3d per week, rising to £7.13.9d in my second year, for a 44-hour week with extra for evening and weekend duties. I was informed later that I had been found board and lodgings for £3 per week with a family in the nearby village of Trumpington, a short bike ride away,

.....

From left, John Gilmour (JSL) director, Peter Yeo, taxonomist and Bob Younger, superintendent in the late 1950s.

The noble black walnut (*Juglans nigra*), seen here in November 2014 close to Brookside in the University Botanic Garden, Cambridge.

and having been transported to Cambridge with my baggage by Bob Ashcroft, one of my former apprentices and now a friend, I used my own bike to reach the Garden on that first morning. All seemed quiet as I sped along Bateman Street, turning right at No. 47 into the Garden's main entrance. I feared I would be the last to arrive until another young man joined me from the opposite direction and we exchanged greetings. He was Jim Plant, a Cambridge man living at Cherry Hinton on the city outskirts.

We found everyone else awaiting our arrival and were welcomed by the Garden's superintendent, Bob Younger, and outside foreman, Peter Orris. Following this we were given a general introduction and brief history of the Garden, plus a resumé of our training and other activities over the next two years. Peter stressed that we would each be given the opportunity of working in as many departments of the garden as practical. Starting with the first to arrive, we were paired off and assigned a department. Being the last to arrive, Jim Plant and I were put to work in the Arboretum and other areas. For the next six months the two of us had a whale of a time among the woody plants, planting, pruning, shaping and propagating a wide variety of species, many of

.....

LEFT An unusual relative of the walnut, *Platycarya strobilacea*, with its striking male catkins in June 2015.

BELOW *Xanthoceras sorbifolium*, flowering in May, is a special favourite of mine first seen in the Botanic Garden.

which I had not encountered in Bolton's parks nor anywhere else for that matter. One such, *Maclura pomifera*, the Osage orange from south and central USA with orange-sized green to pale yellow, pimply-skinned fruits borne on the female tree, was represented by two tall trees, one of each sex.

In the northwest corner of the Garden close to Brookside, which housed the administration offices, grew three special trees, all members of the walnut family, Juglandaceae. The largest of these was a tall-stemmed example of the east North American black walnut (*Juglans nigra*), one of the most noble of hardy forest trees, worth growing for its handsome divided leaves and its rugged greyish-brown, furrowed bark. Not far away was a dense tall-stemmed grove of the Caucasian wingnut (*Pterocarya fraxinifolia*) which had speedily developed from suckers following the demise of the original two mother trees. I loved their large, lush, divided foliage which turned yellow in autumn and the characteristic pendant closely packed chains of winged green fruits. Completing the trio was *Platycarya strobilacea*, an unusual small tree of

.....

botanical and ornamental interest with large, handsome, divided leaves and terminal clusters in July of erect, yellow catkin-like male spikes and small cone-like female seed heads which aged from green to dark brown or black and were retained until the following summer. Years later I was fortunate enough to see all three of these remarkable trees growing in the wild state.

By the pond stood the fast-growing, slender cone of a dawn redwood (*Metasequoia glyptostroboides*), the first specimen I had seen of this famous Chinese conifer. Mr Gilmour informed us that it had been planted here from a private source the year before the arrival of the main introduction via the Arnold Arboretum, Massachussetts in 1948. This was and still remains one of the Garden's signature trees, along with Gerard's pine (*Pinus gerardiana*), the one-needled nut pine (*Pinus monophylla*) and the Cambridge oak (*Quercus × warburgii*), a one-off hybrid between the Mexican *Q. rugosa* and our native *Q. robur*.

Of the many new shrubs seen, *Xanthoceras sorbifolium* from northern China with bold divided foliage and erect panicles of white flowers in May, each with a carmine central stain, followed after a hot summer by large pendant green walnut-sized fruits, became a favourite of mine; so did *Cotoneaster lacteus*, a striking hedge of which had been planted alongside the drive to Cory Lodge, home to the director and his family. It was introduced from south-west China by the Scottish plant hunter George Forrest in 1913, and this cotoneaster's attractive bullate leaves, white flower heads in June and red fruit clusters in autumn identified it in my eyes as one of the best all-round ornamental evergreens in cultivation. After flowering each year its new extension growths would be pruned back to allow the developing fruits to receive full light and indeed the public's admiration. I later saw a similar but even larger hedge of this species in the National Botanic Garden at Glasnevin in Dublin.

A well-rounded education

Mr Gilmour, who was referred to by the staff by his initials, JSL, was a humanist and to us something of a father figure. We were in no doubt that he really cared about us and our welfare and he supported us in so many ways. We hadn't been there long when he invited any students

.....

with musical interests to join the Glee Club, which met at Cory Lodge one evening a week for an hour or so of singing. I found it quite entertaining and given that I had always been one for singing and whistling in the bathroom at home, I came to look forward to these evenings, though not all my fellow students felt the same. Later, especially in summer, JSL and his wife Molly, who were active members of the Cambridge musical fraternity, would invite students to attend the occasional performances of popular operas staged in the Cory Lodge garden; one of the first was Mozart's *Così fan tutte*, a new experience for me, and having enjoyed it I was hooked.

It was JSL who gave the new students our first lecture on 30 September, the subject being Plant Classification, Taxonomy and Nomenclature. For me, with an interest but no formal education in these things, his lecture made it seem straightforward and I found it relatively easy to understand – though, as he wisely cautioned, it can be anything but, as my own experience subsequently confirmed. One

Cory Lodge, then home of the director, John Gilmour, and his family, now the Botanic Garden's offices. It is shown here in July 2015 with *Catalpa speciosa* in flower.

.....

116

thing for certain, JSL's lecture that day opened for me a door to an unending and fascinating world of plant knowledge which over the years has continued to surprise and delight. We were fortunate in having in our director one of the world's leading authorities on plant nomenclature, especially in the fast-developing area of cultivated plants. Before his appointment to the Botanic Garden post in 1951, JSL had served as assistant director at the Royal Botanic Gardens Kew and then director of the Royal Horticultural Society's Garden at Wisley. He was an architect of the 1953 International Code of Nomenclature for Cultivated Plants and he had also served four years as president of the Botanical Society of the British Isles, which I was to join in my first year at Cambridge.

JSL's ability in bridging the gap between the botanical and horticultural worlds was widely recognized and we students were to benefit most notably from his expertise on the regular Garden walks he conducted. Leading us through the plant collections, he would stop regularly to pinpoint a favourite plant, describing its botanical and ornamental features as well as its origins and always telling an interesting story associated with the history of its introduction or economic uses. Alternating with JSL's walks were those led by the Garden's taxonomist, Dr Peter Yeo, a man of shy disposition but with an excellent grasp of taxonomy and the first of that special breed, the horticultural botanist, I had met. I had previously corresponded with him on the subject of eyebrights (*Euphrasia* species), one of his specialities, and he was to become a good friend. His assistant, Clive King, was in charge of the library and like Peter an enormous help to us students.

Following the Garden walks came plant identification tests, based on what we had seen and been taught the previous week. They were normally held in the nearby laboratory with 20 specimens laid out on a bench. Our answers were marked on the plant name – both genus and species – family and country of origin, or garden origin in the case of hybrids or cultivars. We were also marked on correct spelling. In addition to the Garden walks and plant identification tests, we received regular instruction, mostly of a practical nature, from the superintendent, Bob Younger, and his foremen and section heads. There were also visits to

.....

other gardens and nurseries such as Notcutts of Woodbridge and Blooms of Bressingham. Naturally, we were expected to keep notebooks and journal records of plants seen, together with details and comments on their growth, flowering and their ornamental merit and use. I still consult these records when writing plant articles for publication and I constantly find myself referring to plants which I first encountered at Cambridge.

One particular project I started at this time was to keep a record of the host plants of our native mistletoe (*Viscum album*) which occurred on several trees in the Garden, including one of my favourite small ornamental trees, *Crataegus orientalis*. Over the years I have added to the list those new hosts personally seen or in a few cases reported to me by reliable sources. It currently includes 72 different species, varieties and cultivars of plants, mostly trees. Among the more unusual are the Chinese dove tree (*Davidia involucrata* var. *vilmoriniana*), London plane (*Platanus × hispanica*) and *Cotoneaster horizontalis*. On a more recent visit to the garden in April 2016, I was surprised and thrilled to see it growing on the big black walnut, a new host for my list.

Following our period outside with the hardy woody plants, Jim and I were transferred to the Glasshouse Range and a very different world of plants. Quite a number of those grown in the warmer, especially the Tropical and Stove houses and the long corridor I was familiar with from Malaya and the gardens of Singapore while the houses that were nearest in content to my heart, were the Temperate House and the much smaller Alpine House. The former held lots to interest me, including the moon dock (*Rumex lunaria*) a fleshy-leaved shrub sometimes scandent, native to the laurasylva (laurel forests) of the Canary Isles; and *Semele androgyna*, a high-climbing relative of the butchers' broom (*Ruscus*) from the laurasylva of the Canary Isles and Madeira. Many years later I was pleased to see both in their native isles.

By far the most exciting and spectacular occupant of the Temperate House was a *Mahonia* that flowered for the very first time in January 1962. No ordinary mahonia this, but *M. siamensis*, now regarded by some authorities as a synonym of *M. duclouxiana*, a magnificent, large-leaved, corky-barked shrub or small tree of 8ft (2.5m) which grew in a central bed. It had previously grown at Serre de la Madone, the garden

.....

LEFT *Mahonia siamensis*, possibly an original seedling, growing at Serre de la Madone, Menton, France in February 2008.

ABOVE *Mahonia × lindsayae* 'Cantab' (*M. japonica × M. siamensis*) growing in a border at Queens College, Cambridge in February 1998.

made by the American Lawrence Johnston above Menton on the French Riviera. It was Johnston who first introduced this species into cultivation, together with *M. lomariifolia* as seed from the Yunnan/Burma border region in 1931. Following his death in 1958, Johnston's garden was inherited by Mrs Nancy Lindsay who the following year invited Mr Gilmour, accompanied by Bob Younger, to visit the garden with a view to choosing a selection of plants to grow in the Botanic Garden in memory of Johnston. Their choice included a 5ft (1.5m) plant of *M. siamensis*. It was this plant that I first admired when a student.

Many years later, in February 2008, I was lucky enough to visit a newly restored and revitalized Serre de la Madone. To my surprise and delight, I discovered several large specimens of *M. siamensis*, one of which, judging by its size and failing health, I took to be an original. I estimated it to be around 16 x 19ft (5 x 6m). I was particularly pleased to see the handsome, richly scented, multi-fingered inflorescences of golden-yellow flowers, reddish in bud. One curious addition to this story concerns a plant raised at Cambridge from seed collected from another *M. siamensis* at Serre de la Madone which, when it eventually flowered in 1964, was identified by Peter Yeo as a magnificent natural

.....

hybrid between *M. siamensis* and *M. japonica*. This was later described and published by Peter under the name *M. × lindsayae* 'Cantab' acknowledging both donor and the Botanic Garden. It proved itself an excellent ornamental, intermediate in character and size between the parents, while leaning more towards *M. japonica* in hardiness and in the long, lax racemes of the inflorescence with its paler yellow flowers. It received an RHS Award of Garden Merit.

One of the many bonuses of working in the Botanic Garden was the access we had to the University's Botany School, or rather the botanists who worked and taught there, whose field study visits to local native plant locations we students were allowed if not encouraged to join. My first such opportunity was a visit to the chalk pits at Cherry Hinton in October. It was led by Dr Max Walters, who was later to succeed JSL as director. I had been corresponding with him for a few years on his favourite specialist subject, *Alchemilla* (lady's mantle) on which he was a recognized authority and he had identified several species I had sent him from a number of British locations. On this occasion, in the main chalk pit, which he informed us dated from medieval times, he introduced us to a number of wildlings and instructed us on how to recognize them by field characters. I remember seeing *Lonicera caprifolium*, which had been known here apparently since the 18th century, and I was amazed at the blanketing growth of the *Clematis vitalba* (old man's beard) reminiscent of jungle vines. On subsequent visits to this location I saw *Falcaria vulgaris*, a rare member of the carrot family (Umbelliferae) known as longleaf which is naturalized here, while in the chalk hills above grew both grape hyacinth (*Muscari neglectum*) and common star of Bethlehem (*Ornithogalum angustifolium*).

Exploring East Anglia

In the two years I spent in Cambridge I made a great number of field trips, alone or with others, covering Cambridge and its environs in some detail and East Anglia in general. I especially remember the Breckland area of Norfolk and Suffolk, the coastal regions of both counties and specific locations known for their rich flora, particularly

.....

Hayley Wood, south-west of Cambridge, where in May on boulder clay over chalk I was able to enjoy rich carpets of bluebells studded with early purple orchids (*Orchis mascula*), yellow archangel (*Lamium galeobdolon*) and oxlips (*Primula elatior*). Other locations I visited included Wicken Fen for water violet (*Hottonia palustris*) and swamp pea (*Lathyrus palustris*), while at Woodwalton Fen in Huntingdon I saw my first Fen violet (*Viola stagnalis*), Saracen's ragwort (*Senecio fluviatile*) and the rare and impressive marsh sowthistle (*Sonchus palustris*). The last named was originally native there before becoming extinct; the thriving population we saw had been established from a reintroduction.

One of the most striking and instantly identifiable plants I remember seeing for the first time in Cambridge was the blue toothwort (*Lathraea clandestina*), a root parasite from west and south-west Europe which had escaped from the Botanic Garden to become established along local waterways including Coe Fen on the roots of willows, though it also grows on other hosts. Today, a plant I established in my garden on a hedgerow hazel has almost run amok and though its conspicuous low tufts of blue-hooded flowers are a joy in early spring, dying away again after seed shed, its long, scaly, white rhizomes continue to spread underground via the roots of its host. I have twice had to empty my compost bins after they had been infiltrated by them via the roots of a weeping willow in my neighbour's garden.

The blue toothwort (*Lathraea clandestina*), a root parasite from west and south-west Europe, established by the lake in the Botanic Garden.

Scotland

I was in Scotland on two occasions: first in 1961 and again in 1962. The first of these, with student friends from the Botanic Garden in mid-August, ended with a visit to Ben Lawers in Perthshire, a botanist's

.....

mecca, where within three hours I saw native alpine plants I had previously only known from illustrations in books. It had been a long-held ambition of mine to visit this mountain and when I eventually reached its summit I sat down and ate my lunch while contemplating the many plants I had seen on the way up, which included alpine forget-me-not (*Myosotis alpestris*), holly fern (*Polystichum lonchitis*), snow gentian (*Gentiana nivalis*) and the netted willow (*Salix reticulata*). A note in my journal reminds me that I felt on top of the world, the sun shining, a cool wind blowing my hair and a desire to stay there forever.

In early June the following year one of my fellow students, Patrick Hammond, accompanied me on a trip north to join my pal Clifford Heyes on a Scottish adventure, the highlight of which would be a week camping on one of the Rabbit Islands off the coast of Sutherland at Melness, near the mouth of the Kyle of Tongue. Why these islands? It was Clifford's idea – he had been perusing a large-scale Ordnance Survey map of Scotland, and the name of these tiny isles had intrigued him. He had also visited them on a brief reconnaissance. We set off on two scooters, one of which developed a problem at Aviemore, necessitating alternative train and bus transport. To reach our destination we hired a boat from a Mr Mackay in Melness and rowed across the narrow strip of water to the nearest island where, having hauled the boat up the beach, we ascended a steep grass slope. By this time it was dusk and we became aware of myriad storm petrels emerging from their nesting burrows, flitting past our heads like bats before heading out to sea.

During the week we observed and recorded the plants and birds seen, which included rock pigeons, black guillemots, peregrine falcon (nest found) and a family group of great northern divers off-shore. Our best plant sightings were on a day spent on the mainland at Bettyhill, near the mouth of the River Naver, where small white orchid (*Leucorchis albida*), *Primula scotica*, purple oxytropis (*Oxytropis halleri*) and sea sedge (*Carex maritima*) were all new to me. These were just a few of those recorded and more was to come. On our way back to Melness, a brief stop to photograph pastures covered with mountain avens (*Dryas octopetala*) and grass of Parnassus (*Parnassia palustris*) resulted in us

.....

LEFT Using a Kew plant press to dry specimens found on one of the Rabbit Islands, Sutherland, Scotland in June 1962.

RIGHT *Geranium kishtvariense* in the garden at Crûg Farm Plants, north Wales, in August 2001 – my original introduction from Kashmir.

finding a fern I had long dreamed of seeing, the moonwort (*Botrychium lunaria*). It is my experience that this is a plant one only stumbles upon by accident and rarely if ever when one is searching for it, and to prove my point, after returning our boat at Melness on our final day I made to sit down on one of a series of small mounds in a pasture by the harbour in order to write my notes. I was about to settle when I noticed to my amazement several moonworts growing on the mound. On taking a closer look, now on my hands and knees, I found the mound riddled with this fern. In 1.6sq m (2sq yd) I counted a total of 56, some of them robust specimens resembling at a glance the emerging fronds of bracken. Despite subsequent searches in suitable sites elsewhere I have never seen this fern since, though in 1980 I did find the larger *B. virginicum* growing on a mountainside in Yunnan, China.

Following several months working in the Glasshouse Range at the Botanic Garden, I was transferred to the Experimental Area where post-graduate students and others conducted their various research projects. One of my favourite plots of ground here was devoted to Peter Yeo's plants. Known to native plant enthusiasts for his work on eyebrights (*Euphrasia* spp.), few if any of which are grown by gardeners, Peter's popularity with plantsmen and garden designers alike rests on his work with *Bergenia*, *Ruscus* and, most of all, the hardy *Geranium* species and their hybrids and cultivars. His classic work *Hardy Geraniums*, first published in 1985, quickly became the bible for all

.....

those with an interest in the genus and remains so today. I consider myself fortunate in having helped in weeding and caring for these plants and for many years after I continued to send Peter herbarium specimens, seed and details of all three genera that I had found in the wild, including *Ruscus colchicus* 'Trabzon', *Bergenia ciliata* and *B. pacumbis*, plus a number of *Geranium* species. One of these, *G. kishtvariense*, collected at Gulmarg, Kashmir in 1978, turned out to be the first introduction of a species whose original (type) specimen in the Botanical Museum of Berlin-Dahlem had been destroyed by fire when the Allies bombed that city in 1943. This species is now well established in cultivation.

For my final year at Cambridge I lodged with an elderly spinster, Miss Ashberry, and her widowed sister, Mrs Marsh, in a terraced house within easy walking distance of the Botanic Garden. It was a popular digs with students, not least for the meals, especially a traditional roast beef Sunday lunch worth dying for. This included a Yorkshire pudding which had to be eaten quickly before it floated away. Apple pie or crumble with lashings of custard was a regular follow-up, with a creamy rice pudding alternative. So good was this lunch that I regularly agonized over missing it!

The Botanic Garden had a students' lecture society known as the Walkerian and during our two years we were entertained by a number of well-known speakers, including Tony Schilling (an ex-student), Frank Knight, Joe Elliot and Patrick Synge, speaking on 'Arctic Norway', 'The Propagation of Hardy Trees and Shrubs', 'Alpines' and 'Plants of Eastern Turkey and Iran' respectively. Tony later became a good friend and went on to be a successful and highly respected plant explorer.

During their final year students were required to give a lecture of their own, but before this, in March 1961, I was volunteered by JSL to give a lecture to the Science Club of the nearby Perse School for Girls on 'Collecting and Identifying Wild Flowers and the Formation of a Herbarium'. This was to be my first-ever speaking engagement and naturally I was more than a little apprehensive. I sought advice from a staff member at the Botanic Garden who suggested I take a 'wee dram of whisky' before starting, but I decided against this. In the event

.....

I walked boldly into the school science lab carrying a selection of cut material from the Garden plus a plant press, labels and notebook. There was a moment when, faced with the eyes of 40 girls following my every move, I considered turning around and running for my life, then I swallowed hard and got on with the job. Judging by the applause it seemed to have been well received and feeling mightily relieved I headed off to have tea and cake with the headmistress. This experience helped me prepare for my lecture a year later on 'The Pleasures of Plant Hunting' to the Walkerian Society which in the event lasted 1¾ hours, illustrated with 120 slides. JSL's verdict was 'Good lecture but too many slides' and he advised me in future to keep to 50–60 slides before adding 'Cut the jokes.'

First Chelsea Flower Show

It was in May 1962 that JSL enquired as to whether I had any thoughts on what I might be doing on finishing my studentship in September. I had already, at his invitation, visited Joe Elliot's nursery in the Cotswolds and although I liked what I saw I subsequently decided against following such a specialist path. I had not forgotten JSL's comments on the benefits of gaining a broad experience of horticulture and the plant world before settling into a specialist role. Looking back now I guess my horizons never stopped expanding. Anyway, JSL told me of two possible jobs I might like to consider. One was a position in the Herbarium at Kew, which I found tempting but it was another specialist role. He then mentioned that an old friend, Harold Hillier of the famous nursery firm, was looking for someone to help prepare his nursery catalogues and check out plants in his nurseries in Hampshire. This really had me thinking and in order to know more it was arranged that I should meet Mr Hillier at the forthcoming Chelsea Flower Show, where Hillier would be staging their customary large exhibit of trees and shrubs. This was my first visit to the world's greatest flower show and having met up with him, on Tuesday 22 May, Mr Hillier, or HG (Harold George) as he was known to his staff, showed me round his exhibit before inviting me to attend for an interview at the Home Nursery, West Hill in Winchester the following week.

.....

LEFT The main drive to Hillier's home office at West Hill Nursery, Winchester. The borders were full of interesting woody plants, including E.H. Wilson's introductions.

OPPOSITE PAGE Staff and student gardeners at the Botanic Garden in 1962. I am in the back row, sixth from left. Among the staff, front row are Clive King fifth from left, continuing with Peter Orris, Bob Younger, John Gilmour (JSL), Gordon Clarke and Phil Butler.

The Hillier job

On the day appointed I arrived by train at Winchester station and made my way up the steep Romsey Road past Winchester Prison into the nursery entrance. The office was situated halfway along a drive which was flanked by broad borders planted with trees and shrubs, but I had no time to linger. Entering the building beneath the spreading crown of a Chinese dove tree (*Davidia involucrata*), an original E.H. Wilson introduction I was later informed, I was directed along a corridor to HG's office which I was surprised to find rather small and pokey. It was relatively bare except for a stack of old nursery catalogues on the floor in a corner and more of them, together with assorted documents and papers, on a desk behind which the great man sat. Mr Gilmour had referred to him as a walking dictionary when it came to woody plants and I was interested to note on his desk a copy of Rehder's *Manual of Cultivated Trees and Shrubs Hardy in North America*. I was to learn later that his main book collection was at his home, Jermyns House.

Having welcomed me, HG, who would then have been 57, suggested we take a walk along the drive to examine and discuss the trees and shrubs, many of them grown from seed introduced by plant hunters,

.....

notably E.H. Wilson. He told me how, as a young man aged 17 in July 1922, he was privileged to be present with his father, Edwin Lawrence, to welcome the great English plant explorer when he visited the nursery, where he spent the day reminiscing about his travels and plant adventures. He clearly enjoyed seeing so many of his Chinese introductions flourishing on the shallow chalk soil at West Hill and left HG and his father with an abundance of stories.

As we strolled along the drive HG pointed out a number of his favourites, some of which I knew from Cambridge. As a final test we stopped by a shrub with small pinnate opposite leaves and clusters of small, white, slender-tubed flowers. I had not seen its like before but something about it reminded me of a lilac and I said so. To my relief, I had guessed correctly and that is how I first met with *Syringa pinnatifolia* which, 23 years later and 82 years after Wilson first discovered it, I was to see for myself in China's Sichuan province. HG wouldn't say whether I had passed the test but he did offer me the job. On leaving the nursery for the station I could not get over the fact that I had just shaken hands with a man who had once shaken hands with my hero, 'Chinese Wilson'. A few days later I received a letter from HG saying he was

.....

127

pleased to confirm my appointment and that he looked forward to my joining the firm on 22 September. He also confirmed that I would be paid the sum of £10 per week.

My final months at the Botanic Garden were spent in the Alpine Department, which included the limestone and sandstone rock gardens beside the lake. Looking back on my two years in Cambridge, my mind fills with so many happy memories: the excitement and fun of living in a university city thronging with young people and older heads brimming with knowledge and a desire to share it; the Orchard Tea Rooms at Grantchester and the Sunday breakfasts I enjoyed there beneath the apple trees in spring bloom and the ripening fruits of autumn; those many moments punting with friends on the Cam; the concerts both classical and jazz in the Guildhall; evensong at King's College Chapel; and last but not least, the plants and plant people I first met in the Botanic Garden, my alma mater. As for the cricket, well, I did take part in an occasional friendly match but never for or against a University Eleven.

The dream makers

King Alfred the Great (849–99) and his battles against the invading Danes was one of the many chapters in England's history I recalled from my school days. I would not have believed then that one day I would be living in his ancient capital. My first weekend in Winchester was busy and exciting. I had been found accommodation with a Mr and Mrs Stevens in an end of terrace house right next door to Hillier's home nursery at West Hill.

Only a hedge separated the two properties. I could hardly believe my luck. I also noted the close proximity to Winchester Prison!

Both the Stevens were long-time employees of the company. Arthur was then foreman at their Chandler's Ford Nursery while Evelyn worked in their shop down the road in the city. They were a kindly couple and having no children of their own, treated me like a son. Having settled in with my belongings I then made a preliminary tour of the nursery before heading down the Romsey Road to explore the city centre. I visited most of the historical sites, the West Gate, King Arthur's Round Table in the Great Hall and Winchester Cathedral among them, ending the day on St Giles Hill for views of the city, especially the High Street with its familiar statue of King Alfred.

A metal bench slowly being enveloped by a London plane in the grounds of Winchester College in 1962.

The following day, a Sunday, I continued my exploration with a visit to Winchester College, noting its portrait of the Trusty Servant and on the cricket field the curious sight of a metal bench slowly being enveloped by the massive stem of a London plane (*Platanus* × *hispanica*);

.....

St Catherine's Hill offers some of the best views of Winchester and supports a rich chalkland flora.

by 2016 the bench had virtually disappeared. From here I followed the River Itchen south through the water meadows to the Hospital of St Cross, one of whose Masters was Henry Compton (1632–1713), later to become Bishop of London. A keen patron of botanical and horticultural activities and a sponsor of plant-collectors, he assembled in his garden at Fulham Palace a notable collection of new and rare foreign plants including many trees and shrubs from the New World (East North America). His name is commemorated in *Comptonia peregrina*, sweet fern, a small, suckering, deciduous North American shrub related to our native bog myrtle (*Myrica gale*) with aromatic fern-like leaves. Many years later I saw it growing wild in the coastal sand dunes of Cape Cod, Massachusetts.

Dominating the Itchen valley and offering excellent views of Winchester and its environs is St Catherine's Hill (318ft/97m), which was my final destination. It supports a rich chalkland flora including round-headed rampion (*Phyteuma orbiculare*), my first sight of this rare British native, and autumn gentian (*Gentianella amarella*) as well as a medley of butterflies. From this vantage point I was struck by the frequency of trees in the city and not just their numbers but, as subsequent investigation revealed, the many exotics planted in gardens, public places and quiet corners. The Cathedral precincts supported both Chinese and American evergreen magnolias in *Magnolia delavayi* and *M. grandiflora* respectively and my eye was caught by another

.....

evergreen, *Ligustrum lucidum*, the Chinese tree privet, a British and Irish Champion according to the Tree Register of Britain and Ireland (TROBI) before it succumbed to a disease. Shortly after, it was replaced by another specimen which is itself now a notable presence.

The grounds of Winchester College boasted massive examples of London plane, while in private gardens around the city centre I came upon noble specimens of weeping silver lime (*Tilia tomentosa* 'Petiolaris'), *Ginkgo biloba* and sycamore (*Acer pseudoplatanus*). There were more unusual trees, including Indian bean tree (*Catalpa bignonioides*) and the Chinese *C. ovata*, empress tree (*Paulownia tomentosa*) and Judas tree (*Cercis siliquastrum*) and it required no serious research to conclude that Winchester's gardeners enjoyed a local source for such specials, namely Hilliers.

This Chinese tree privet (*Ligustrum lucidum*) by the main entrance to Winchester Cathedral Green was a British and Irish champion.

Since first learning of my appointment I had had plenty of time to think about the challenge of joining one of the gardening world's most famous nurseries. As I was soon to discover, it was regarded by many authorities to have taken on the mantle relinquished at the beginning of the century by the celebrated Veitch Nursery of Chelsea as the major supplier of woody plants hardy in the temperate regions. HG's grandfather Edwin Hillier, the founder of the family nursery at Winchester in 1864, had himself worked for Veitch in the 1850s. In retrospect, I consider myself fortunate to have joined Hillier and Sons when I did. The 1960s and 1970s are considered by many as being the company's glory years in terms of the number and variety of plants being grown and made available to the public.

First day at Hilliers

So it was with a feeling of expectation that I reported for duty on that first Monday morning, having been fortified with a full English breakfast by Mrs Stevens. HG told me that I would be working under

.....

Ron Hoskins, the nursery foreman at West Hill Nursery in the stock office. Each year during summer, a count was made by foremen in the various nurseries of the plants considered ready and available for sale the coming season. The names and quantities available were entered by hand in large stock ledgers. Given that Hilliers at this time had several nurseries situated in a triangle between Winchester, Romsey and Eastleigh, the total number of different plants involved was considerable.

Woody plants (trees, shrubs, hedging plants, climbers and bamboos), roses, hardy perennials and alpines were all being grown, while bulbous and aquatic plants were sourced from specialist growers. The names of plants in each category were entered in the stock books in alphabetical order, each name followed by the total number of plants available for sale. As orders were received by post or phone or given verbally at flower shows (since of course there was no email then) the totals for each plant were reduced until the stock was exhausted, at which point orders subsequently received would be placed on an Await Supply List.

The wedding cake tree (*Cornus controversa* 'Variegata') with its characteristic tabulated branching, seen here in a garden near Wells Cathedral, June 2016.

For those desirable plants difficult or slow to increase (bulk up is the commercial term), most customers would be happy enough to be on the AS List and to pay the special price such plants commanded. One of these was the so-called wedding cake tree (*Cornus controversa* 'Variegata'), a charming white-variegated form of a Chinese tree admired for the tabulated nature of its branching which can be emphasized by selective pruning. It is relatively slow-growing and was then scarce in the trade, being propagated by grafting. Only small plants were available and only a few each year, hence the name given it by a gardening journalist – 'the pound an inch tree'.

.....

Plant catalogues

The following year the stock books were replaced in favour of a cabinet system with sliding trays housing individual cards for each plant. This required extra staff and a new office. I found it a tedious job, but at least it ensured that I became familiar with a great number of new names which over time I came to match with the plants themselves. I was also given a job helping a colleague, Dennis Woodland, gardens adviser in the Landscape Department, in compiling and revising the plant catalogues. At that time, Hillier issued ten catalogues and lists covering the whole range of plants, bulbs and seeds on offer. Dennis was a fine plantsman, Wisley-trained and generous with his expertise and advice. Thanks to him I became familiar with the succinct style required for plant catalogues; he advised me to try to visualize, if not actually view, the plant when describing it and to keep in mind those reading about it for the first time. Dennis also encouraged me in writing articles for the horticultural press, especially the *Gardeners' Chronicle* and the *RHS Journal*.

The publications we were working on at this time had special significance. The company would be celebrating its centenary in 1964 and the main catalogue that year would be a bumper edition with many additional plants offered for the first time. Referred to as the *Centenary Catalogue of Trees and Shrubs including Climbers, Conifers and Bamboos*, this green-covered descriptive publication (Trees & Shrubs 100) when completed contained 203 closely packed pages listing around 4000 woody plants and sold for 7s 6d. A companion catalogue in a pale blue cover, *Hardy Perennial and Alpine Plants including Hardy Ferns and Ornamental Grasses*, cost 3s.

One bonus of my involvement on the catalogues was the need for me to visit the nurseries on a regular basis in order to see the living plants and prepare the appropriate descriptions. Initially I was asked to check the nursery stock for rogues, that is, plants growing in the wrong rows. Normally, the nursery staff themselves would be the first to spot 'wrong-uns' and occasionally the 'wrong-un' would turn out to be something special, as when Reg (Alf) Alford, foreman at the Eastleigh Nursery, noticed a branch sport on one of a row of round-leaved

.....

beech (*Fagus sylvatica* 'Rotundifolia'). The sport had smaller, more rounded leaves than the parent and when grafted on to a common beech stock it developed a more erect habit. With Alf's agreement, we named it 'Cockleshell'.

The dream makers

Over many years the company benefited from a long succession of talented and skilled nursery foremen and propagators who not only honed their skills while germinating, rooting, grafting, budding and

growing a huge range of plants – many of them rare or difficult – but also passed on their expertise to others. Not satisfied with simply increasing or growing plants, many extended their interests into plant breeding, to which the Hillier catalogues and today's *Hillier Manual of Trees and Shrubs* bear ample testimony. These individuals, whom I nicknamed the 'dream makers', were valued by HG who, like his father and grandfather before him, had an eye for a good plant and just as keen an eye for ability, active or latent. No wonder so many of his staff, encouraged by his example and his enthusiasm, took more than a working interest in the plants they were growing.

Harold Hillier, known to his staff as HG, had a good eye for a plant and for recognizing ability in a person. Here he is in his arboretum, aged 75, in 1980.

The first of the Hillier propagators I met was Arthur Prior at the West Hill Nursery. I was told that he was one of the old school who kept his propagation methods close to his chest but I always found him helpful with information, especially when it came to the wide range of tender plants from the world's Mediterranean and warm temperate regions under his care. Another propagator was Peter Dummer, a Devonian who had spent several years as a cowman on a Hampshire farm before joining Hilliers, where he worked in several of their nurseries including a period of propagation at West Hill before being sent to the Chandler's Ford Nursery. Here he became assistant to the legendary propagator Vic Pawlowski, who helped hone his grafting skills while working on

.....

Japanese maples and a host of other specialist woody plants including magnolias as well as rhododendrons, azaleas and other ericaceous plants.

Vic Pawlowski, who later worked as chief propagator for the Rothschilds at Exbury Gardens on the Solent, was an inspirational and pioneering tutor in propagation techniques. Several of those who worked with him later went on to make names for themselves elsewhere, including John Bond, who eventually became keeper of the Savill and Valley gardens at Windsor, and Douglas Harris, who became a senior horticultural adviser with MAFF,

The 'dream makers', Peter Dummer (*left*) and Reg (Alf) Alford; between them they raised a wealth of new hardy, woody plants.

now DEFRA, before moving to Exbury Gardens as manager. Finally, with his wife Margot, he established his own nursery at Penwood near Newbury in Berkshire. Another beneficiary of Pawlowski's skills was Brian Humphrey, a founding member of the Plant Propagators' Society of Great Britain and Ireland, who rose to become Hillier's nursery manager and director before leaving in 1986 to join Notcutts Nursery at Woodbridge in Suffolk.

It was at the Chandler's Ford nursery that Peter Dummer picked out a seedling of *Hamamelis vernalis*, the Ozark witch hazel, which produced brilliant orange and flame shades in its autumn leaves instead of the normal yellow. He named it 'Sandra' after his daughter. Peter enjoyed a long and successful career at Hilliers, latterly at their Jermyns Lane Nursery, as a master propagator and hybridizer. He is remembered especially by those who worked with him, staff and students alike, as a generous and patient teacher with a wicked sense of humour. Of the many new hybrids

The late summer-flowering *Hypericum × dummeri* 'Peter Dummer', one of many new hybrids and selections raised by this master propagator.

.....

FAR LEFT Peter Moore with his new hybrid *Sarcococca hookeriana* 'Winter Gem' in February 2013.

LEFT *Daphne bholua* 'Jacqueline Postill', raised in 1982 by Alan Postill and named for his wife. It is one of the most popular winter-flowering shrubs.

and selections he raised, *Hypericum* × *dummeri* 'Peter Dummer', *Phygelius* × *rectus* 'Salmon Leap', *Gaultheria* × *wisleyensis* 'Pink Pixie' and *Abutilon* × *suntense* 'Jermyns' are among the most well-known. Several of them earned the RHS Award of Garden Merit, while *Cotinus* 'Grace' in 1983 and *Berberis* 'Goldilocks' in 1991 earned him the Reginald Cory Memorial Cup for the best new hardy plant raised and shown to the RHS as a deliberate hybrid.

Following on in Peter's footsteps, two of his young protégés who joined Hillier on leaving school have since made their own contributions to the world of garden plants. One of them, Peter Moore, used his skills and imagination in producing, among others, an excellent and popular evergreen flowering shrub in *Choisya* × *dewitteana* 'Aztec Pearl' as well as the sweetly fragrant *Sarcococca hookeriana* 'Winter Gem', both AGM plants. Alan Postill, meanwhile, will forever be remembered by shrub enthusiasts for *Daphne bholua* 'Jacqueline Postill', named for his wife, who joined Hilliers having travelled from New Zealand in order to learn more about plant propagation. This exceptional evergreen has since proved to be one of the best-selling winter-flowering shrubs in Britain and another recipient of the RHS Award of Garden Merit. Although officially retired, Alan, like Peter, is still producing new hybrids, two of his most recent being *Cotinus* 'Candy Floss' and *Choisya* × *dewitteana* 'Aztec Gold'.

.....

'Alf' Alford, both in the Eastleigh Nursery and in his own small town garden, raised plants many a breeder would have been envious of. One of these, *Sorbus* 'Eastern Promise', a small tree with fiery autumn foliage and rose-pink fruits, was awarded the RHS Reginald Cory Memorial Cup in 1994, while *Lonicera* × *purpusii* 'Winter Beauty' and *Deutzia* × *hybrida* 'Iris Alford', named for his wife, are just two of the many flowering shrubs he was responsible for. Alfie was born in the village of Mortimer on the Hampshire-Berkshire border, later moving to Sherfield-on-Loddon and joining the church choir, where he became known as the boy with the golden voice. His interest in nature and growing plants was encouraged by his grandfather and on leaving school he worked as a gardener with several local estates before joining the Royal Navy at the outbreak of war. On leaving the navy at the war's end he joined Hilliers, eventually becoming foreman at the Eastleigh Nursery.

Lonicera × *purpusii* 'Winter Beauty' raised by Alf Alford in 1966 – an excellent winter-flowering shrub.

I enjoyed living in Winchester with its many opportunities and attractions, not all of which were plant-related. On one occasion I attended a classical concert in the cathedral given by the Hallé Orchestra, which I had first heard at the Victoria Hall in my home town, Bolton. It was a varied programme beginning with Vaughan Williams's Fantasia on a Theme by Thomas Tallis. I was sitting in the back row of seats below the great west window and I recall closing my eyes and feeling the swelling power of the music surging down the nave to overwhelm me.

Winchester flora

On that same day I purchased in a secondhand bookshop a slim volume entitled *List of Flowering Plants and Ferns found within seven miles of Winchester*, compiled and revised by F.I.W., whom I later discovered was a Mr F.I. Warner, a Hampshire amateur botanist. It was a simple list of some 750 plants with their botanical names and locations and had been published by a local printer and publisher, Warren & Son. As

.....

The Neptune steps with attendant Canary Island palms (*Phoenix canariensis*) in Tresco Abbey Gardens, Isles of Scilly in April 1981.

The stunning muscular piebald stem of a Chilean myrtle (*Luma apiculata*) in Tresco's Abbey Gardens.

I had found in Bolton, there is no more enjoyable way of getting to know an area than compiling a flora and that is what I decided upon. Given that Mr Warner's book was published in 1872, I reckoned it would be an interesting challenge to compile another list to publish in 1972, a century later. Accordingly, I bought a map covering the Winchester area and drew a circle on it defining the 7 miles (11km) radius. I then divided the area into segments which I could visit in turn. It helped that a pioneering work, *An Atlas of the British Flora*, had recently been published and I was in possession of a pack of record cards produced by this project to enable recorders in the field to tick off those species found in a particular area.

For the next few years I spent occasional weekends and many long summer evenings on foot or bicycle exploring my target areas and recording the plants, but it was a slow job. In the summer of 1963 I had help from a fellow Hillier employee, Michael Hickson, who took me riding pillion on his scooter to search for wild flowers as well as visiting gardens and nurseries. Towards the end of the year he left to become head gardener for Sir John and Lady Heathcoat-Amory at Knightshayes Court above Tiverton in Devon and his place at Hillier and as my help and occasional transport was taken by Len Beer, a Devon man whose motorbike was instrumental in getting us to many peripheral locations. In the event I never got to finish the recording as other work and events

.....

overtook it. However, some of my records were incorporated in *The Flora of Hampshire*, published in 1996.

South West of England

It was Len who invited me to join him on a week's holiday visiting gardens and wild places in Devon and Cornwall in October 1963 and never having been to the South West I needed no second asking. Starting with Dartington Hall, where Len had previously studied horticulture, we moved on to Slapton Sands, Plymouth Ho, Land's End and then to Penzance, where we boarded a ferry to the Isles of Scilly and thence to Tresco and the Abbey Gardens whose then head gardener, John Smith, had been a fellow student of mine at the Botanic Garden in Cambridge. He invited us to stay with him and his wife in the gardener's cottage and had also arranged for us to meet Commander Dorrien-Smith, who lived in the Abbey House. It was the end of the day and slightly misty when we set out towards the Old Abbey ruins, where we spied the Commander in a white jacket and peaked cap, moving through the tropical foliage like a spectre. We met and he bade us welcome before strolling ahead, intent on showing us something of the garden's collection before darkness enveloped it. This was the first of many visits I was to make over the years and I can still see in my mind's eye the huge New Zealand pohutukawa (*Metrosideros excelsa*) rising above me, the stately Canary Island palms (*Phoenix canariensis*) and the exotic piebald stems of *Luma apiculata*, a Chilean myrtle, all new to me.

Returning to the mainland, Len and I visited three famous Cornish gardens. The first was Trengwainton, near Penzance, where the owner, Colonel Sir Archibald Bolitho, showed us around. Next came Trewithen Gardens near Truro, where we were welcomed by Mrs Alison Johnstone, accompanied by her head gardener and his deputy. One of the many highlights of Trengwainton was a giant *Eucryphia cordifolia* from Chile in magnificent bloom, while at Trewithen the *Acer wardii* with its beautiful yellow-tinted, three-lobed and slender pointed leaves was the jewel in the crown for me. This specimen, now long gone, was probably the last remaining example in cultivation of the Scottish plant hunter George Forrest's 1914 introduction from the Yunnan-Burma border.

.....

Our final visit, to Caerhays on the coast near St Austell, completed a memorable week. Here, we were introduced by the owner, Mr Julian Williams, to a veritable Aladdin's cave of rare trees and shrubs, principally from Eastern Asia. I especially remember numerous maples as well as meliosmas, magnolias, rhododendrons, camellias (none in flower of course), evergreen oaks (*Quercus* species) and two remarkable stone oaks, *Lithocarpus fenestratus* and *L. pachyphyllus*, the last named bearing curious shillelagh-like clusters of strangely contorted fruits, one of which, now dried and wizened, I still have as a keepsake. Indeed it makes a regular appearance at Christmas parties in a 'guess the object' game!

The following year I again found myself in Cornwall, travelling with Arne Jakobsen, a Danish student at Hilliers, and Keith Courtney, a Liverpudlian who was then working at Warrens, the printers in Winchester. Although professing no particular interest in plants, Keith helped in staging a Hilliers exhibit at an RHS London Show and on many occasions turned out for the Hilliers cricket and football teams. He became a firm friend and remains so today. Unlike my first visit, this one took place in March and in arranging our trip HG kindly agreed to write to the garden owners beforehand, all of whom he knew, to help smooth the way.

This time we began with Caerhays and both Julian Williams and his head gardener, Philip Tregunna, were our guides. The camellias were in full bloom and we were shown *C.* × *williamsii* 'J.C. Williams' and the original 'Mary Christian' plus a number of rhododendrons and the big magnolias, including the Wilson introduction of *M. sprengeri* var. *diva* and a magnificent *M. sargentiana* var. *robusta* in full bloom which took our breath away. At one point we were admiring a tall group of evergreen *Michelia doltsopa*, now regarded as a *Magnolia*, when Mr Williams commented that one of them was suspected to be different. I thought no more of it at the time but on a subsequent visit, again with Len Beer in April 1967, I asked if I might collect a flowering specimen to check it out and on being given the go ahead I proceeded to climb bear-style up one of the two main stems to reach it, above a fork. This was a big mistake. Rain had fallen overnight and the stems were greasy. To cap it all I was wearing wellingtons and had ascended to a height of around

.....

The curious fruit clusters of the rare evergreen stone oak, *Lithocarpus pachyphyllus*, at Caerhays Castle, July 2004.

Julian Williams (right) and head gardener Philip Tregunna admiring *Rhododendron* 'Golden Oriole' at Caerhays Castle, March 2004.

20ft (6m) when I suddenly found myself sliding back down the stem with my arms still wrapped around it. Seconds later I was hanging upside-down with one leg jammed in the fork, my head less than 12in (30cm) from the ground! Len rushed to my assistance, anxiously asking, 'Are you all right?' All I could think of saying by way of a face-saver was, 'I bet Wilson never fell out of a *Michelia*.' This tree was eventually identified as *Magnolia floribunda* (formerly *Michelia floribunda*), which enjoys a wide distribution in the wild from south-west China into Burma and Thailand south to Vietnam.

When we departed Caerhays in 1964 we headed for Penjerrick, another famous woodland garden above the coast near Falmouth. On arriving we knocked on the door of a nearby cottage whose smoking chimney was a hopeful sign of occupancy. It turned out to be the home

.....

of Bert Evans, the recently retired head gardener, whose predecessor Samuel Smith raised many *Rhododendron* hybrids in the early 20th century, for which he was awarded a Veitch Memorial Medal by the RHS. He was also an early recipient of the RHS Associate of Honour. Mr Evans was expecting us and generously gave the whole morning to taking us round, describing the history and stories associated with the garden and its plants, one of which, a huge Chilean aromatic, evergreen tree, *Laureliopsis philippiana*, possessed a broad, multi-stemmed, semi-weeping crown. This was only the beginning.

Now warming to his role, Bert took us to see the original plants of Penjerrick's most notable *Rhododendron* hybrids, *R.* 'Cornubia', *R.* 'Cornish Cross' and *R.* 'Barclayi Robert Fox', the first with blood-red, bell-shaped flowers, the second with narrowly bell-shaped, waxy blooms mottled rose-pink and the third with flowers of a glowing deep crimson. All three were showstoppers and I can still picture them today, their blooms glistening in the morning sun. He next led us past groves of Australian tree ferns (*Dicksonia antarctica*), one with a 21ft (7m) stem, to see two impressive bamboos, *Chimonobambusa quadrangularis*, the square-stemmed bamboo, and *Phyllostachys edulis*, both of which were forming extensive colonies beneath the canopy. It was an exciting conclusion to our Cornish gardens tour but we still managed to visit a further two notable gardens on our return home, both in Devon.

The first of these was The Garden House at Buckland Monachorum, whose owner, Mr Lionel Fortescue, a former Master at Eton, had designed and planted a lovely garden filled with fine plants tastefully displayed. We then hastened to Knightshayes Court above Tiverton, home of Sir John and Lady Heathcoat-Amory, where Keith and I were pleased to meet up again with our friend head gardener Michael Hickson, who since our Hillier days had married Lena, a Danish girl he had first met at The Garden House. I was to see a lot more of them over the years. Back at work the following morning, I gave HG a resumé of our adventure showing him my notes of plants seen, most of which he knew from his own visits in earlier years.

By this time I had become familiar with most if not all of the trees and shrubs growing in the West Hill Nursery. An original Wilson

.....

collection of the Chinese *Emmenopterys henryi* had grown slowly on the shallow chalk soil and had yet to flower, though its distinctive bronze-tinted foliage was more than attractive. Another Wilson introduction, *Tilia oliveri* became a favourite of mine for its handsome silver-backed leaves and broad rounded canopy. It still thrives and dominates an open, grassy space to the rear of what is now a Hillier Garden Centre.

Another tree of note was a maple raised from seed of the Japanese *Acer miyabei* growing at the Royal Botanic Gardens, Kew some time before 1935. It had developed a pleasing rounded crown and displayed rich butter-yellow autumn tints. Examining the leaves and fruits with HG one day, we came to the conclusion that it was a hybrid between the above and *A. cappadocicum*. On a subsequent visit to Kew I found the two parents growing within pollinating distance. The same hybrid later occurred in a paddock at Hergest Croft Gardens, home of the Banks family at Kington in

Tilia oliveri, an original E.H. Wilson (Veitch) introduction of 1900, still thrives at the rear of the Hillier Garden Centre at West Hill, Winchester.

Herefordshire. HG allowed me to publish the name *Acer × hillieri* for the West Hill tree accompanied by the cultivar name 'West Hill'. Later, a yellow-leaved seedling was raised and selected by Peter Dummer which we named 'Summergold', its *A. cappadocicum* parent being the cultivar 'Aureum'.

Of the many shrubs of interest raised at this nursery, both *Buddleja* 'West Hill' (*B. davidii* × *B. fallowiana*) and *Viburnum* × *globosum* (*V. davidii* × *V. calvum*) are of note. The latter was brought to my attention by propagator Ray Murphy, who distinguished several seedlings of sturdier growth in a box of *V. davidii* seedlings. The parent plants grew in close proximity by the nursery drive. An original seedling named

.....

LEFT *Buddleja* 'West Hill', raised as a chance seedling in the old Jail Border at Hillier's West Hill Nursery. Here it is flowering in the Centenary Border at the Sir Harold Hillier Gardens in October 2014.

BELOW The *Hillier Centenary Catalogue of Trees and Shrubs*, published in 1964.

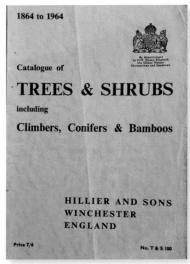

1864 to 1964

Catalogue of

TREES & SHRUBS

including

Climbers, Conifers & Bamboos

HILLIER AND SONS
WINCHESTER
ENGLAND

Price 7/6   No. T & S 100

'Jermyns Globe' still grows in the Sir Harold Hillier Gardens.

One other shrub worthy of mention is *Lonicera setifera*. A single plant of this late winter-flowering species grew in a border below the high outer wall of the neighbouring prison. It had been raised from seed collected by the Austro-American collector Dr Joseph Rock in China in 1924 and was then rare in cultivation. One night an escaping prisoner climbed over the wall, dropping on the nursery side slap bang on poor old Joseph Rock. HG was not amused. Luckily the prisoner was recaptured and the damaged shrub soon recovered.

Hillier centenary

In 1964 two things occurred which contributed significantly to the future course of my career and life. Hilliers celebrated their centenary with a number of special events, one of which was an invitation to horticultural friends, including members of the gardening press and other guests, to join them on 11 June for a tour of seven of the company's

.....

nurseries. This was followed after lunch by a visit to the garden and arboretum being developed around HG's home, Jermyns House at Ampfield, near Romsey. It was an unforgettable occasion on a fine day, with many of the great and the good of the horticultural world in attendance. The highlight was the recently completed 'Centenary Border', a central grass vista 260yd (237m) long flanked by beds of woody plants (including species roses) and perennials, which was officially opened by Lord Aberconway, President of the RHS, who marked the occasion by planting a 10ft (3m) tall Dawyck beech (*Fagus sylvatica* 'Dawyck') at its eastern end. Close by grew a venerable sweet chestnut (*Castanea sativa*), which had obviously been pollarded in the past. The comparatively short bole, clothed with a thick, deeply fissured, reddish-brown bark, had an impressive spiral twist. Not long after, it was found to have a hollow and diseased centre and pronounced by some authority, I know not who, to be a potential risk to the public. I returned from a holiday one morning to find it had been removed. A ring count of the cut stump confirmed the tree to be 150 years old.

Guests were supplied with copies of the newly published green-backed *Centenary Catalogue of Trees and Shrubs*. As a comparatively new member of staff I felt a certain pride in being part of the team and the role, albeit small, I had had in putting the catalogue together. To see so many of the important guests that day thumbing through its pages gave me a buzz and I still treasure my original working copy with blank page interleaves for additions and corrections. Many were the generous articles written by members of the press following this event including, in the *Gardeners' Chronicle*, a four-page illustrated account of the Dwarf Conifer Collection written by one of the doyens of the day, Reginald Corley.

However, it was two comments made by HG that day which particularly impressed me. In answer to a reporter's question, 'What is your opinion on plant conservation?', he replied, 'I will tell you what I think of it – while others are talking about it I am doing it, roots in the ground, planting, planting, planting.' Earlier, in a speech, he had told his guests that 'with a staff of about two hundred and twenty we believe we are growing a greater variety of plants hardy in the temperate regions

.....

Jermyns House, former home of Sir Harold and Lady Hillier, now Administrative Centre of the Sir Harold Hillier Gardens at Ampfield.

than any other nursery in the world'. It was a proud comment but he wasn't a boastful man – he was simply stating a fact.

Some months later, shortly before Christmas, HG decided that he wanted me based at the Arboretum permanently, which is how I came to find myself ensconced in the billiard room at Jermyns House. It was the only room then available and the impressive full-sized billiard table it housed took up most of the space. HG's wife Barbara didn't like this arrangement one bit, especially when, after only a week, I had covered the table, protected by a white sheet, with myriad cut specimens of holly (*Ilex*) and box (*Buxus*) cultivars which I was then checking out. The following year I transferred to a proper office newly prepared for me in an outbuilding which, I was told, had once housed pigs. It proved most convenient and was spacious enough to accommodate an assistant, Hatton Gardener, whom I had come to know at West Hill Nursery while working in the stock office and later the landscape department.

Hatton had previously worked for the Roads Beautifying Association in an office below Charing Cross Railway Station in London and before that with an estate agent for a large private estate. During the Second World War he had been employed by the Forestry Commission, assessing plantations countrywide for timber to use as pit-props in the mining industry, which is how his interest and expertise in recording and measuring large or otherwise notable trees developed. He was an older man than me, a bachelor with a passion for recording and

.....

research, especially concerning trees. He was also a skilled tree measurer and had travelled widely throughout Britain, recording large, old and historical trees.

When I was told by HG that he wanted me to record the woody plants in his Arboretum, checking their identities and labelling them accordingly as well as preparing descriptions for a new publication he had in mind as a supplement, if not a successor to the centenary catalogue, I had requested that Hatton might be allowed to join me. HG agreed and here we were, the two of us, in our own office with a 12-year collection of trees, shrubs and much else to catalogue. Hatton quickly settled into the recording role in addition to preparing labels for those plants I identified or confirmed. All planting and gardening operations were then the responsibility of the head gardener, Jack Brice, a long-time and respected professional of the old school, who from the age of 14 had worked his way from garden boy then journeyman to become head gardener on a number of large estates in Surrey, Sussex and Berkshire before heading to Pembrokeshire to run a market garden.

In 1961 he was invited by HG to take on the job of working head gardener at Jermyns in charge of a small staff. He tackled the job with gusto and by the time I became involved he was well established and totally trusted by HG. A disciplinarian, he was seen as something of a martinet by the company's propagators when, armed with secateurs and large plastic bags, they combed the Arboretum for cuttings, scions and seed to meet their annual targets. He didn't harass them, but he kept a close eye on their activities. Like most gardeners, Jack would admire a tree or shrub for its ornamental quality alone while a propagator, or some of them at least, would be looking to see how many cuttings it might provide. I suspect Jack viewed my activities with a certain reservation given that I wasn't actually doing anything really physical like digging or pruning, but he gradually accepted and respected my role and Hatton's and we became good friends.

I remember him once telling me how, in his years as a journeyman, he would look forward to the day when he, like certain other head gardeners of the day, would get to wear a bowler hat and manage enough staff to enable him to take life a little easier. Sadly it never happened and

.....

Jack Brice, head gardener at the Hillier Arboretum, with one of his favourite camellias, *C. × williamsii* 'Donation', in the 1960s.

he continued working hard until the day of his retirement when, to commemorate the event, he and HG each planted a specimen of a conifer Jack had found as a chance seedling in the Arboretum. Its name is *Cupressus lusitanica* 'Brice's Weeping'. I prefer to remember him for the mass displays of camellias and deciduous azaleas he and his staff planted, which are much enjoyed by visitors to this day.

Naming new cultivars
One of my most enjoyable roles was naming and describing new cultivars of plants discovered or raised on the nurseries. I had noted that many such had previously been named either after the company or one of its nurseries, *Viburnum × hillieri* and × *Halimiocistus wintonensis* being just two. This was logical enough but staff members were constantly discovering new sports and seedlings which I reasoned might be named after them or something even more adventurous. I began cautiously with names such as *Laburnum × watereri* 'Alford's Weeping', *Tsuga heterophylla* 'Laursen's Column' and *Pinus parvifolia* 'Adcock's Dwarf', gradually extending the choice to include more fanciful and descriptive names such as *Prunus* 'Pink Shell', *Sorbus folgneri* 'Lemon Drop' and *Helianthemum* 'Coppernob'. A seedling Knaphill azalea, with flowers of a blackish-red in bud opening to a smouldering nasturtium-red overlaid crimson, I christened 'Dracula'. I was never quite sure what HG would allow me to get away with given

.....

Prunus 'Pink Shell', one of the loveliest spring-flowering Japanese cherries in a genus full of treasures.

that his tastes were more traditional and cautious, but then things began to change.

HG was spending a few days in a nursing home recovering from a minor operation when I sent him, via a family member, a few cut specimens from the Arboretum. They included a *Cotoneaster salicifolius* seedling with an abundance of berries at first yellow becoming pink-flushed with age. I thought it might cheer him up and occupy his thoughts if I asked him to suggest a suitable cultivar name. The next day the specimen was returned to me with a note from HG which read 'why not 'Pink Champagne'! This from a man who, according to John Hillier, his elder son, only ever drank an occasional cider and maybe a small dry sherry at Christmas. I was surprised, as was his family too. Having started, he continued in a similar vein with *Sorbus* 'Pearly King', *Ulmus parvifolia* 'Frosty' and so on. Eventually, those staff finding or raising their own hybrids or selections were encouraged to come up with their own names, many of which are in common use today.

First dawn redwood

One of the first trees that HG had planted following his purchase of Jermyns House in 1951 was a dawn redwood (*Metasequoia glyptostroboides*). Hillier was the first British nursery to offer this famous deciduous conifer commercially when, in their 1949 *Catalogue of Trees and Shrubs* they advertised 'seedlings which have grown with surprising

.....

The strongly fluted base of the dawn redwood planted close to Jermyns House. This was one of the first seedlings raised by Hilliers in 1948.

vigour having survived their first winter outside' at 21 shillings. The above seedling was planted by the drive to the house, where today it has made a tree with an openly-branched habit, not unlike mature specimens in China but lacking their size, due no doubt to the relatively dry conditions of its site. This contrasts with the more vigorous columnar and shapely younger trees in the moister soils below the house and in nearby Ten Acres. It does however, possess an impressive buttressed base.

By now I was lodging in Brentry House, which served as a most convenient accommodation for those students, British and overseas, working in the Arboretum and nurseries. It was built on a slight rise across the road, Jermyns Lane, from the Arboretum entrance which allowed those so inclined to spend their free time studying the plant collections. When I stayed there (for a year only) it was surrounded by a plantation of tall-stemmed Scots pine with a dense undergrowth of *Rhododendron × superponticum*. Over a period of years many of the pines were culled or blew down and the rhododendron thicket was cleared. In their place a goodly collection of species and hybrid rhododendrons and azaleas together with *Pieris* species and cultivars and other ericaceous shrubs were planted, bolstered by a wide variety of broad-leaved and coniferous trees including a Japanese red maple (*Acer pycnanthum*), by 2016 a TROBI British and Irish Champion at 52ft (16m), the flaky barked Chinese *Abies squamata*, the Mexican sacred fir (*Abies religiosa*), famous in its native country as providing a winter roost for migrant monarch butterflies, and a goodly collection of oaks both deciduous and evergreen. King among them today is a magnificent loquat oak (*Quercus rysophylla*) from Mexico which when last measured (2013) proved to be the TROBI British and Irish Champion at 67ft (20.5m).

Not far from Brentry House an old sand pit offered a home for a variety of less hardy shrubs, *Mahonia acanthifolia* and *M. lomariifolia*

.....

among them, as well as a family of badgers which I occasionally visited at dusk, sitting in an overhanging oak the better to observe them. It was in Jermyns Lane in a damp ditch that I saw my first glow-worm and in nearby Ampfield Wood that I heard a nightingale singing. An old Hillier employee, Michael Marsh, from the nearby village of Ampfield, told me that he remembered as a boy hearing as many as seven nightingales singing when walking the length of the same lane. Today they are no more.

In case I have given the impression that my life was all work and no play, I should say that I led a busy social life too. It was a work colleague, Steve Berry, and I who started a Hillier Social Club with weekly meetings on winter evenings in a local church hall and coach visits

Quercus rysophylla; this Mexican loquat oak growing in Brentry plantation is the British and Irish Champion.

A Hillier Cricket XI versus a Wisley XI at West Hill School, Winchester (1 September 1963). It includes Steve Berry, Keith Courtney and Len Beer (first, second and fifth from left standing) and me, Maurice Pritchard and Michael Hickson (first, second and fifth from left crouching).

.....

through the year to well-known gardens such as the Savill and Valley Gardens at Windsor Great Park, Wisley, Kew, Sheffield Park and the Westonbirt Arboretum, to mention but a few. We also found enough volunteers to play cricket and football matches against Kew and Wisley and friendly matches against local opposition. We were allowed to use the cricket pitch at West Hill School next door to the Hillier Nursery for our home matches and on one occasion there we soundly beat a farmers' eleven, only to be annihilated by them in a return match in a farm paddock which had previously contained a herd of cattle. All was forgotten, however, when they entertained us to a hearty meal in a nearby barn with a plentiful supply of beer. For a year or two, the traditional staff cricket matches were revived, a President's XI captained by HG and including his elder son John versus a Staff XI captained by his younger son Robert.

Meanwhile, having joined the Hampshire Field Club and the Hampshire and Isle of Wight Naturalists Trust and being already a member of the Botanical Society of the British Isles, I spent many weekends on field outings in search of native flora. I shall never forget one such occasion with the last named when a large group of members met up in a woodland in the Chilterns to witness two boffins, both grass experts, one from Kew, the other from the British Museum (Natural History), discussing the differences between two closely related grasses, the hairy brome (*Bromus ramosus*) and the lesser hairy brome (*B. benekenii*), both now included under *Bromopsis*. One of the experts was convinced they were distinct enough to be regarded as separate species while his colleague wasn't so sure. We gathered around as they examined specimens of the two while discussing the minutiae of hairs, ligules, scales, angle of branching and so on before retiring to the nearby downs to eat our sandwiches. It was quite exciting and, from my point of view, good entertainment.

One of the members I met that day was Eric Clement, himself to become a respected amateur taxonomist and an authority on native flora. Later, with a colleague, he wrote a book entitled *Alien Plants of the British Isles* which, to my disappointment, excluded grasses. His name was given to a group of popular perennial garden tree mallows, *Lavatera*

.....

× *clementii*, he being the first to establish their hybrid origin as *L. olbia* × *L. thuringiaca*. 'Barnsley', 'Burgundy Wine' and 'Rosea' are just three of the many named selections currently available.

In search of the ghost

Several times in my life, exciting events or experiences have presented themselves at the end of a telephone line. One day, in mid-July, the phone rang in my office and on my answering, a man's voice announced 'I have just seen a ghost.' This was followed by a number with a GR prefix. I found the grid reference, which appeared to pinpoint a wood near Marlow in the Chiltern Hills in Buckinghamshire. Puzzled, I scratched my head and then recalled that a few years before I had been on a field meeting with the Botanical Society of the British Isles and had fallen into conversation with a man who, when it came to plants, seemed to know his onions, or in this case his orchids. He told me he had once seen the ghost orchid (*Epipogium aphyllum*), one of Britain's rarest natives, growing in a wood in the Thames valley area. He promised that if he ever saw it again he would let me know. Naturally, I gave him my contact details. So, this was it, at last.

As luck would have it, the next day was a Saturday, so with no time to waste I made an early morning start and drove to the location, parking my car in a quiet place beside a narrow road before heading into the wood, which was of beech. The ghost orchid, or spurred coral-root orchid, is a saprophyte – that is, a leafless plant without chlorophyll, living on dead or decaying woodland debris such as leaf mould. It is extremely rare in England, though distributed through most of Europe to Russia and the Caucasus.

In his classic account *Wild Flowers of the Chalk and Limestone* (1950), J.E. Lousley claimed it to be Britain's rarest plant, having been found in only two small locations and only about half a dozen individuals recorded since its first discovery in 1842. Its flowering is spasmodic and many years can pass before it next blooms. The erect inflorescence can carry four or five nodding flowers of a fleshy, pale yellowish or pinkish white, easily missed in the darkness of a beech wood. The chances of finding it myself were not good, but I might never have another one.

.....

I decided to walk slowly on a zigzag course and several times my eyes fixed on a likely candidate only to discover on closer examination it was a fungus. I had been told by my informant that it was imperative to protect the secret of its location and not to do anything to attract unwelcome attention. Accordingly, I kept my eyes peeled but the only people I saw were walkers with or without dogs. But could they, like me, have other things in mind? I tried to vary my deliberate quartering of the ground but found myself wondering what the others were about. Was that man apparently tying his shoelaces really examining the orchid? Was the dog walker only watching me? It was crazy but I couldn't be sure. I seemed to have covered the whole of the target area and was slowly making my way back to the car when I saw yet another fungus. I decided to check it out and that's when I had my 'Eureka' moment: a single spike a few inches above the leafy woodland floor and I had no doubt that I too had at last seen the ghost. I lingered no more than a minute after furtive glances all around before wandering apparently aimlessly back to my car, stopping occasionally to examine nothing in particular before driving home on cloud nine.

Work on the proposed new Hillier catalogue of trees and shrubs progressed slowly over the late 1960s due to competing activities and it wasn't until 1970 that a sense of urgency was injected into the project. HG continued to discuss with me plants he wished to have included and many is the time he would emerge from his small study in Jermyns House, a letter, note or plant specimen in hand as he set off to find me. The inevitable outcome, having discussed the matter in hand, was that we would then wander off together discussing other plants. HG was an inveterate letter reader and writer; I would often pass the French windows of his study as evening descended and catch sight of him still poring over heaps of correspondence, mainly letters, complimentary or otherwise, written by customers. He took it as his duty to reply to anything addressed to him personally or simply to the head of the company. I believe this responsibility in part prevented him from ever writing the kind of book his knowledge and experience justified.

The only time he started and actually finished writing what was to be the first in a series of Penguin gardening books, this one on trees and

.....

shrubs, the bundles of typed descriptions and text stored in a large cardboard box mysteriously went missing before it could be delivered to the publishers. One rumour was that it had inadvertently been misplaced in a general tidy up and ended up on a bonfire. Whether he lost heart after his loss I do not know, but apart from occasional articles and a descriptive booklet based on a lecture he had delivered on the subject of dwarf conifers, he never to my knowledge attempted a book again except for the new catalogue, of which more to come.

By 1970 I had been with the company for eight years and though I was undoubtedly learning more about woody plants every day there were other issues both private and professional that had me considering the options of moving on. I still wasn't sure how important my present role was in the company's eyes nor what my future expectations might be. On one occasion, a senior member of the company brought a group of American horticulturists into my office and on introducing me to them, struggled to explain my exact function before asking me 'What do we call you?' He was genuinely unsure and I was genuinely embarrassed. I had been regarded by HG as a sort of horticultural botanist, though I had no academic training as such.

I was answerable directly to HG and I was more than happy with that, but I sensed that times were changing and changes in the commercial nursery industry would undoubtedly be felt and acted upon by Hilliers. What was to be my role in the future of the Arboretum and the Arboretum's role in the future of the company? Naturally, I was aware of some of the opportunities available should I decide to seek pastures new. I had already had a favourable indication from a friend at a well-known and respected arboretum in the USA that a senior position there might be made available to me and there were other possibilities too, both in the USA and New Zealand. It was all very tempting but first I needed to make my feelings known to HG, which I did towards the end of November that year.

He took seriously my request and arranged for me to meet him in his study, where he gave me a sympathetic hearing before suggesting I write a list of my concerns and requests which he would discuss with his partners – his sons John and Robert – before responding. On

.....

5 December 1970, my thirty-third birthday, I was offered by Hillier and Sons a new contract which went a long way towards satisfying my desire for change. One of these, important to me, though it seemed to puzzle HG, was that I should have an official job title and my preference for 'curator' had been accepted. There was also a clarification of my duties, giving me a greater latitude to use my creative instincts in remunerative outside work such as lecturing, literary and advisory work as agreed with the partners as well as reasonable freedom to attend conferences, horticultural shows and gardens relevant to my work. An unexpected but welcome clause stated that in the event of the retirement or death of H.G. the curator should assume responsibility for the Arboretum and gardens under the direction of the continuing partners. As a bonus I was offered a raise in salary to £1600 per annum. I could not but rejoice at this turn of events, which had arrived at a critical and stressful period in my life and career.

I spent that Christmas with my friends the Hicksons and their children in Devon, where I relaxed by reading J.R. Tolkein's *The Lord of the Rings*. At night I lay in bed wondering what the year ahead would bring and what my future might be.

CHAPTER SIX

The catalogue to end all catalogues

Apart from meeting my future wife on 9 January, I shall remember 1971 for two other major events, the publication of the *Hillier Manual* and my participation in a three month plant hunting expedition to the Himalaya. An account of the expedition was published in 1981 under the title *Plant Hunting in Nepal*.

For several years, work on what HG referred to as a new extended catalogue of trees and shrubs had rumbled on. It was a tale of stops and starts as more pressing work intervened on a regular basis. Taking the Centenary Catalogue as a base, we worked on revising the nomenclature and descriptions of the 4000 plants already included while providing descriptions of all those other plants grown by Hilliers, often in smaller numbers, most of which had never before appeared in their catalogues. As a guide, HG determined that to be eligible for inclusion, a new plant must be represented in the nurseries by at least ten saleable individuals. This made sense in theory but proved difficult in practice, as the temptation to include certain plants available in lesser numbers was hard to ignore and I was the biggest culprit.

The plan of action agreed by HG was this. I would review and where necessary revise the 1964 text and prepare descriptions for the additional plants. Hatton, meanwhile, now known as Arboretum Recorder, worked zealously on researching information on those new plants referred to in the literature, including each and every volume of the *Gardeners' Chronicle* since its first publication in 1841. He achieved this by means of an arrangement with the RHS Lindley Library, which allowed him to take out on loan one volume at a time. Being a bachelor, Hatton chose to devote much of his free time to research and he was a dedicated list-maker. I wrote all the new text in longhand before passing it to our secretary, Mrs Parsons, who typed it up ready for the attention of HG. This he read through whenever he could find the time, mostly in the

.....

FAR LEFT The Hillier Manual of 1971 was a team effort led by Harold Hillier with Hatton Gardener (left) and me, seen here with *Magnolia delavayi* at Jermyns House.

LEFT Desmond Clarke, chief editor of the eighth edition of Bean's classic *Trees and Shrubs Hardy in the British Isles*, at his Surrey home in September 1988.

evenings or at weekends in his study, before returning it to me. I then dealt with any comments, queries, additions or deletions he had made.

Initially, I found that many of the descriptions from the Centenary Catalogue which I had increased from two or three to four or five lines, HG had reduced with a blue pencil. It was the same with my additions. He kept reminding me that this was to be a catalogue, not a book. Because the company was anxious to move things on, HG urged me to send the early entries from A to C to our printers, Yelf Brothers Ltd of Newport in the Isle of Wight, whose experienced and dedicated manager, Mr Alfred (Alfie) Daish, was to become a good friend. He was a man of integrity and unlimited patience, blessed with a ready sense of humour, all of which he needed in steering the project through to fruition.

Birth of the Hillier Manual

It came to a point, however, when I felt strongly that we owed it to our customers to provide them with more detailed information, at least for those plants of special interest. I decided one evening to bite the bullet and discuss this with HG. When I put it to him that here was an opportunity to further educate and even inspire the reader, he began to have second thoughts. He then asked 'If it isn't to be a catalogue, what

.....

are we to call it?' 'Why not a manual?' was my reply. To my relief he agreed, and from then on the descriptive text increased. I was delighted when he began to include brief anecdotes and personal comments which added considerably to the manual's value and attraction.

The botanical aspects of identifying and describing plants, known as taxonomy, fascinated HG and he once told me that if he had his time over again he would have gone to university and studied for a botany degree. He was the only nurseryman I ever saw using a hand lens. A favourite tome on woody plants was Alfred Rehder's *Manual of Trees and Shrubs Hardy in North America*, which was ever-present on the desk in his study. Another favourite, especially for its practical comments, personal anecdotes and historical information, was *Trees and Shrubs Hardy in the British Isles* by William Jackson Bean (1863–1947), who was in charge of the Arboretum and eventually curator of the Royal Botanic Gardens, Kew. Known to woody plant aficionados simply as 'Bean', this three-volume masterpiece was then being revised for an eighth edition by Desmond Clarke as chief editor, helped by a panel of experts and specialists, one of whom was HG. The general editor for the project was Professor George Taylor, the director at Kew. As it happens, the first volume of this edition covering the letters A–C had been published only the year before (1970) and volumes 2 (D–M), 3 (N–Rh.) and 4 (Ri–Z) were to follow in 1973, 1976 and 1980 respectively, followed by a hefty supplement compiled and written by Clarke and published in 1988.

Desmond Clarke's work was respected by HG and in preparing our manual we were kept informed of any major changes, especially in nomenclature, proposed by him for the new 'Bean'. In fact, we enjoyed a generous and mutually beneficial sharing of information which enriched both publications. Over this period I came to know Desmond quite well, though by nature he was a man of retiring nature who disliked crowds. He often came to the Hillier Arboretum and several times I visited his garden in Haslemere, Surrey, which boasted many interesting and rare trees and shrubs, including those collected by him as seed on visits to Kashmir and Chile. For close on 20 years I supplied him with notes, lists, seeds and plants relating to my own trips to the

.....

A galley proof of the Hillier Manual returned by the printers, with a request that it be donated to the Printers' Museum.

world's wild places and on several occasions I joined him and others on garden visits to Exbury, Abbotsbury, Kew and Borde Hill in Sussex. Following his death, aged 76, in 1991 I was surprised and honoured to find that he had left me in his will a handsomely bound copy of the three-volume *Plantae Wilsonianae*, an account of E.H. Wilson's woody plant collections for the Arnold Arboretum of Harvard University made in Western China during the years 1907, 1908 and 1910, edited by the Arboretum's director, Charles Sprague Sargent. A book-plate in the inside front cover of Vol.1 told me that this copy had originally belonged to Gerald Walter Erskine Loder, the 1st Lord Wakehurst, one time president of the RHS and a member of the famous Sussex garden dynasty whose home and garden, Wakehurst Place in Ardingly, is now managed by the Royal Botanic Gardens, Kew.

The final stages in the Manual's preparation found Hatton and me almost fully occupied with proofreading. In order to help the Yelf staff to interpret our corrections, Hatton decided to use pens with different-coloured inks to denote additions, deletions, corrections and so on. Some of the galley proofs looked quite colourful, but they were viewed with alarm by Yelf. One particular proof was returned to us after correcting with the request from Mr Daish 'Please preserve'. In a separate note he wrote, 'If you don't intend keeping this, we would like to donate it to the Printers' Museum or no one will ever believe it.' In another despairing note he ended with the comment 'I think the Manual will not be published in my lifetime' and sadly this was to prove true. He died aged 59, having steered it through virtually to the end.

.....

HILLIERS' MANUAL

OF

TREES & SHRUBS

HILLIER AND SONS
WINCHESTER
ENGLAND

FAR LEFT On the day
the *Hillier Manual
of Trees and Shrubs* was
launched in London
I was in Kathmandu,
Nepal – a dream
come true.

LEFT 'The catalogue
to end all catalogues' –
the first edition of the
green-backed *Hillier
Manual of Trees and
Shrubs* of 1971.

On 20 August that year I received one of the first copies off the press, just in time to include it in my rucksack when I set off the following month as a member of the University of Bangor (North Wales) Expedition to East Nepal. My absence abroad prevented me from attending the launch of the *Hillier Manual of Trees and Shrubs*, which took place at the Royal Horticultural Society's Great Autumn Show at Vincent Square, London on 20 September. On the same day, I was visiting the Botanic Garden at Godavari near Kathmandu where, on the wooded hillside above, I enjoyed seeing for the first time in the wild *Daphne bholua*, *Quercus lamellosa*, *Hydrangea aspera*, *Rosa brunonii*, *Rhododendron arboreum* and the striking *Roscoea purpurea* – and that was for starters.

Making gardening history

Naturally, I was delighted on returning home to hear from HG how well the Manual had been received, with reviews ranging from 'a horticultural bible' to 'the catalogue to end all catalogues'. The RHS president, Lord Aberconway, had described its publication as 'making gardening history'. The then doyen of gardening journalists Arthur Hellyer wrote in the *Financial Times*, 'Never has there been a catalogue quite like this, written entirely for enthusiasts, crammed with information and with no pictures

.....

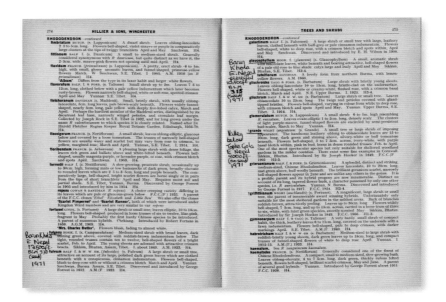

or other concessions to popular taste. It runs to 576 closely printed pages, contains descriptions of over 8000 plants representing 638 genera and with much of the tight-packed information expressed with telegraphic brevity.' Looking again at my copy, now dog-eared from constant use in the field, I was pleased by the number of Himalayan plants described which I had seen in Nepal and those I had noted to include in a future edition.

At first the Manual was published in hardback and soft cover editions costing £1.75 and £1.25 respectively. It was all text with no pictures. Today, with an eighth edition recently published, it is still referred to fondly as the 'greenback' edition. In 1979 the Manual went with me on my first visit to China, and when on one occasion I was confronted by a man waving a copy of Chairman Mao's 'Little Red Book', I responded by flourishing Hillier's 'Little Green Book', which he examined but could make neither head nor tail of!

Eminent botanists

One of the duties I most enjoyed at the Arboretum was accompanying visitors around the collections, especially those who were experts in a particular genus or group of plants. For several years in succession we hosted groups from the Botany Department at the British Museum

.....

OPPOSITE PAGE Pages from the first copy of the Manual, with three of the 24 *Rhododendron* species we saw in East Nepal underlined.

RIGHT Botanists from the British Museum (Natural History) visit the Hillier Arboretum; Professor William Stearn (fourth from left) and Dr Norman Robson (green shirt) talking to H.G. Hillier (far right), August 1974.

(Natural History), whom I encouraged to collect specimens to add to their Horticultural Herbarium of dried material. They welcomed the opportunity of a day in the country, as they viewed it, and their herbarium collections benefited too. These groups were usually led by a senior member of staff, of which the two most notable were Dr Norman Robson and Professor William Stearn. Norman was, and still is, the world expert on *Hypericum*, of which there are currently around 500 species worldwide. He also possessed a sound all-round knowledge of the rest of the plant world and together with his wife Eve he had planted their garden with a variety of interesting as well as ornamental plants, including of course hypericums. Over a period he checked and named all the hypericums grown in the Hillier Arboretum and nurseries and the account of the woody species in our Manual was based on his advice and research. He later did me the honour of naming a Chinese species *Hypericum lancasteri*.

William Stearn, who died in 2001 aged 90, I have previously mentioned as the author of one of my favourite and oft-consulted reference books, *Stearn's Dictionary of Plant Names for Gardeners*. Botanists, however, especially those engaged in the fields of taxonomy, nomenclature and bibliography, remember him as the man who wrote the book others thought impossible – *Botanical Latin*. First published

.....

in 1966, it is described on the inside cover as 'the first comprehensive guide and handbook to this essential language' and those are just the first two lines. My copy is signed by the author, the simplicity and modesty of his signature belying the mind-boggling erudition of its content, though it says much about the man. A world authority on Linnaeus and the genera *Paeonia* and *Epimedium* and author of numerous books and scientific and horticultural papers, this much-honoured scientist was a man I found always eager to share an anecdote or some fascinating snippet of information. More than once when I visited him in the Kew Herbarium he would suggest we continue our conversation over lunch at his favourite pub, the Rose and Crown on Kew Green, where a pie and a glass of beer added to the conviviality of the meeting.

Professor William Stearn with *Epimedium davidii* at Blackthorn Nursery, Hampshire, in April 1991. His book on the genus was eventually published posthumously in 2002.

On one such occasion I asked him about plant classification – how does it work? Using the cutlery on our table as an example, he described the concept as follows: 'Let's start with the family, in this case cutlery. Just as the rose family Rosaceae is divided into genera *Rosa*, *Potentilla*, *Spiraea* etcetera, so is cutlery divided into spoons, knives, forks, and so on. Genera in turn contain species, such as *Rosa canina*, *R. moyesii*, *R. rugosa*; so too with spoons. There are soup spoons, tablespoons, teaspoons, for example.' He would, I am sure, have continued had it not been for our puddings arriving – apple crumble drowned in hot custard. 'We mustn't let it go cold,' he said.

Apart from Frank Ludlow (1885–1972), who the year before he died had advised me to look after my feet and my stomach when travelling in Nepal, the only pre-war plant collector of note I ever met was Harold Comber (1897–1969), who visited the Arboretum in the 1960s. I was invited to accompany him and HG on a tour which included a small private garden on the west side of Jermyns House where HG had planted some of his most treasured shrubs. It was while approaching a low raised bed that Comber doffed his hat to a

.....

Olearia phlogopappa (Splendens Group) 'Comber's Pink', introduced by Harold Comber from Tasmania in 1930. Here it is seen flowering in the RHS Garden at Wisley in May 2008.

carpeting evergreen shrub studded with small white flowers. There was no need for HG to name it, for it was Comber who had introduced *Leptospermum rupestre* from his expedition to Tasmania in 1930, along with the colourful but less hardy daisy bush *Olearia phlogopappa*. Today, three colour clones of the *Olearia* known as the Splendens Group are represented in cultivation by 'Comber's Pink', 'Comber's Mauve' and 'Comber's Blue'. Arguably the most spectacular of Comber's introductions in terms of flower is a Chilean fire-tree, a selection of *Embothrium coccineum* collected as seed by him in the Ñorquinco Valley in the Argentinian Andes during his visits to Chile and Argentina in 1926 and '27.

Harold Comber's father, the legendary James Comber (1866–1953), was one of our head gardener Jack Brice's heroes. He had started his

Harold Comber plant-hunting in the Andes near Lake Huechulafquen in the province of Neuquén, Argentina, in 1926.

.....

career working for James Veitch and Son before being appointed head gardener in 1894 for Lt Col. Leonard Messel at Nymans in Sussex, where he worked for the rest of his life, the longest-serving head gardener in the same garden employ. He was also a successful hybridizer and skilled propagator. His achievements earned him the RHS's highest award, the Victoria Medal of Honour.

In the same private garden and in the same bed as the *Leptospermum* grew the dwarf or carpeting *Sorbus pygmaea* (now *S. poteriifolia*) which Harold enjoyed showing to special visitors whom he knew would be impressed. It was, HG would tell them, the world's smallest mountain ash and as far as he was aware his was the only one in cultivation. A low-growing, suckering shrub with minuscule glossy green leaves, pink flowers and pink fruits ripening to white, it had been introduced by the English plant hunter Frank Kingdon-Ward from north Burma (now Myanmar) in 1926 and required a moist, acidic soil if it was to thrive. The one problem, HG found, was that its fruits seemed to be infertile and the nursery had to rely on increasing it by suckers. Then one day in 1975 I had a visit from a young botanist named Dr Hugh McAllister from Liverpool University's Botanic Garden at Ness in the Wirral, previously the home of Arthur K. Bulley (1861–1941), a Liverpool cotton broker and keen gardener who employed both George Forrest and Frank Kingdon-Ward to collect plants in China. McAllister was at that time working on the genus *Sorbus* and later, in 2015, published the definitive work on the subject. As it happened, HG's *Sorbus poteriifolia* was in fruit. On hearing of the problems our propagators had experienced, he begged a handful of fruits which I helped him to pick. When I later told HG what I had done he wasn't best pleased and asked me to write down McAllister's details. I didn't dare mention his name again until the following year when I received a package in the post from McAllister containing a dozen healthy seedlings of the *Sorbus*, the seeds of which he had extracted from their fleshy coats, placing them in a fridge at -5°C where they remained for eight months before germinating. The key to solving the problem, McAllister told me, was to prevent the seeds from drying out. He had cracked it. When I delivered the seedlings to HG he was both surprised and impressed, writing immediately to thank

.....

McAllister and asking if he could spare any more, for which he would be happy to refund postage.

The Hillier Nurseries counted a good number of famous people among its clientele, including the late George Harrison of the Beatles and the great actor Sir Laurence Olivier, with whom I corresponded briefly in May 1971 over the identity of a Japanese cherry he had sent me a specimen of in a plastic bag. The reputation of the Arboretum and the nursery was such that many applications were received from British and foreign students seeking employment, usually for a year. We had two or three each year at work in the Arboretum, lodging in the Brentry House hostel across the lane. Most of them proved more than satisfactory and left at the end of their term having gained valuable experience, practical and otherwise, in the cultivation of woody plants. For several years I organized trips for them to see other gardens and collections as well as field trips to study native plants.

A former Hillier Arboretum student, Holly Harmer went on to become executive director of the US Botanic Garden below the Capitol in Washington DC. She is seen here in July 2008.

Lectures and other plant activities including plant idents were held in Brentry House on winter evenings. Among those students I particularly remember an American, Holly Harmer. On the day of her arrival she prepared a herbal tea for her two fellow students using the roots of a sassafras tree (*Sassafras albidum*) growing by Jermyns House. I tried it too and quite enjoyed it, even though I could not get out of my mind how sassafras oil was once used as a treatment for head lice! It was in the Arboretum that she first met her future husband, Osamu Shimizu. On leaving she enjoyed further work experience at a nursery in Germany and then the Arboretum Kalmthout in Belgium, concluding her European training at the RHS Garden, Wisley. She went on to become curator of the famous Herb Garden at the National Arboretum in Washington DC and finally executive director of the United States Botanic Garden below the Capitol.

An earlier American student was Paul Meyer, 'Tall Paul' as we called him. Among his many talents he excelled in the plant idents. On

.....

Paul Meyer, currently
executive director of
the Morris Arboretum
in Philadelphia, with
Microbiota decussata
on a visit to the
Sir Harold Hillier
Gardens in
November 2014.

returning home he went on to become head of collections then director and finally executive director at the Morris Arboretum, one of America's finest, in Philadelphia. He also travelled widely on behalf of the Morris as a plant collector and accompanied me in 1981 on a plant trek to west Sichuan in the Tibetan border region. A beautiful specimen of a maple, *Acer triflorum*, collected as seed by Paul and his colleagues in South Korea and planted here in 1984, lights up my garden each autumn with its old gold, red-tinted foliage.

Susyn Andrews, an Irish student trained at the National Botanic Gardens at Glasnevin in Dublin, was a fellow student and friend of Paul's at the Hillier Arboretum and a keen competitor in the plant idents. After leaving the Arboretum she worked for a time at a nursery in Germany, eventually joining the Herbarium at the Royal Botanic Gardens, Kew, where she realized her ambition to become a horticultural taxonomist. She also became a specialist on hollies (*Ilex*) to such an extent that she is often referred to in gardening circles as the 'Holly Queen'. She eventually left Kew to pursue a successful freelance career.

Trip to Iran

In 1972 Hillier and Sons received their biggest-ever order for the supply of woody plants to the Aryamehr Botanic Garden (now the National Botanical Garden of Iran) then being made a few miles west of Tehran, capital of Iran. One story had it that Princess Fatima, daughter of the Shah, had been thumbing through a lavishly illustrated book on botanic gardens of the world and finding no mention of an Iranian garden had approached her father about having one made. Whatever the truth in that, the plan for a garden was real enough and so were the trees and shrubs being lifted and packed into a large container in November, the first of several consignments planned over

.....

the next three years. The designer of the garden was Edward Hyams, who had accompanied Dr Sabeti, the newly appointed director of the garden, on a preliminary visit to Hilliers in May when they were given a tour of the nurseries and the Arboretum before conferring with HG about the choice of plants. The eventual order is reputed to have contained three of every tree and shrub described in the Manual which the above three considered might be suitable for the new site.

I could hardly believe my good fortune when HG told me I was to fly out to Tehran ahead of the container and help supervise the unloading and planting of its contents on their arrival. With a TV film crew and local news reporters recording the event, the container on its trailer began the long journey overland to Iran which would take 14 days. Three days later, on 23 November, I arrived in Tehran by plane late in the evening. Edward Hyams was staying at the same hotel and the next morning he drove me out to see the Botanical Garden site, an area of 247 acres (1 square kilometre) of steppe situated south of the Elborz Mountains whose uncompromising slopes dominated the northern horizon. We were met by Dr Sabeti, George Cobham, a young ex-student of Hilliers who had secured the job of curator and working

Site of the new Aryamehr Botanic Garden with the southern slopes of the Elborz Mountains in the background, November 1972.

foreman, and Ann Ala, the English wife of a senior Iranian surgeon who saw it as her duty and pleasure to welcome any garden-lover visiting from the old country. She was a charming and gracious woman who over the following weeks did her best to see that I met other people including her family. She also promised me that before I left Iran she would try to arrange for me to visit the ancient forests on the northern slopes of the Elborz, above the Caspian Sea.

The weather during my visit was mostly warm and sunny by day becoming colder at night, especially so as winter approached and the

.....

From left, George Cobham, Ann Ala, Edward Hyams and Dr Sabeti at the Aryamehr Botanic Garden in north Iran, November 1972.

first snow appeared on the mountains' upper slopes. I found several officials based in a cluster of buildings which looked stark and isolated on the endless plain. I was told that the men employed to prepare the site, 200 or more of them, were villagers from Azerbaijan who had been given the job of raking up the stones into little heaps before raking them into bigger heaps and so on for which they were paid 150 rials (less than a £1) a day. They were accommodated on site in large tents but otherwise exposed to the elements. I would see them returning from local bakers in the morning with several large flat-breads known as nan-e sangak thrown over their shoulder, enough for each member of their tent. They were a rugged breed and needed to be, given the hard work in less than ideal conditions. They were overseen by a burly foreman with a permanent scowl who, it was rumoured, had once killed a man and on another occasion had wrestled with a bear and survived. As unlikely as that seemed, he was not a man I would wish to meet in a narrow alley at night.

Some planting had already been accomplished, mostly poplars to form a perimeter screen and windbreak. Shallow trenches had been dug to facilitate irrigation in summer when temperatures soared. On one side of the site trenches had been dug to provide a temporary nursery for incoming plants. Some native trees and shrubs had already

.....

arrived from collections made in other areas of Iran and I noted *Quercus brantii*, *Colutea buhsei* and *Populus euphratica*. Further trenches were being prepared to receive the Hillier plants.

A brief visit one weekend to the nearby town of Karaj allowed me to botanize on nearby dry, stony slopes which is where I found *Rosa persica*, a species requiring heat and perfect drainage and rarely seen in Western cultivation. Famous for its solitary, brilliant yellow flowers with a scarlet-stained base to each petal, it was common here, forming dwarf, suckering, thorny bushes often in the company of a sumach, *Rhus coriaria*, and the wild pistachio (*Pistacia vera*) whose fruits are the pistachio nuts of commerce.

Bringing back the day's bread supply (nan-e sangak) for his fellow workers on the bleak Botanic Garden site.

On the last day of November the weather was awful, with torrential rain causing extensive flooding and in places snow fell. A few days later I suffered stomach pains which Edward Hyams called 'Tehran Tum' and he recommended I drink a stiff vodka before having an early night. It seemed to have worked, for the following day, 5 December – my birthday – I felt well enough to celebrate at a dinner hosted by Ann and her husband Firouz at their home. More snow fell through the night, leaving the garden site very wet and muddy and difficult to work, but the men were out in it all day as the snow continued. The following day, however, the men remained in their tents despite orders from the director to report for work. When they did not respond he tried to drive away to get help but one of the men lay on the ground in front of the jeep to prevent him from leaving. I sympathized with the men and their grievance but the director was not yet finished. A message must have been sent, for a while later an army truck arrived and a detachment of soldiers jumped out, led by an officer. Off they marched to the tent lines where the men were turned out and forced to listen to the officer who read them the riot act. Reluctantly but resigned to the situation they gathered their tools and went to work.

.....

The container of Hillier plants finally arrived in Tehran on the 10th of December but was held overnight before we obtained its release. When the container doors were finally opened we found that some of the plants had frozen to the floor due to bitter nights crossing high passes towards the end of their journey. Once those defrosted, everyone set to placing their root balls in the trenches and protecting them until they were needed for planting. Later, I noted how many of the shrubs and trees were being planted in large communal pits, together with a plentiful supply of camel dung.

Caspian forests

My final weekend in Iran was now approaching and Ann told me that she had managed to arrange for a driver and jeep to take us to the Caspian forests. We left Tehran on the 16th of December, a Saturday, to spend three days in what turned out to be a paradise on earth. In terms of geography, the main range of the Elborz Mountains stretches some 270 miles (434km) east-west above the Caspian shore and varies in width between 45 and 55 miles (72–88km), with high ridges averaging 12,000–15,000ft (3657–4572m), effectively dividing the Caspian Sea in the north from the steppe and desert areas to the south. Its composition is mainly volcanic with outcropping calcareous formations and even coal.

The route we followed to reach the town of Chalus on the Caspian coast begins at Karaj at around 3200ft (975m) on the south side of the Elborz Mountains, from where it winds its way upwards through the lower river valleys, eventually crossing the range via the Kandavan Pass at around 10,700ft (3260m) and then through valleys on the northern flanks of the range down to Chalus. Compared with the wetter, northern slopes, which are densely forested in places, the south-facing slopes are drier, receiving around 12in (30cm) of rain annually, and this is reflected in the flora. Our driver, Mr Ebrahimi of the Aryamehr Botanic Garden, was a native of the Caspian shore and knew the area extremely well. I noticed a pile of wheel chains in the back of his jeep for use on the icy or snow-covered roads which we were sure to experience over the weekend.

.....

By late afternoon we were approaching the pass, the stark whiteness of the snow-covered upper slopes relieved only by the occasional thrust of emergent rock and the scattered dark green mounded forms of a juniper, *Juniperus polycarpos*, with some tree-like specimens reaching 16–23ft (5–7m). Crossing the pass, we resisted the temptation to stop given the rapidly fading light and the threat of snow, hurrying north through narrow gorges and along precipitous roads, the final stretch a muddy forestry track to Anjou Lodge, our accommodation for the night. It was a large log cabin with a welcoming fire crackling and spitting in the hearth. I fell asleep quickly after the long day and consequently was up like a lark the following morning, tramping through the snow to examine a large, lone specimen of *Zelkova carpinifolia* I had spotted whose characteristic besom broom crown I was familiar with in Western cultivation. A quick stroll through the forest revealed more *Zelkova* which here occurred as a relatively small tree with a short, stout, piebald stem. There occurred also a hornbeam,

The southern slopes of the Elborz Mountains from the town of Karaj, where our journey to Chalus on the Caspian Coast began.

. . . . .

its leaves now turned brown, which on examination appeared intermediate in character between those of the common species, *Carpinus betulus*, large trees of which we saw later, and the more shrubby, smaller-leaved oriental hornbeam (*Carpinus orientalis*). We were told later by a forester that it was a distinct species named *C. schuschaensis* and we collected its seed. It subsequently proved to be, as we suspected, a hybrid between the above species which made sense given their close proximity. There are now two fine trees established in the Sir Harold Hillier Gardens.

A spindle bush, *Euonymus velutinus*, with grey, velvety-hairy young shoots was also new to me. *Colutea buhsei*, which I had previously seen cultivated in the Botanic Garden, was on view as a large, hardy shrub which when it flowered in the Hillier Arboretum from seed collected at this time caused a good deal of interest, its yellow pea-flowers being abundantly produced. On the road again after breakfast we drove down a valley in snow, passing beneath several fine trees of the chestnut-leaved

Carpinus × schuschaensis, a hybrid hornbeam (*C. betulus × C. orientalis*) on the southern slopes of the Elborz Mountains.

oak (*Quercus castaneifolia*) and the bold-leaved *Q. petraea* subsp. *iberica*. Near the bottom of the valley by a river we came across a grove of the Caucasian wingnut tree (*Pterocarya fraxinifolia*) with 50–65ft (15–20m) stems, its leaves just changing to yellow, while close by were huge Caucasian alders (*Alnus subcordata*) and an Iranian version of our pussy willow (*Salix aegyptiaca*), 16–20ft (5–6m) tall. We cultivated a male form of this species in the Arboretum and its yellow catkins on grey-felted shoots were sensational in late winter.

Shortly afterwards we arrived in a neighbouring valley known as Dasht-e Nazir where the steep slopes, composed of a conspicuously white soil, a chalk marl, supported scattered populations of the Mediterranean cypress (*Cupressus sempervirens*), the wild form var. *horizontalis* with a spreading crown, unlike the better known and columnar Italian cypress 'Stricta' which is unknown in the wild. Many of the

.....

LEFT Heavy snow covers cherry laurel and holly in the Elborz Mountains, December 1972.

BELOW Snow in the Elborz Mountains and a superb specimen of *Fagus orientalis* soars above our forest ranger guide.

larger veterans, some growing from rock fissures, resembled mature firs (*Abies* spp) or cedars from a distance. Ten years later I was to see this same variety again in the White Mountains of Crete, where it grows with the shrubby *Zelkova abeliacea*.

Turning eastwards we now travelled on slush-covered roads heading for the remote Veysar and Camarlou forests which lie between 5600 and 7200ft (1700–2200m). Here, in a deep valley we found some of the finest trees of their kind I have ever seen. Common hornbeam, Caucasian alder (*Alnus subcordata*), oriental beech (*Fagus orientalis*) and *Acer velutinum* var. *glabrescens* were the dominant species, the last three with individuals over 100ft (30m) tall with impressive girths. They were a breathtaking sight standing in the snow yet, sadly, felling was taking place and in a nearby logging camp we saw large stacks of maple and beech awaiting transport.

We now followed a road used by logging trucks, eventually pulling off to proceed on foot into the deep forest. Here the snow lay heavy, shrouding bushes and smaller trees alike. A gentle tap of a forester's axe was enough to dislodge the snow, revealing to our surprise cherry laurel (*Prunus laurocerasus*) and a curious holly (*Ilex spinigera*) with small, boldly spined leaves and bright red berries, some of which we collected, introducing

.....

Ilex spinigera, a common understorey plant in the Caspian forests of the Elborz Mountains, here growing at the Hotel Dunloe Castle Gardens in Ireland.

this species for the first time to our knowledge into British cultivation. I currently have two bushes in my garden, a male and a female.

Hillsides aflame with parrotias

We spent that night in a small hotel in Chalus, where I eventually slept soundly having lain awake for a time replaying in my mind the experiences of the day. Waking to a fast rising sun and the sound of the Caspian Sea below my window, I hurriedly dressed in anticipation of another good day, our last. Oranges are plentiful in these parts and for breakfast we enjoyed wafer-thin slices of bread spread with marmalade made with honey. Suitably replenished, we drove east out of town along the coast road with oranges gleaming like Christmas baubles in the dark green orchards. The morning wore on and the sun rose higher, causing whole hillsides to ignite in a flame of parrotias (*Parrotia persica*) and golden hornbeams. The Swedish botanist Per Wendelbo (1927–1981) wrote that the South Caspian (Hyrcanian) forests most probably survived the ice ages of the Pleistocene; he believed both *Parrotia* and the Caspian locust (*Gleditsia caspica*) were undoubtedly Tertiary relics. We saw the locust growing on the shore along with wild pomegranate (*Punica granatum*) in dense thickets interspersed with pink siris or Persian silk tree (*Albizia julibrissin*), a scrubby plum (*Prunus caspica*) and scrambling masses of summer jasmine (*Jasminum officinale*). The pomegranate and plum were not the only fruiting plants we saw that day. In the nearby forest we also found wild medlar (*Mespilus germanica*),

.....

a small-fruited, spiny-branched bush, a vine (*Vitis vinifera* subsp. *sylvestris*) considered as the wild ancestor of the domestic grape, a wild fig (*Ficus carica* var. *genuina*) and the date plum (*Diospyros lotus*), which had us believing we had stumbled upon the Garden of Eden – and we were not yet done!

The dominant trees were *Acer velutinum* var. *glabrescens*, one with a girth of 16ft (5m), and *A. cappadocicum*; *Tilia dasystyla* ssp. *caucasica*, referred to by Iranian botanists as *T. begoniifolia*; and *Quercus macranthera* and *Parrotia persica*, the Persian ironwood, common here as a tree of 50–66ft (15–20m) or more, many of them hosting large bunches of mistletoe (*Viscum album*). In the shrubby layer beneath the canopy we found Alexandrian laurel (*Danae racemosa*), cherry laurel (*Prunus laurocerasus*), *Rhamnus grandifolius*, *Ruscus hyrcanus* and *Buxus hyrcana*. Scrambling into trees was the powerful horse briar (*Smilax excelsa*), the females with red fruits, while forming ground cover in places and climbing trees and rocks were two ivies, the Persian ivy, bold-foliaged *Hedera colchica*, and a new one to me, *Hedera pastuchovii*, with leaves of variable shape. I selected a distinct and ornamental form of the last for its long, spear-shaped, dark glossy-green leaves with pale veins which I later named 'Ann Ala' in memory of Ann's part in making this dream come true.

A distinct long-leaved selection of an an ivy, *Hedera pastuchovii*, which I named for Ann Ala who arranged my visit to the Caspian forests.

As for perennials, many ferns and violets and a native British grass, *Melica nutans*, were common while a primrose relative, *Primula heterochroma*, had yet to open its flowers, which can vary from white to blue and yellow. The star perennial on show, however, was *Cyclamen elegans*, an appropriate name for a beautiful species with attractive silvery-grey marbled, kidney-shaped leaves crowned with rose, lilac or white flowers. It flourished in the deep leaf litter, forming low mounds and carpets in the forest shade.

Reluctantly we dragged ourselves away for our return journey to Tehran. Mr Ebrahimi drove like the proverbial wind, leaving the Caspian behind and

.....

hurtling along the road through the forest. I glimpsed Caucasian wingnuts along the river bank but my shouts failed to distract him. After what seemed like hours later, high on the mountain, we met with snow and lurching timber traffic and only then did he stop to fix the snow chains on his wheels. Again we were off but more slowly now and more cautiously given the poor light until, while Mr Ebrahimi was eating an apple, it slipped from his grasp and to my horror he groped around to locate it using both hands while steering the jeep with his chin! At this point I closed my eyes and tried to imagine the good things HG might have to say when I returned with my seeds and cuttings.

New plants for British gardens

The next day, standing on the flat brown site of the Aryamehr Botanic Garden, I studied the now snow-covered southern slopes of the Elborz and pinched myself again and again. Only my notes and memories would remind me of the mountain chain which separated me from paradise. Having said all my goodbyes, I left Tehran at midday on 20 December, arriving in London the same evening. The following day, a Wednesday, I couldn't get to the Hillier Arboretum fast enough to meet an equally excited HG for a long debriefing on the Botanic Garden, the Hillier plants, the people and finally the Caspian adventure. As I had expected, he was thrilled with the seeds and cuttings, which were immediately taken to master propagator Graham Adcock in the nursery. In all, I returned with 40 separate collections listed under A&L (Ala and Lancaster) numbers, many of them new to British cultivation.

There was some talk awhile of my returning to the Elborz, but sadly it came to nothing. Interestingly, a concerted effort was mounted the following year by the Aryamehr Botanic Garden to persuade me to join them as official botanist. There were plans afoot to create a second garden in the Caspian forests and others elsewhere in Iran but I decided against it, a wise decision perhaps, given the changes to come in that country.

It was in August 1974 that HG was invited to visit a hotel garden in Ireland to advise on a new planting scheme. The Hotel Dunloe Castle (now The Dunloe) lies near the village of Beaufort on the outskirts of

.....

Killarney in Co. Kerry, a relatively new hotel of no particular character or charm. With its bland white-painted exterior it could have passed off as a hospital. Yet it had the most stunning views looking south across green-hedged paddocks and fields to the Gap of Dunloe, a defile in the mountains long popular with visitors and tourists. To the left (east) of the Gap are Tomies Mountain (2411ft/735m) and Purple Mountain (2736ft/834m) while away to the right (west) rise the several peaks and ridges of the Macgillycuddy's Reeks, culminating in Ireland's highest mountain, Carrauntoohil, at 3412ft (1040m). But why was HG being called in? It transpired that the builder and owner of the hotel and estate was Killarney Hotels Ltd, owned by a German industrialist, Mr H Liebherr, who had already built another hotel by Lough Leane in Killarney as well as a factory manufacturing cranes.

Liebherr had purchased the estate with its house in 1960 on the death of its owner, a Miss Petitt, who in her turn had purchased it from Howard Harrington, an American who was mainly responsible for the many ornamental and unusual trees and shrubs planted there from the 1920s to 1936, when he returned home due to ill health. Liebherr had the house demolished but stopped short of razing an old walled garden and its associated arboretum. The remains of the castle, an Anglo-Norman keep, he made safe but little more. He next sought advice from a friend, Count Bernadotte, about the importance and quality of the trees – were they worth keeping? Bernadotte, owner of Mainau, a world-famous garden on the Bodensee in Germany, urged Liebherr to contact Dr Gerd Krüssmann, director of the Dortmund Botanic Garden and an internationally known dendrologist and author. Krüssmann visited the hotel to compile an inventory of its trees and significant shrubs with a view to labelling them for the benefit of the hotel's guests. It so happened that Krüssmann was also a good friend of HG; the two were long-time members of the International Dendrology Society (IDS) and not surprisingly, he recommended to Liebherr that he invite Hilliers to update the collections and do whatever work was necessary to rejuvenate the garden and rescue it from neglect. When HG flew to Dunloe via Cork in August that year he took me with him to make all the necessary notes.

.....

179

We met Krüssmann, like HG silver-haired though five years younger, in the hotel lobby and following coffee we all three set out on a tour of the collections accompanied by head gardener Sean Sweeney, who had worked for the estate's previous owner, Miss Petitt, since leaving school. It was quite exciting and educational for me to follow in HG's and Krüssmann's footsteps as they examined the collection, commenting upon it and occasionally disagreeing with each other on the identities of some individuals, but of one thing they were in total agreement – it was undoubtedly a collection of merit with many rare and unexpected treasures. We were told later that Howard Harrington had acquired a good number of his special trees from Hilliers, which Krüssmann teasingly claimed gave HG an unfair advantage.

Special tree collection in Ireland

Some of the species I had met with previously in Cornish gardens and many of them I had first seen as young saleable plants in the Hillier nurseries but there were others quite new to me, such as *Corylus × colurnoides*, a hybrid between the Turkish and the common hazel, the strikingly creamy-yellow variegated *Thuja plicata* 'Irish Gold' and *Acer × diekii*, a hybrid of German origin between Lobel's maple and Norway maple which Krüssmann identified. The walled garden was packed with interesting trees including *Maytenus boaria*, *Weinmannia trichosperma* and *Laureliopsis philippiana* from Chile; *Magnolia delavayi* from China, *Acer campbellii* and *Rhododendron arboreum* subsp. *cinnamomeum* from the Himalaya and *Gymnocladus dioica*, the Kentucky coffee tree from the USA, while in an open grassed area stood a superb *Cornus controversa* 'Variegata', a large specimen of perfect proportions. We also noted many poorly shaped, dead or dying trees and those in need of thinning.

It was only on a later visit I discovered a fine specimen of the Chinese pond cypress (*Glyptostrobus pensilis*). It was growing by a stream concealed from above by a dense thicket of bamboo and birch scrub which I subsequently had cleared. This rare deciduous conifer proved to be a TROBI British and Irish champion at 33ft (10m) and was at its most eye-catching when the foliage turned a rusty gold before

.....

Glyptostrobus pensilis, the rare Chinese pond cypress, growing by the River Loe at Hotel Dunloe Castle gardens in August 1999.

falling in autumn. Sadly, many years later it fell victim to honey fungus, which was rife at Dunloe.

That same evening, at dinner, HG and Krüssmann were in good form as conversation moved on from the day's delights to their tree experiences elsewhere. It was then that Krüssmann asked me if I was interested in alpines and I mentioned having seen my first blue trumpet gentians growing in the Swiss Alps. He followed this with a story about his experience in Greece as a young officer in the German army and how he was once requested by his commanding officer to go into the mountains to pick flowers for the officers' dinner table. He continued with his war-time reminiscences concerning plants before finally relating how his transport company was part of a large force assembled on the French coast awaiting orders to cross the channel. Everyone was ready and then one day a general arrived, ordered Krüssmann's unit off the beach and he ended up in Norway instead. He then paused for a moment and I noticed that HG, who had served with the Home Guard during the Second World War (his favourite TV series was *Dad's Army*), had stopped eating and was looking just a little uneasy. Without thinking, I asked Krüssmann what he would have done if the invasion had gone ahead and he had landed in England. Without hesitation he replied 'Well of course, I would have headed to Winchester and Hillier Nursery.' We all three chuckled at this and thankfully the conversation moved on to our plans for the next day.

HG admired Krüssmann for his sound knowledge of woody plants, having served before the war as botanist with the famous German nursery firm of Spaeth in Berlin which, together with Vilmorin in France and Veitch in England, was regarded as one of the greatest and

.....

most influential nurseries of their day. He authored many books, including in 1976 the magisterial three-volume *Handbuch der Laubgehölze* (*Manual of Cultivated Broad-leaved Trees and Shrubs*) and in 1972 *Handbuch der Nadelgehölze* (*Manual of Cultivated Conifers*).

As a result of our visit to Dunloe, HG was asked to prepare plans for a new planting scheme around the hotel with beds and borders of shrubs and to supply new and interesting trees and shrubs to refresh the collections already established in the arboretum and walled garden. He agreed to this and instructed me to take charge of the project, which he believed would take at least two years. In the event it involved me in an advisory role for the next 30 years, during which time, with Sean Sweeney's help, I planted a huge number and variety of trees and shrubs including many new to, or rare in, Irish cultivation.

HG was full of surprises, especially those concerning plants. One morning he burst into my office carrying a brown paper package. He was visibly excited and reminded me of a schoolboy carrying his tuck box. He had received a very special plant from his friend Lord Talbot de Malahide of Malahide Castle near Dublin and could hardly wait to open it. Eventually, with the aid of a small penknife, he cut the string binding and slit open the wrapping. He then opened the lid of the box before carefully inserting his hands. Like a magician, he produced its contents. It wasn't a rabbit or a dove but a small, loose-limbed conifer in a plastic pot. 'Have you any idea what this is?' he asked. I knew by

Sean Sweeney, long-serving head gardener at Hotel Dunloe Castle Gardens near Killarney in Co. Kerry, Ireland. Here he is admiring *Berberis valdiviana* in April 2002.

.....

the triumph in his voice that this had to be something I had never seen and probably never even heard of. I was right on both counts. It had the look of a juniper or a cypress but no, this was my first sight of the Tasmanian endemic *Diselma archeri*. It looked to be in a parlous state; how long had it been in the box? Having handled it I gave it back to HG, who took it to the propagation unit and placed it in the capable hands of Graham Adcock. Graham not only kept it alive but successfully propagated it from cuttings. I later had the good fortune to see this rare conifer wild on Cradle Mountain in Tasmania where it grows with another Tasmanian endemic conifer, the dwarf, prostrate *Microcachrys tetragona*, also represented at the Hillier Arboretum.

Fighting crime

Both the Arboretum and the Hillier Nurseries suffered from occasional thefts over the years and one in particular caused HG distress. It was late autumn and I had just returned from travels abroad to find him in a troubled mood. He immediately briefed me on a series of thefts involving dwarf conifers in the Arboretum. The culprit had been wrenching them out of the ground. HG insisted that I accompany him on a tour 'to see the crime scenes'. We walked along a perimeter path bordering Jermyns Lane, HG pointing out holes where conifers had once been. Reaching the far end of the path close to the perimeter fence, we came upon a small cache of recently lifted dwarf conifers placed as if for collection at the base of the fence and within easy reach of someone on the roadside. He immediately told me to conceal myself where I might see if not catch the thief and hurried off back to Jermyns House to recruit help to replace me should it prove a long wait.

I decided to climb into a nearby tree from where I had a good view of the conifers and the road. It was the end of the day and dusk was drawing in as I sat there, noting every movement on the road including members of the Arboretum and the nursery staff heading for home in cars or on bicycles. It was quite dark when, feeling cramped and with no sign of a replacement, I decided to leave my perch, climb over the fence and walk back along the road to the Jermyns House entrance. I had almost reached the entrance when I was passed by several cars, the

.....

last one of which slowed down as it passed the cache site. I stopped and watched as it then did a three-point turn and slowly headed back. I ran through the entrance gate and down the perimeter path as fast as my legs and the darkness would allow. I had almost reached the cache when I heard a car door or boot slam shut and on reaching the fence I found the conifers gone. I just had time to see part of the poorly lit registration number as the car pulled away. I then ran to Jermyns House, repeating out loud what I had read, to find HG having his supper. The staff having left and darkness descending, he had assumed I would have given up and gone home. I could hardly believe my ears.

Although it was only a partial number I had seen, when the thief, emboldened by his luck so far, struck again a week later at the West Hill Nursery in Winchester, the suspicions of a member of staff were raised and he made a note of the car registration which matched that which I had seen. Having traced the owner of the car the police attended his home address where they found a greenhouse filled with the stolen plants all potted on. The culprit, an avid amateur gardener and collector, was employed as a teacher at a local school.

A new era for the Arboretum

It was during the early 1970s that HG gave serious thought to the future of his Arboretum, though I wasn't party to what he had in mind. It seems he had considered offering it to the National Trust or maybe the Forestry Commission, but without a substantial endowment to maintain and develop it there was no likelihood of either of them taking it on. In 1974 he had a preliminary discussion with Lord Porchester, then chairman of Hampshire County Council, which led to further protracted discussions with the council with a view to him gifting the Arboretum to them. It was another three anxious years, however, before in 1977 an agreement was finally reached and on 26 September that year I received confirmation of my new appointment with HCC. In preparation for the change of ownership, all the Arboretum staff had been 'invited' to be interviewed by a senior officer in the Council's Estates Department who had been given the responsibility for this new addition to their portfolio.

.....

When my turn came, it was immediately made clear to me that whatever rung of the ladder I might occupy in my profession, when compared with his profession, I would be starting at the beginning. I was somewhat taken aback by this and concluded that it spoke more of his insecurity than his self-confidence. Some time before this, when negotiations were at a critical stage, I had been told in confidence by a senior member of the Hillier Nursery management that he hoped for my sake the agreement would be forthcoming because if the company were left with the Arboretum on their hands they would probably have to reduce it from the present 115 acres (50 hectares) to around 10 acres (4 hectares) around Jermyns House and my present role would be changed accordingly. It was with some relief therefore that we heard an agreement had been reached, though I had no illusions about the changes that might still follow. But now there was much to be done and to look forward to, especially given the exciting news that Her Majesty Queen Elizabeth the Queen Mother had graciously consented to accept HG's gift on behalf of Hampshire County Council at the official opening of the Arboretum, now registered as a charitable trust following its transfer to the trusteeship of the County Council.

The day of the official opening, 9 May 1978, dawned bright and beautiful and the Arboretum, thanks to Jack Brice and his staff, was in

The Queen Mother at the Hillier Gardens, guided by Harold Hillier (left) with his wife Barbara following and Lord Porchester, Chairman of Hampshire County Council behind (right).

.....

My wife Sue and I
are introduced to the
Queen Mother.
Head gardener Jack
Brice looks on.

immaculate condition with magnolias, viburnums, rhododendrons, azaleas and myriad other springtime ornamentals in bloom. Groups of local schoolchildren, friends and colleagues from the horticultural world and a happy wave of well-wishers joined the Arboretum staff, local dignitaries and many others in welcoming the royal visitor as, accompanied by Lord Porchester, Her Majesty was conducted on a tour of the Arboretum by its creator. She was introduced to and shook hands with the Hillier family, all members of staff, the many VIPs and members of the recently appointed Arboretum Management committee. For everyone she had a warm smile and a gracious wave of the hand. None of us present that day will ever forget it.

For me it was a pleasure doubled because with me on this occasion to meet the Queen Mother and share in the joy of a great garden occasion was my wife of six months, Sue. We had married on 5 November the previous year at her family church in the Shropshire village of Hopesay in the Clun Valley. The day before the wedding, I had driven to her home with a boot-load of cut material from the Arboretum, mostly autumn foliage and fruits, which I used to create colourful arrangements in and around the church. One such, placed in the porch as a welcome to guests, combined the sword-shaped leaves of New Zealand flax (*Phormium tenax*) with a large ruff of the rich red leaves of *Mahonia japonica*. Sue was still employed as a teacher at a Winchester school and other than spending our wedding night in a hotel nearby in the Stretton Hills we had decided to delay our honeymoon until the New Year, when at the kind invitation of one of

.....

my then Arboretum students, Princess Isabelle Wolkonsky, and her father Prince Peter, we spent several days at their home in St Cloud, Paris, welcoming in the New Year in the Champs Elysées.

In addition to the must-see sights of the city we visited the home and garden of Roger de Vilmorin at Verrières-le-Buisson, followed by the famous Arboretum established by Maurice Lévêque de Vilmorin (1849–1918) on his family estate, the Domaine des Barres. It was Maurice who received and germinated many of the seeds sent from China by the French missionaries to the great French botanist Adrien Franchet, who was his friend. Two of the many special trees I remember seeing at Verrières that day was a massive wingnut (*Pterocarya × rehderiana*), a hybrid between the Caucasian and the Chinese wingnuts (*P. fraxinifolia × P. stenoptera*). Just as exciting was what was claimed to be the original tree of *Halesia diptera* 'Magniflora', planted in 1920. It was then around 33ft (10m) tall, while another impressive example grows in the Arboretum Kalmthout in Belgium. At the Arboretum des Barres I recall *Tilia henryana*, a fine tree of 36ft (11m) planted in 1940, and more nettle trees (*Celtis* species) than I knew existed.

Sue and I had purchased a house on a new development behind HM Prison in Winchester, though our address of Poet's Way, Greenhill, gave correspondents no hint of the true significance of its location. Here, on a shallow chalk soil, we planted our first garden, starting with a striking white peeling-barked birch seedling, *Betula utilis* var. *jacquemontii*. We planted it in an island bed toe deep in winter flowering heaths, *Erica carnea*, where it could be enjoyed by all who passed by. We had collected the seedling on our visit to Kashmir in June 1978, later naming it 'Kashmir White'. It seemed a fitting start to our future life together.

.....

CHAPTER SEVEN

Spreading my wings

To begin with, I found life at the Arboretum under the new regime exciting; I was presented with fresh challenges and responsibilities. On 26 October 1978 our long-serving head gardener Jack Brice retired and we organized a party at the Arboretum for him and his wife, attended by HG and Barabara Hillier and all the staff at Hilliers. His leaving signalled the end of an era and we knew the Arboretum would be poorer for his departure. He was one of the old school who, like my former boss at Moss Bank Park in Bolton, believed that if a job was worth doing it was worth doing well. His knowledge, his skills and his thoroughness and patience gathered from a lifetime working in the private gardens system was demonstrated to all who worked under him, and though not all of them realized it at the time it was the making of them.

Under the County Council I was given day-to-day responsibility for the Arboretum including staff. Best of all, along with Jack's former deputy Bill George, now acting head gardener, I was made responsible

Staff and students at the Hillier Gardens in April 1978. For head gardener Jack Brice (on my right) this was his final year; he retired in October.

.....

for all planting projects, the first of which was the new public entrance and car park. A pair of dawn redwoods marking the entrance to the car park was one of my first decisions and they are there still. The long-drawn-out negotiations and the resultant will they, won't they scenario leading up to the Council's acceptance of HG's gift of the Arboretum had made me aware of the strength of opposition to it from some individuals at the Council. It was said that one head of department had expressed disbelief that they should be considering taking on a garden and he wasn't the only one to voice disapproval, if not outright opposition. Fortunately, wiser heads prevailed, but it left me determined to remind doubters that far from being any old garden, the Hillier Gardens as it became known (now the Sir Harold Hillier Gardens) was a huge living collection of international repute whose ornamental, educational and scientific value should be viewed as a jewel in the Council's crown.

Plant committees

The previous year I had been invited by the RHS to become a member of one of their plant committees – Committee B (now the Woody Plant Committee), which met on the mornings of the Society's flower shows held in Vincent Square, London. I viewed it as an honour and a privilege to be invited and following the new procedure I requested permission from my line manager, which was granted so long as it did not unduly affect my work at the Hillier Gardens. Other invitations followed, one of which was my attendance at what was to prove a pioneering meeting at the RHS Halls to debate the conservation of garden plants. I attended the meeting along with a large number of gardeners and garden-lovers, professional and amateur, as well as members of the botanical fraternity. This led to my being invited to join the working group charged with setting up what became known as the National Council for the Conservation of Plants and Gardens (NCCPG), now known internationally and thankfully more succinctly as Plant Heritage. These were exciting times and I believed it important that the Hillier Gardens, already a major player in the conservation of woody plants, should be involved and supportive of this new initiative.

.....

RIGHT The snow gum, *Eucalyptus pauciflora* subsp. *niphophila*, a popular tree with visitors, here with Allen Coombes, the Gardens' botanist, in September 1995.

BELOW The snow gum was especially appreciated by the partially sighted, who enjoyed feeling the stem; April 1979.

One of my favourite trees in the Hillier Gardens and also popular with visitors, especially children, was the snow gum (*Eucalyptus pauciflora* subsp. *niphophila*) from the Australian Alps of New South Wales. Planted small from a pot in 1962, it had achieved a height of around 19ft (6m) with several branches but had a distinct lean, enabling small children to sit astride its lower stem. Its exfoliating bark exhibited several shades of green, creamy-white and silvery-grey which I used to liken to the skin of a python. It

was also solid and cool to the cheek, especially so on a hot summer's day. On one occasion I introduced a group of partially sighted visitors to this tree, encouraging them to stroke or hug the stem and to listen to the sound of the scimitar-shaped, leathery leaves shaking in the breeze. It was a special moment for them and for me. Nearby grew a tall-stemmed Apache pine (*Pinus engelmannii*) from Mexico, whose spreading branches sported huge, drooping terminal clusters of long, grey-green needles. The pine is today a TROBI British and Irish Champion, while the snow gum, despite being supported, eventually blew down in a gale.

.....

Other gums in the gardens included the fast-growing *Eucalyptus dalrympleana*, with a tall, slender stem and drooping, matt grey leaves to 8in (20cm) long. It had been planted in 1957 by John Hillier and a staff member, Bert Compton. It featured in a series of challenges I set visiting horticultural students as a break from information overload. It began with 'Hug-a-Bear', which had competitors ascending the gum tree bear-style as high as their strength and technique would allow. Next was the 'Bamboo Crawl', which entailed threading your way on your belly, snake-like, through a particularly large and dense bamboo thicket. Competitors were timed. This was followed by 'The Leap of Faith' which I would lead in jumping across a broad ditch. The finale was 'The Centenary Border Dash', a race down the central grass strip of the border. On one occasion when I was about to signal for the competitors to start their dash from the far end of the border, they jumped the gun and were already on their way when a voice from behind me boomed 'What is going on here?' It was HG, looking a little puzzled. All I could think of by way of an explanation was

'They are students from Merrist Wood College, Mr Hillier, and they are so keen to see the next plant.' It was a pathetic excuse and he knew it, but to my relief he simply instructed me to stop them running and moved on. Apart from Merrist Wood the Arboretum Challenge was enjoyed by student groups from Kew and Wisley, who welcomed this opportunity to mix education with a bit of fun.

Sharing enthusiasm for plants
The County Council's input to the Gardens was considerable. Apart from the financial aspect there was a significant injection of help and advice from its collective expertise, especially in marketing, planning and design. The many facilities made available proved of great benefit to the Gardens and the staff in the process of facing the new era. Both Bill George and I found ourselves on regular guide

Merrist Wood College students testing their skill and stamina in the Hug-a-Bear round of the 'Hillier Arboretum Challenge' in May 1977.

.....

duty as garden clubs, professional organizations and school parties requested tours, and with the help of Council staff we began planning themed trails and preparing pamphlets and other illustrative material to assist our visitors. It was great fun and I never tired of my involvement, whether it be with the elderly or very young, the amateur gardener or the expert. On one occasion I was surprised and honoured to meet the famous astronomer Professor Sir Bernard Lovell, who was visiting the Gardens with friends. He was a customer of the Hillier Nurseries and was planting his own arboretum around his Cheshire home. We had a most enjoyable stroll and I was impressed with his knowledge of trees while I knew little or nothing about the mysteries of space. He wrote to me shortly afterwards, inviting me to come and visit the Nuffield Radio Astronomy Laboratories at Jodrell Bank to see their radio telescope. Just as important to me was a letter I received from a teacher at Bishopwood County Junior School near Basingstoke addressed to 'Roy the Tree'. He thanked me on behalf of his class for taking them round the gardens: 'They thoroughly enjoyed it and certainly caught your enthusiasm.'

On the subject of publicity, I was keen to seek every opportunity of drawing the public's attention to this very special garden and resource in Hampshire's green acres. To this end I tried to keep the local media informed of any new developments or special flower or plant events. On such things, as with my writing, I was required to seek my line manager's permission before taking any action. This I began to find irksome as he did not always share my enthusiasm for such things and seemed not to trust my judgement when dealing with the press. Whatever the reasons, his reticence and sometimes refusal to allow me to deal with such matters began to weary me. It all came to a head one day in autumn 1979 when I read in a national daily newspaper a story suggesting a probable rise in the cost of our morning cuppa due to a dispute between plantation owners, traders and tea-pickers over rates of pay. It was also mentioned on a BBC radio news bulletin. This reminded me that we had in the Gardens in a border close to Jermyns House a group of three large bushes of a wild tea (*Camellia sinensis*) which had originally been introduced from Yunnan province, south-west China,

.....

early this century by the Scottish plant hunter George Forrest. This had proved hardy, in milder counties certainly, and though its small white flowers in no way competed ornamentally with those hardy larger-flowered, many-coloured garden selections and hybrids of *C. japonica*, *C. saluenensis* and *C. reticulata*, it was the real McCoy. The quality of this wild form could never match that of the teas used commercially from sources in the east such as Darjeeling and Sri Lanka, but nevertheless it gave me an idea. There was no time to delay, such opportunities are fleeting, so I hatched a plan.

I would contact local press, television and radio sources and invite them to come to the Hillier Gardens the next morning to see what a tea plant looked like. While they were writing their notes and photographing or filming the bushes, I would signal my previous secretary, Mrs Parsons, watching from her office window, and she would prepare and deliver cups of piping hot tea made from these very bushes. I planned to pick the leaves and dry them overnight on radiators. The story would be 'Why not grow your own tea?' Having discussed it with our new Council secretary, who was unsure about it, I then phoned the media, with whom I enjoyed good relations. Their response was favourable. I again spoke to our secretary, who urged me to discuss it with my line manager. I was reluctant to do this but she did it, and I then found myself having to explain my plan to an irate and concerned boss who ordered me to ring round and cancel the event. He had spoken to his head of department and had his support.

Naturally, I found it humiliating to do this and the media were not best pleased. They quite understood my predicament but one or two decided to contact the Council direct and the next thing I knew the chief executive had become involved. To cut an already long story short, I was summoned to the office of my head of department at The Castle in Winchester, where he told me that he would not condone these things any longer. I had been making waves and if I was to continue in my job I wasn't to make so much as a ripple. I returned home that day depressed but determined to stay positive and discussed the situation with Sue. We decided the choice was either to continue as curator of the Hillier Gardens and keep a low profile or change my job. We thought

.....

193

long and hard about it over the following weekend and reached the conclusion that if I really wanted to be myself and decide my own future then I should resign and pursue a freelance career. Given that Sue was nearing the end of her first pregnancy, we decided it would be wise to wait until after the baby arrived before making my decision known. In the event, our son Edward was born on 5 November and I then served notice of my resignation. Interestingly, 20 years later, in 1999, the first successful plantings of *Camellia sinensis* as a commercial crop in Britain were established on the Tregothnan Estate, home of the Boscawen family near Truro in Cornwall. This was followed in 2006 by the first marketing of an English tea grown on English soil.

Freelance life begins

There were those who were surprised if not concerned about my decision, including the chief executive who, at my leaving party on 1 February 1980, suggested I had chosen a difficult time to be contemplating a freelance career, especially with a baby to care for. A collection had been made by the staff and we had been asked for suggestions as to a suitable gift. Sue, ever the practical one in our partnership, suggested a calculator and some sherry glasses. In presenting them to us, the chief executive said he hoped we would find a use for them. I was even more determined that we would!

The one person I was most anxious to share my decision with was HG. I found it hard and hoped he would not feel that I was letting him down. We were in my office at the time looking through the window at the scree and heather garden beyond. He said he quite understood why I had come to the decision but expressed unease about my going freelance as he had never regarded me as having a head for business. I assured him that Sue had more of a feel for this than I and that together we would make a good team. At least we were not intending to move out of the area and HG requested that I keep in touch and visit the Gardens whenever possible. Curiously, once I had left the Gardens and both Hillier's and the County Council's employ he began all his letters to me with 'Dear Roy', which signalled a new chapter in our relationship and one I warmly welcomed.

.....

Over the Christmas period Sue and I had had plenty of time to think and talk about how I would earn a living. I remember us sitting down and making a list of the areas which I hoped to explore. It was an exciting time and an anxious one too, but we were both determined to make a go of it and we did. Writing, lecturing and advisory work would be my main sources of income and Sue had already done a typing course to help me with my articles. I was still writing everything longhand and I do even now as I find it relaxing and therapeutic.

A friend had told us that it can take ten years to establish a freelance career and in our case we can only agree. We had our highs and lows and our share of scary moments, but thanks to Sue's practical nous and work ethic we made it a success. My first job as a freelance was an advisory visit to the witch hazel plantations run by Optrex, the eye lotion company, near Basingstoke. Our long-time friend David Hutchinson, then employed by MAFF (now DEFRA) as a nursery stock adviser, had recommended me as being just the man to help them with problems regarding their present stock. I spent a morning touring the plantations with an official and was able to offer plenty of advice. Having seen the common species *Hamamelis virginiana* growing wild in the woods of the north-east of the USA I suggested that through my contacts there I could easily search for new selections for their trials to improve or replenish their stock. I was asked to send them a report on all that we had discussed and I headed for home believing that I had convinced them of the wisdom of inviting me. The report was duly prepared and carefully typed, and together with my invoice for services rendered it was posted the next day. Apart from an acknowledgement of its receipt I heard no more from them. It took several weeks before, with the help of our friend David, the invoice was honoured. It seems they thought that I had visited them as a favour. It was an early lesson and so nearly our first bad debt.

In the meantime I had been requested by a Yorkshire nursery that grew conifers to check out their proposed catalogue prior to printing. It duly arrived in the post and on reading it I could hardly believe the number of errors both in nomenclature and descriptions it contained. I virtually had to rewrite the whole publication before returning it with

.....

our invoice to the sender. This time, the customer wrote to thank us by return of post and included a cheque – our first earnings as a business and our first excuse to use those sherry glasses.

As we had hoped, lectures and writing provided my main source of income but payment for articles did not always immediately follow publication, nor were fees always forthcoming at the end of a lecture. Some societies and clubs had a schedule regarding when to pay while one or two proved more difficult. Having agreed in writing to pay my fee and travel expenses for a talk, one treasurer subsequently rang up to ask me to cut the amount, to my surprise. Despite my protestations he continued to try to persuade me to reconsider. I was now annoyed, so I asked him what he did for a living himself. He hesitated before answering, 'I'm a solicitor.' A friend of mine had a similar experience when at the end of his lecture, after he had driven a good distance to get there and would be making a late-night return, the treasurer tried to persuade him to forego his travel expenses. My friend, mentally exhausted after his talk, refused. 'But we are a charity,' was the reply. 'So am I,' my friend retorted, 'and I have a long drive ahead of me.' I hasten to add that such incidents were few and in my experience involved particular individuals and not the clubs and societies they represented. I have always found audiences welcoming, understanding and a pleasure to be with.

Speaking engagements
The variety of venues I have spoken in is enormous, from potting sheds and marquees to state-of-the art public and university lecture theatres. By far the majority, however, have been village halls in their varied guises. At one time most of my lecture invitations were for evening meetings, usually in winter; now they are mostly daytime occasions, often at weekends. Conferences, symposiums, workshops, garden societies, student groups and children's groups all have their challenges and pleasures and I have always sought to prepare a lecture to suit my audience. Naturally, given my experience as a plantsman who loves storytelling, my preference has leaned towards plants in the wild and in cultivation rather than garden or landscape design, ornamental plants

.....

rather than fruit and veg and lawn care. My personal preference is for plant exploration, which should not be surprising given my travels. I especially enjoy giving illustrated lectures and for many years it was with the use of slides, over which, having my own projector, I had total control – well, not always.

My biggest disaster and one I shall never forget befell me when I was preparing to give a lecture one evening in a village hall in Berkshire. I was all set up, my projector with a full magazine of 80 slides settled firmly on its stand in the central aisle, and a full house of garden enthusiasts waiting expectantly on either side. The club secretary checked I was ready and I nodded. Just then, we noticed a late arrival, an elderly lady, her back bent and using a stick. We waited and watched as she walked slowly and shakily down the aisle, heading for a seat reserved for her on the front row. As she was negotiating the projector stand she stumbled and fell, sending the projector crashing to the floor with bits and pieces flying off in every direction. After my initial shock I ran down to help her to her feet. She was confused but otherwise unhurt and a friend offered to take her home to recover, which she accepted. Only then did I attempt to locate and collect my projector parts, including the slides scattered under people's feet. Of course they helped me but the projector was kaput. In the event the secretary remembered they had a spare projector which he retrieved from the attic. 'I don't know when we last used it,' he said, blowing the dust off its box. It was an antique compared with mine but it did work, just.

Today, I give PowerPoint presentations thanks to a digital camera Sue bought me several years ago. I have never been technically minded, so it pains me to share an office with four metal cabinets containing thousands of slides, the best of them superior in quality to any digital image, none of which I have used for several years except for publishing purposes.

One of my first-ever lectures was to a local gardening club in the north country. It was held in a community centre which on the night was extremely busy, so much so that the main room had been divided by a large, dark curtain to accommodate two events. I had been delayed by traffic and arrived in a rush to be met by the secretary, who helped me set up my projector and screen. Eventually, I was ready and after a

.....

quick introduction I asked for the lights to be switched off. As I was about to begin a loud voice cried out, 'Are you there?' I presumed it was someone in my audience and replied, 'Yes,' before showing my first slide. Again the voice rang out, 'Can you hear me?' I then realized that the voice emanated from the other side of the curtain and I was quite perplexed when the lights were switched on and the secretary came to apologize, explaining that the other half of the room had, without their knowledge, been booked for a séance by a spiritualist group and I would just have to speak louder!

On another occasion, in Boston, USA, I had just begun a lecture to the Massachusetts Horticultural Society in their impressive headquarters when I noticed two police officers had entered the room. Having spoken to them, the Society's secretary announced that due to a bomb alert we had been requested to vacate the room and relocate to the concert hall next door, which we did in an orderly fashion. Here I found myself speaking from the stage in the famous home of the 'Boston Pops'. Having set up the projector I continued my lecture from where I had left off, but for a second time I was interrupted by an announcement, this time informing us that it was now safe to return to where we began, in the Society's hall. Here I managed to finish my lecture without further disruption.

I have several times found my lectures interrupted by a member of the audience fainting or otherwise feeling unwell and long ago decided that the best strategy, given that there is invariably a doctor in the house, is to carry on unless requested not to in the belief that my stopping would only encourage unwanted curiosity, further embarrassing the victim.

In the university lecture theatre in Kunming, in China's Yunnan province, I once gave a lecture on Chinese plants in Western cultivation to an audience of students. It later emerged that they knew little, if any, English but they had enjoyed the slides. For a lecture I was to give to a Japanese audience it was requested that I speak slowly. It took me one-and-a-half hours, but given the need for someone to translate my every word into Japanese the lecture lasted three hours and that did not allow for questions.

.....

Nearer home, I was standing on a stage at a West Country venue with an in-house bar when the lights went out before I was quite ready. I began my lecture but decided I needed a glass of water. Signalling to a man standing off stage I whispered my request for a drink. A few minutes later a glass was handed to me in the dark and on taking a sip I realized I had been given a pint of beer, a strong local bitter!

My favourite story concerns a series of lectures staged annually over a ten-year period by a group of keen gardeners headed by the late Billy Douglas, long-time nursery and show manager for Sam McGredy Roses of Portadown in Northern Ireland. The lectures were held in nearby Craigavon Civic Hall and Billy had invited the speakers to deliver what he ambitiously advertised as the Horticultural Lecture of the Year. Geoffrey Smith was one of the speakers and I was another. For the final lecture in March 1999 and to celebrate the ten years, Billy invited all the previous speakers to attend for a Grand Finale. We were given approximately 15 minutes each to speak on 'The Romance of Plant Life'. The hall was full to bursting and as always the stage was full of plants including trees, shrubs, perennials, flowers and foliage which had been supplied and arranged by local nurserymen. It looked like a scene from *A Midsummer Night's Dream* as one by one we speakers came on to perform.

At the end of the show, Billy took to the stage once more, a short, thick-set man with a ruddy face and a Churchillian gift for the big occasion. I once asked if he had ever kissed the Blarney Stone, to which his wife replied 'No, he swallowed it!' He stood there, a stout blackthorn stick in one hand, and delivered a speech worthy of Falstaff. He thanked everyone, his committee, the volunteers, the audience, the mayor and his special guests, the nurserymen and the good Lord. He then called for the speakers to join him, introducing each one of us with words of extravagant praise, his voice trembling and rising all the while, his hand stomping the stage with his stick. What we didn't know was that the sound of the stick was a signal to an accomplice beneath the stage to start releasing dry ice. Soon, a vaporous cloud emerged from the cracks in the floor, the effect accelerating in response to Billy's evangelical delivery and the thumping of his stick. Within ten minutes the stage

.....

was filled with mist. We could hardly see a thing and neither could the audience, but Billy's voice and his thumping were finally stilled as the audience loudly cheered and applauded.

Horticultural veterans

One thing I look forward to when lecturing is the unexpected meeting with someone I haven't seen in years or conversely someone of special interest I have never before met. It happens quite a lot and I never know who might be in the audience. At the end of my lecture for Billy Douglas, I was approached by two men, one a good deal older than the other. The younger man was Archie Bingham, one time manager of the famous Slieve Donard Nursery in Newcastle, Co. Down. His white-headed companion was Harry Bryce who, it turned out, had served since 1928 at Donard as chief propagator. Archie informed me that he was my host for the night and that we could all have a good talk about plants and things. I could hardly wait and for two hours or so I listened to Harry's at times moving story of his long career propagating and selecting plants, some of which, *Deutzia* × *elegantissima* 'Rosealind' AGM, *Escallonia* 'Apple Blossom' AGM and *Potentilla fruticosa* 'Tangerine' to name but a few, were raised by him. Equally famous in gardens are the original seedlings raised by Harry of *Mahonia* × *media* (*M. japonica* × *M. lomariifolia*), a chance hybrid which occurred in the Donard Nursery in around 1950. The first to be named, by Sir Eric Savill at the Savill Gardens in Windsor Great Park, was 'Charity'. Donard subsequently named another 'Winter Sun', an AGM plant.

The more Harry reminisced the more silent I became. Born in 1897, he began his career aged 15 as a boy probationer at the Royal Botanic Garden Edinburgh, where his interest in plant propagation developed. Along with many of his colleagues he served in the First World War, surviving a bullet wound below his eye. Fortunately, this did not affect his ability to spot a new plant nor his propagating skills. Returning to continue his training at Edinburgh, he left in 1921 to join Hillier and Sons as head propagator at their West Hill Nursery. He recalled the day in 1922 when Edwin Hillier, HG's father, introduced his son of 17 years to him in the nursery, instructing Harry to teach him about propagation

.....

and ensure that he did not pick up any bad habits. HG later referred to Harry as 'the cat's whiskers'. I stayed in contact with Harry and was privileged to be with him in London on the day in January 1989 when he was honoured by the RHS as an Associate of Honour. 'It was the proudest moment of my life,' he said. Sadly, he died in July the following year aged 93.

Another famous gardening veteran I was privileged to meet was Captain Collingwood Ingram, known as 'Cherry' to his friends in acknowledgement of his expertise on those popular ornamental trees, especially the Sato Sakura or Japanese flowering cherries of garden origin, though his plant interests were wide-ranging. In the 1960s and '70s he was a familiar figure to me at RHS London and Chelsea flower shows, where he was often to be seen exhibiting plants including dwarf rhododendrons he had raised. In 1980, his hundredth year, I was commissioned by the *Gardeners Chronicle & Horticultural Trade Journal* to write an article on him. Uppermost in my mind as I travelled to his garden in the village of Benenden in Kent was the thought that he had been born in 1880, the year that saw the death of the great Scottish plant explorer and gardener Robert Fortune and the births of two other notable gardeners and collectors, Reginald Farrer and William Purdom, who had died in 1920 and

ABOVE Congratulating Harry Bryce on his becoming an Associate of Honour of the RHS aged 92 in February 1989

BELOW Captain Collingwood ('Cherry') Ingram in his hundredth year, showing me around his garden at Benenden in Kent in August 1980.

.....

TOP A valley in the Organ Mountains near Petrópolis, Brazil, in March 1990.

ABOVE The unmistakable silvery-hairy canopy of *Cecropia glaziovii* in the forests around Petrópolis.

1921 respectively. Yet here I was, about to meet this amazing survivor who spent several hours showing me round his garden with non-stop comments and anecdotes as he poked, prodded and pointed out the many treasures. Two friends who had accompanied me, Alan Hardy and Douglas Harris, suggested we treat him to lunch at his local hostelry and on entering I asked Cherry if I might buy him a drink. 'Thank you,' he said, 'say who it's for and that I'll have my usual tipple.' This I did and I couldn't help smiling when I saw the landlord reaching for a bottle of The Famous Grouse, a whisky I had enjoyed myself. After we finished our meal Cherry insisted that we return to his garden to finish our tour, which we were only too pleased to do. My article was published on the last day of October that year, just in time, as the following year he passed away.

Destination Brazil

In March 1990, I found myself on a flight out of London, leaving a cold grey landscape for one of blue skies and golden sunlight. A couple of months earlier I had picked up the phone in my study to hear a lady called Nariko Ford inviting me to give a talk to a flower arranging society. I would be paid all expenses plus a fee and be well looked after. It sounded promising. I then asked where the talk was to be held. Her reply 'São Paolo' left me momentarily speechless. Eventually I responded 'That's in Brazil, isn't it?' It was indeed. I quickly revised my thinking and asked if I might come for a week. Her answer

.....

'But of course' had me reaching for my diary. As it turned out, the society was hosting a special gathering of flower arrangers and gardeners countrywide. It was agreed that I should fly over a few days before the talk and head for Rio de Janeiro, where I was to be met by Vicki Walker, who would be hosting me until my talk. On my arrival Vicki suggested I might like to escape the heat and blinding sun and head for the old Imperial city of Petrópolis which lies 42 miles (68km) north-east of Rio at 2749ft (838m) in the Serra dos Órgãos, known to the Victorian plant explorers, especially the orchid hunters, as the Organ Mountains. The great Veitchian collector William Lobb, a Cornishman, visited here in 1841 and again in 1845 and it was with this thought in mind that I looked forward to this unexpected opportunity.

The first plant to catch my eye in the forest canopy was *Cecropia glaziovii*, a fast-growing pioneer tree whose broad-spreading crown of huge, long-stalked, horse chestnut-like, silvery-hairy leaves stood out a mile. Equally striking were the rich purple-flowered crowns of *Tibouchina granulosa* and the smaller *T. mutabilis*, of which the flowers change from pale purple to white. Golden yellow was provided by *Cassia multijuga* and other species and pink by the large orchid-like blooms of massive kapok trees (*Chorisia speciosa*), which I first saw planted as a street tree in Funchal, Madeira. I was amazed to see *Bougainvillea speciosa* scrambling high into forest trees. The flora, especially around Petrópolis, was bewildering in its variety: native species and planted exotics, some of which had gone wild, such as the

Flowering trees planted in the gardens near Petrópolis include *Cassia multijuga* (yellow), *Tibouchina granulosa* (purple) and, far right, *Chorisia speciosa* (pink). The first two are native in local forests.

.....

203

white-flowered *Hedychium coronarium* from Asia which, with busy-lizzie (*Impatiens walleriana*) from Africa filled roadside ditches. Curiously, there were colonies of golden rod (*Solidago canadensis*) or similar and everywhere we went we saw huge butterflies in blue, white and black and bromeliads of all kinds encrusting rocks and in trees. A purple-leaved shrub, *Euphorbia cotinifolia*, resembling a smoke bush (*Cotinus coggygria*) at a glance, was commonly planted as a hedge, while in forest glades we spied a palm, *Syagrus romanzoffiana* (previously *Arecastrum romanzoffianum*), native here but commonly cultivated in tropical and warm temperate regions of the world.

Roberto Burle Marx

The next day I was taken to see the Botanic Gardens in Rio, which boasted some fine trees including an impressive avenue of old mango trees (*Mangifera indica*) and an equally impressive avenue of royal palms (*Roystonea regia*). Other trees to catch my eye were cannonball trees (*Couroupita guianensis*) in heavy fruit, sausage trees (*Kigelia africana*) in flower and nutmegs (*Myristica fragrans*). Before we left, Vicki introduced me to the superintendent, an elderly gentleman who lived for the garden. We stayed that night with Vicki's mother-in-law in her beautiful apartment in Rio. Over our meal we discussed our plans for the next day. Vicki offered three options: a tour of local gardens, a return to the mountains or, if she could organize it, a visit to see Roberto Burle Marx's garden. My eyes lit up at the mention of this famous Brazilian landscape architect who was recognized internationally for his designs for parks and gardens. What I wasn't aware of then were his other talents as a painter, printmaker, ecologist, naturalist and musician. As if this weren't enough, Vicki mentioned his pioneering efforts in highlighting the destruction of Brazil's forests and the urgent need for conservation. At least 50 plant species, she added, had been named in his honour. Not surprisingly, I chose the third option – but would Burle Marx want to see us? Vicki went to make the call, returning shortly after to confirm that he would be pleased to meet us the next day. I could not sleep that night.

Early next morning we drove south along the coast road beyond Ipanema, which had me singing 'The Girl from Ipanema' in the car,

.....

A meeting with Roberto Burle Marx at his home, the Sitio de Santo Antonio da Bica estate in the hills of the Barra de Guaratiba. His garden was awash with exotic plants, mostly native to Brazil.

much to my companion's amusement. Eventually we arrived at Burle Marx's estate in the Sitia da Santo Antonio da Bica in the hills of Guaratiba. My first impression on approaching his garden was that it was hard to separate it from the surrounding vegetation, but on passing through a security gate into the garden proper, distinct areas were revealed. One of them, around the house, was filled with exotic plants in which bromeliads of many shapes and sizes dominated. We drove to the house, a long single-storeyed building with a stone-paved veranda looking out over a sunken lawn with several groups of multi-coloured plant stands – a quite remarkable sight. Burle Marx was being interviewed and filmed by a TV crew, but once they departed he came to find us. He was of full figure with a broad face, a moustache and a shock of flowing silver hair. Following introductions I presented him with a copy of my book *Travels in China: A Plantsman's Paradise* and he then led us on a tour of his 'collections', which were extensive and diverse. I was informed later that they contained more than 3,500 different plants.

Philodendrons, begonias, orchids and myriad other exotics followed, some in drifts of a single kind, others as large individuals. Passing through one shady area, I noticed the minuscule nest of a humming bird in a bush. It contained what I first took to be a hairy

.....

brown caterpillar which turned out to be a chick. Out host pointed out many rare plants, some of which were new species collected by him. He also showed us a moonlight cactus (*Selenicereus wittii*) that had belonged to the late botanical artist Margaret Mee, who had been a friend, along with her anthurium collection. Finally, we climbed the slope above the house to see his 'castle', the reconstructed shell of an impressive stone-built house he had found and bought in Rio, which he intended to make into a 'grand studio'. 'I will have my coronation there,' he said with a smile. On taking his leave he urged us to continue higher to see his new plantings, which included bamboos, palms and yet more bromeliads.

On returning to the house we were served glasses of chilled passion fruit juice on the veranda before following him inside to view his private collection of religious and native artefacts and his paintings, some of which featured bold tropical foliage and flowers. By now we were thoroughly at ease and were surprised and delighted to be invited to stay for a meal while listening to CDs of his favourite music, which included Ravel. I shall never forget the experience of sitting in that fine room surrounded by paintings and artefacts, quiet but for an occasional story from our genial host and the sounds of the night outside. Two days later I finally got to deliver my lecture, 'The World is My Garden', to an appreciative audience of ladies, some of whom were from Argentina, representing the Buenos Aires Garden Club which boasted, I was told, 2000 members.

Trip to Jordan

When it comes to advisory visits I have had my fair share of unusual requests, but the prize for the most curious must go to one, again received by phone, from a man who asked me to fly to an unnamed Middle Eastern country to advise someone he wasn't allowed to name about a dying tree. All he wanted to know initially was if I could I do it and if so would I do it as a matter of urgency. This was in July 1990, prior to the Gulf War. I was intrigued and asked for further details, upon which I was told I would be heading for Amman in Jordan and I should stay for 3–4 days. I was excited, while Sue was less sure. In a follow-up

.....

conversation with my nameless contact I confirmed my interest which is why, on 7 August, five days after Saddam Hussein's Iraqi forces occupied Kuwait, I found myself on a flight to Amman, arriving at night to be met beyond the passport desk by a military officer who instructed me to follow him. I ended up in a car which transported me to a city centre hotel. The officer told me to check in while he waited in the lobby. On completing this I turned to find the officer gone.

The following morning, expecting to be summoned, I was up and breakfasted early. I then waited in my room until late morning, when a call from the desk informed me that someone was waiting. It was not the officer but a civilian who introduced himself in English as a senior official in the Jordanian Forestry Department and asked me to accompany him. He drove without any attempt at conversation through the busy city, finally entering the gates of a large building, past the security guards and into a courtyard. My host then led me round the outside of the building into a large garden, where he pointed to a tree which I recognized as an oriental plane (*Platanus orientalis*) and asked me why it was dying. Apart from some twig die-back I could see nothing to suggest that the tree was in trouble. I examined its base and stem and checked its foliage but I still couldn't see any reason to be concerned. 'Why do you think it is dying?' I asked him. 'It is losing its bark,' he replied, looking me in the eye, his face without a hint of a smile. 'But plane trees do that, it is normal,' I explained. I had no doubt that he knew it too – a shrug of his shoulders told me so. 'We were instructed to bring in an expert from the UK for a second opinion,' he admitted. I then realized his predicament – an order is an order. To spare us both further embarrassment I suggested that I take photographs and include my findings in my report. Having saved face, he visibly relaxed and became more informative.

He told me that the garden was that of a royal palace and if I was interested he would take me to see other royal gardens, which he did. In each one I found plenty to advise him on, including a group of 16–23ft (4.8–7m) tall evergreen trees which he said had 'stopped growing'. I asked him to carefully dig a hole above the roots. This revealed the root balls still encased and restricted in their canvas wrapping. He also

.....

mentioned another palace garden in the south of the country at Petra, asking if I had been there. I hadn't and to my surprise he offered to take me the next day. I had noticed as we drove around that groups of people were increasingly gathering in the streets, huddled around radios which, from the sound of it, were broadcasting news of the military situation in Kuwait and Iraq. My host switched on his car radio and gradually his mood and demeanour began to change. Next thing we were back at my hotel and before I could properly thank him he was gone. Most of my fellow guests had packed their bags and departed that morning, so it was a strange atmosphere in which I ate my evening meal while mulling over my options. I doubted that I would hear any more from my host, so having been denied my trip to Petra I decided I would spend my last day visiting some of the local historical sites and hopefully doing some botanizing as well.

The next morning after breakfast, with no messages forthcoming, I took a taxi and visited first the Greco-Roman city of Jerash with its Street of Columns, Forum, Theatre and Temple of Artemis, a breathtaking sight in a dry, stony landscape. The only plant life I recognized here apart from a shrubby oak (*Quercus ithaburensis*) known as the Tabor oak, which assumes tree size in suitable sites, was an *Ononis*, a *Centaurea*, a thistle, a *Verbascum* and the caper bush (*Capparis spinosa*). From here I was taken to see the hilltop Ajlun Castle, built by Izz al-Din Usama ibn Munqidh, one of Saladin's generals, in AD 1184–85 against the threat of Crusader attacks. At the hottest time of the day we crossed the Jordan valley to the shores of the Dead Sea. In the valley I noted pink-flowered oleander (*Nerium oleander*) crowding stream gullies and *Populus euphratica*, whose juvenile leaves are oblong while its adult leaves are ovate or rhombic. In drier places *Zizyphus lotus*, a thorny shrub, and a most striking globe thistle (*Echinops viscosus*) with large, globular, spiky heads of blue flowers above deeply divided, spine-toothed foliage were common. The obligatory bathe in the Dead Sea followed but far from refreshing me I emerged feeling like a steamed and salted shrimp and was thankful to return to the cool of my hotel room before dinner, which I again ate alone. The following day I made my own way by taxi to the airport for my return flight home.

.....

In the footsteps of Carl Linnaeus

In total contrast to my brief adventure in Jordan was an exhausting but exciting 17-day journey through Sweden and Norway in June 1999. A good friend of ours, Gertrude Looi, had invited Sue and me to accompany her in the footsteps of the great Swedish naturalist Carl Linnaeus. Basically, she wanted me to help her locate and identify those native plants seen and named by Linnaeus on his travels in the above countries in the 18th century, in particular his Lapland journey from May to October 1732. She had already hired a driver and car to transport us from Copenhagen. Sue and I had travelled in Scandinavia previously, but this trip had a compelling purpose and as things turned out it proved to be one of the most memorable journeys of its kind I have experienced. It was also on occasions one of the most frustrating, as our driver had no particular interest in plants and became increasingly difficult about us stopping to look for them.

On entering Sweden we headed for Lund and then to Bjuv, which was celebrating the 250th anniversary of Linnaeus's visit in 1749. The castle gardens at Gunnarstorp was our main destination, where we met an old friend, Kenneth Lorentzen, who acted as our guide and took us to inspect the old box hedges 'seen and touched' by Linnaeus as well as a fine clipped hornbeam tunnel which was already 100 years old when Linnaeus visited on three occasions in July 1749. I noted three-nerved sandwort (*Moehringia trinervia*) thriving in the shade of the box. Continuing our Linnaeus theme, we stopped to view the church at Stenbrohult where his father had been rector and where a statue of Linnaeus stands in the churchyard. Next was the village of Råshult, where stands the log cabin that was Linnaeus's birthplace in 1707. Here we noted the turf roof supporting houseleek (*Sempervivum tectorum*), heartsease (*Viola tricolor*) and other native plants. Our hotel that night was a mock castle I shall remember for the persistent singing of a thrush nightingale keeping me awake and for my first sight the next morning of wild Swedish whitebeam (*Sorbus intermedia*), a commonly planted street tree in Britain. Later in our journey we found the related *S. hybrida*, which is thought to have originated as a cross between *S. rupicola*, a whitebeam, and the mountain ash or rowan, (*S. aucuparia*).

.....

Calypso bulbosa, an exquisite little ground orchid in a pine and oak woodland in north-east Sweden in June 1999.

On reaching Uppsala we headed for the University's Linnaean Gardens to be met by the recently appointed director, Magnus Lidén. It was at the University of Uppsala that Linnaeus, as Professor of Botany, reigned supreme and in the country nearby at his farm, Hammarby, too. During the next few days we found and photographed many of the classic Scandinavian plants including the twinflower (*Linnaea borealis*) named for and by Linnaeus, which also occurs in Scotland. Here, it was growing in woodland with pink-flowered dwarf *Rubus arcticus* and other woodlanders. It was in a pine and oak woodland near Mjällom in north-east Sweden that we found a plant quite new to me in *Calypso bulbosa*, an exquisite little ground orchid with a bulb-like tuber, a single, stalked leaf and a solitary, charming, pink and white bloom with a yellow-stained, slipper-like lip. A careful sweep of the wood revealed around a dozen of these individuals in flower, along with the lesser butterfly orchid (*Platanthera bifolia*) and *Hepatica nobilis*.

We crossed the Arctic Circle just south of Jokkmokk and later, on our way north to our overnight stop at Abisko, we saw drifts of globe flower (*Trollius europaeus*) by a roadside lake, reminding me of my first meeting with this beautiful buttercup relative in a stream valley north of my home town Bolton in the 1950s. The Abisko National Park offered us a wealth of arctic alpines including *Rhododendron lapponicum*, *Cassiope tetragona* and *Phyllodoce caerulea*. We drove on across the border to Narvik in Norway before heading south along the coast, where we stopped to have a picnic on the edge of a pine wood. We relaxed surrounded by carpets of dwarf cornel (*Cornus suecica*) in full flower, each cluster of tiny dark purple flowers surrounded by four white bracts. In places it formed mounds, sometimes enveloping old tree stumps. That night we stayed at Bodø from where we were treated to spectacular views of the Lurfjelltinden (mountains), which apparently are even more impressive when viewed from out at sea, according to Gertrude.

.....

Next day our route led us south through several rock tunnels to the Junkerdalsura Gorge near Storjord, home of the National Park Centre. It was here that I enjoyed one of the really special moments of my plant life when I realized a lifelong dream in seeing lady's slipper orchid (*Cypripedium calceolus*) in the wild. It was all the more enjoyable because it was totally unexpected. First a group of three flowering stems by the trail which had me standing transfixed before reaching for my camera; I then found myself threading my way carefully around boulders and scrub on a steep hillside where the lady's slippers grew in profusion, individual clumps with as many as 10–15 flowers gently trembling in the breeze. At one point I sat down on a rock and drank in the wonderful display. Nothing I had seen before could match this, especially in emotional terms. How long I stayed I do not know, but it suddenly occurred to me that Gertrude and Sue must be wondering where I had got to, so I took yet more images to finish off my film before heading

One of my favourite perennials is the globe flower (*Trollius europaeus*), here flourishing by a lake north of the Arctic Circle in Swedish Lapland.

Cornus suecica, the dwarf cornel, was abundant in Norway, here enveloping an old tree stump.

.....

My eureka moment in seeing *Cypripedium calceolus*, the lady's slipper orchid, wild and abundant in Norway.

back down the slope towards the trail. I hadn't gone far when, while fiddling with my camera, I tripped on a rock and lurched forward towards a large boulder. Split seconds later I found myself on my knees with my face against the rock and nothing to show for it but a grazed and sore cheekbone. I slowly got to my feet, expecting to feel pain somewhere, but nothing. Agreeably puzzled, I glanced down at my camera which hung from its strap on my chest. It had taken the full force of my fall and the impact had pushed the lens into the camera body. It was a close call, but I had to wait until our return home before discovering that the film had suffered no damage.

That could have been the end of our adventure for me but there was more to come. Returning to the car with the song of a willow warbler in the air and those of a fieldfare and a brambling nearby, we drove across the border into Sweden and a long journey south to Östersund, where we again headed west on the Trondheim road, recrossing the border into Norway. It had been raining for hours and the rain followed us as we drove down a valley where waterfalls of creamy, coffee-coloured water rushed to the main river. Our driver had no intention of stopping, staring resolutely ahead, no doubt thinking of the warm and dry hotel room awaiting him in Trondheim. The road was busy, narrowing at one point to pass through a gorge where the vertical rock faces were plastered with large numbers of arching, conical panicles of white flowers. I recognized them as belonging to a saxifrage (*Saxifraga cotyledon*) which I remembered growing in the rock garden at Moss Bank Park in Bolton in the early 1950s. This spectacular, crevice-dwelling plant produces a

.....

dense rosette up to 4in (10cm) across of broadly obovate to oblong, finely white-toothed and slightly fleshy leaves and when sufficiently mature it has a multi-branched inflorescence which can reach anything up to 28in (70cm) long, containing as many as a thousand small white or pink-speckled flowers. This was another plant named by Linnaeus and I asked our driver to take the first exit. He totally ignored me and with his eyes fixed resolutely on the road ahead drove on. Several times I requested him to pull off the road so that we could view and photograph the saxifrage in all its glory but my voice fell on deaf ears. Even Gertrude's plea failed.

Not long after, we reached a village whose name was defiantly displayed on a red roadside sign, HELL. The name, apparently, is derived from Old Norse, meaning overhang or cliff cave, referring perhaps to the cliffs we had so recently noted. Eventually, we arrived at our hotel in Trondheim where I could hardly bring myself to speak to our driver. Despite having seen, no thanks to him, the glory of the lady's slippers, I could not stop thinking about the article that might have been 'The Saxifrage from Hell'!

CHAPTER EIGHT

Spreading the word

'More and more I am grateful that circumstances combined to make me a gardener. Just think, I might have become a politician.' Those were the words of Yorkshireman Geoffrey Smith, a good friend with whom I corresponded for over 40 years until his death in 2009 aged 80. We had first met in spring 1967 when I paid an advisory visit on behalf of Hillier to a private estate, Rudding Park, close to Harrogate. At his suggestion we met at a pub in town for 'a pie and a pint' before going on to the Northern Horticultural Society's Garden, his beloved Harlow Carr, where he was then superintendent. We finished the day visiting the gardens of Parcevall Hall near Skipton, a particular favourite of his, where he showed me a wealth of plants introduced by some of the famous British plant hunters. He then took me to see a view from outside the garden, of Upper Wharfedale, 'God's Country' he called it. Geoffrey even pointed out a grassy ledge on the steep bank below us where he would sometimes come to sit, a sort of bolt-hole, when he needed to 'get away from it all' and 'commune with nature'. It was dark when we left Parcevall, returning to Geoffrey's local pub and then his home, where we continued discussing plants until the early hours.

Like me, Geoffrey had wide interests in both native and cultivated plants and in wild places and natural history in general. He was a hands-on professional gardener and a natural communicator and raconteur, so it came as no surprise to me when he eventually left Harlow Carr to pursue a freelance career in radio and television and as a writer, in all of which he excelled. He soon attracted a huge fan base and when Peter Seabrook left BBC TV *Gardeners' World* in 1979 Geoffrey became one of its main presenters. It was in this role that, out of the blue, he rang me one day in January 1981 to ask if he might bring the *Gardeners' World* cameras to our garden the following March. I must admit to

.....

being taken aback and responded that mine was a new garden with relatively small plants, few of which would then be in leaf, let alone flower. His reply was typical of the man: 'If you and me can't find enough to talk about in a garden then it will be a sad day', and he had a point. So, I agreed to his suggestion that we meet the day before filming for a private recce and chat. This proved satisfactory and the following morning, Geoffrey arrived with an outside broadcasting unit and film crew and introduced me to the producer, John Kenyon.

A visit from Geoffrey Smith and the BBC TV's *Gardeners' World* team in March 1981 led to my own career as a presenter.

BBC TV's Gardener's World

We began with Geoffrey's introduction and opening question, 'When did you start the garden?' It was a gentle, easy way into the interview which followed, but I was still a tad nervous until Geoffrey, sensing this and well aware of my passion for plants and their stories, pointed to a dwarf spreading juniper-like conifer with sprays of foliage, which were a bright green in summer but were now caramel-coloured with a purplish tint. 'What is that?' he asked. '*Microbiota decussata*,' I replied, explaining that it had no English name and was relatively rare in cultivation, though bone-hardy and suitable for most soils. Geoffrey claimed that he had never heard of it, let alone grown it, and asked me where in the world it came from. Now I had the bit between my teeth, having once researched this plant for the Hillier Manual. 'In the wild apparently it only grows on wind-blasted, rain-drenched, mosquito-ridden heaths somewhere to the east of Vladivostock,' I said, to which Geoffrey exclaimed, 'My goodness, any further east and it would fall off the edge of the world.' This ready quip had me chuckling and from there on we didn't stop talking.

Microbiota decussata, then a rare conifer, attracted Geoffrey Smith's attention when filming in my garden. Here it has a dusting of hoar frost in the Sir Harold Hillier Gardens in November 2014.

.....

Clay Jones admiring
Pieris 'Forest Flame'
in the garden at Pine
Lodge, St Austell,
Cornwall with Shirley
Clemo, May 1987.

John Kenyon seemed pleased enough with the interview and asked me if I might consider doing more in future. 'I believe in horses for courses,' he said, 'and there are gardens we visit where your specialist knowledge and your enthusiasm would be welcome. How about it?' He wasn't asking for a specific commitment, but I made it known to Geoffrey that I would be happy to contribute in a plantsman's role on ornamental plant-related topics. What I wasn't aware of then was Geoffrey's intention to leave *Gardeners' World*, which he did the following year. He went on to present his own series for BBC Television, including *Mr Smith's Vegetable Garden* and *Mr Smith's Flower Garden*, both proving popular with the public. Then followed the pioneering *Geoffrey Smith's World of Flowers*, which had him travelling to countries worldwide. Sadly I never got to do another programme with him.

Clay Jones
Luckily for me, Geoffrey's co-presenters Clay Jones and Geoff Hamilton took me in hand and thanks to their encouragement and patience and that of the directors and production teams, I thoroughly enjoyed the next eight years as an occasional presenter visiting gardens in Britain and Ireland and meeting a lot of keen and knowledgeable amateur and professional gardeners along the way. In Clay Jones, I found a real gentleman whose wonderful warm Welsh baritone voice was a joy to listen to. Aged 17 he had been invited to join the D'Oyly Carte Opera Company, but thankfully for horticulture his mother had other ideas.

.....

Clay's all-round knowledge and experience of gardening from the science to the practical aspects of growing plants, especially vegetables and ornamentals from seed, was his great strength. He was, in his own words, 'In my true element with people and plants' and those programmes I was privileged to share with him, most of them in the gardens of amateur enthusiasts, I will remember for his skill and gentle manner when interviewing garden owners, especially those unnerved by the presence of an outside broadcasting unit on their patch with its scanners, cable layers and crew filming and recording their every move and word.

On one occasion we were filming at Wallington, the National Trust garden in Northumberland. It was a lovely summer's day and while I waited to record a sequence in the lower garden I could hear via the nearby scanner van Clay being shown around the conservatory by the head gardener, Mr Geoffrey Moon. At one point, on being told that a tall, magnificent flowering plant of *Fuchsia* 'Rose of Castile Improved' was 75 years old, Clay exclaimed, 'Well, if I look like that when I am 75, I'll be well pleased.' Due to the almost inevitable technical hitches, he was required to repeat his comment several times before the sound engineer was satisfied. Even now, when I think about it, I can still hear his rich tones emerging from the scanner. I could have listened to him all day.

Geoff Hamilton

I was sorry when in 1985 Clay decided to leave *Gardeners' World* to concentrate on his radio work. He had been a member of BBC's popular *Gardeners' Question Time* panel since 1976, becoming its chairman in 1984. Sadly, he did not quite equal the Wallington fuchsia's longevity, dying after a heart operation in 1996 aged 73. Tragically, in the same year, Geoff Hamilton, who had given the eulogy at Clay's funeral, died following a heart attack during a charity bike ride in the Brecon Beacons. He was just a few days short of his sixtieth birthday. In the eight years I was a presenter on *Gardeners' World*, most of my appearances were shared with Geoff. Some of these were at his Barnsdale gardens, old and new, where I was usually involved in practical demonstrations concerning hardy ornamentals and their cultivation. Much as I enjoyed these sessions, I enjoyed more those programmes filmed in locations

.....

Geoff Hamilton in the garden of Clive Jones near Carnforth in Lancashire in August 1986.

countrywide where I was really in my element talking about a wide variety of long-established gardens and their ornamental plants, which included discussions with the garden owners.

One such was a plantsman's garden north of Carnforth in Lancashire. As usual we visited the garden the previous day for a recce, Geoff and I strolling round with the director, in this instance John Kenyon, and the garden owner, Clive Jones, an enthusiast who was eager to show us the results of his endeavours. Both Geoff and I were looking for those plants or features close to our hearts and in my case, specialist interests. Geoff's wide-ranging expertise allowed him to speak on anything and everything in a garden but he was particularly keen on the practical aspects, especially those where he could demonstrate how (or how not) to do it. As usual on these occasions, on completing our tour Geoff and I discussed with John which particular plants or subjects we would like to film. These discussions would be finalized over or after our evening meal so that the following morning we would arrive at the location with a pretty good idea of our roles and the plants to be featured.

It so happened that just to the east of this garden was a massive hill, Hutton Roof Crags (899ft/274m), which supports one of England's largest areas of carboniferous limestone paving and an interesting native flora to go with it. Geoff had never before seen such a feature and when I suggested we visit it after filming he was more than up for it, as was John. Those who have picked their way across limestone paving will be familiar with the large, flat rock slabs (clints) of the surface and the deep fissures (grikes) which divide them. These grikes offer a perfect refuge for plants such as the black-berried baneberry (*Actaea spicata*), bloody cranesbill (*Geranium sanguineum*), lesser meadow-rue (*Thalictrum minus*) and limestone polypody (*Gymnocarpium robertianum*). To Geoff,

.....

this was a revelation and when I told him that such places were under threat from exploitation by those intent on making easy money from removing and selling the limestone for use in rock gardens and landscaping features, he was incensed. We explored the paving until poor light forced us to return to our hotel. The following morning at breakfast we again discussed the limestone paving problem and Geoff, who had been mulling it over all night, told me he was determined to do something about it. From this experience was born Geoff's subsequent and successful campaign to highlight the despoliation of these precious natural heritage features and to dissuade gardeners from fuelling the demand by recommending cheaper and more easily obtained artificial alternatives.

Over time, Geoff and I became good pals with a comfortable working relationship and when in 1989 I made the decision to leave *Gardeners' World*, due principally to impending changes I didn't like the sound of, he tried to persuade me to change my mind. We had been filming in a garden in Dorset and Geoff and I were the only members of the team staying the night at a nearby hotel. During a long discussion over our meal he reasoned that as we were such a good partnership it would be a shame to end it. I really had enjoyed working with Geoff, but having thought long and hard about it I knew in my heart that the rumoured changes to the programmes would not be to my liking, nor did I much care for the 'hatchet man' who had been drafted in by the BBC to make those changes. Geoff understood and respected my decision and wished me the best of luck.

My last appearance on *Gardeners' World* in July 1989 was with Beth Chatto, one of my favourite gardeners and plantswomen. Here she is seen at a later meeting in October 2004.

My final programme in July that year happened to be filmed at one of my favourite gardens, Beth Chatto's in Essex. I felt I could not have chosen a better garden in which to say my goodbyes and interviewing Beth was the icing on the cake. There is much that I

.....

haven't detailed here about the *Gardeners' World Specials* I enjoyed doing, which included visits to Scotland for the 600th Anniversary programme and for one glorious week in May 1986 to the gardens of Lake Maggiore in Italy, both directed by Dennis Gartside, all of which was great fun.

In Search of the Wild Asparagus

Running parallel with my appearances for BBC *Gardeners' World* through the 1980s were two series of my own, made by Granada Television for Channel 4. Following my return from an expedition to China in the early summer of 1981 I was approached by Arthur Taylor, who at that time was producing a long-running countryside programme called *Down to Earth*. He wanted to film a short piece with me about my experiences as a plant explorer from my early days in the Bolton area up to my recent travels abroad. It was a 'local boy made good' sort of story and turned out to be an experience I much enjoyed. Following this, Arthur came up with the idea of a full-blown series of return visits to some of my old haunts in search of native flora. The six programmes were to be aired on Channel 4 and directed by Neil Cleminson, who had previously worked with the BBC Bristol Natural History Unit and had been responsible for several *World About Us* series. Filming took place during the summer of 1982 at locations in Lancashire and Hampshire. Arthur asked for ideas on a suitable title for the series and I came up with *In Search of Wild Flowers,* obvious but unambiguous. However, he was looking for something more intriguing and having recently read a book called *Stalking the Wild Asparagus* by American author Euell Gibbons, published in 1962, he suggested it as a working title. I was a little unsure about this, especially as truly wild asparagus (*A. officinalis* subsp. *prostratus*), a low-growing, prickly shrub, is rare as a native in Britain. I had only ever seen it once, growing on fixed sand dunes in Jersey. In the event, we filmed feral plants of the garden asparagus (*A. officinalis*), which is commonly found naturalized as a garden or allotment escapee on sandy soils, especially near the sea, which is where we located ours at Ainsdale on the south Lancashire coast.

.....

The series was eventually transmitted under the title *In Search of the Wild Asparagus*. Locations ranged from a weedy allotment in Bolton to a rubbish dump in Salford, a disused railway line and station near Newbury, a canal in Oldham, the river Itchen below Winchester and Highgate Cemetery in London. I also wrote a book to go with the series which was based entirely on my own experiences of botanizing with no connection to Gibbons' delightful account of his lifelong experiences in searching for wild edible plants together with their preparation. In fact, it was many years later when staying with American friends in the Adirondack Mountains of upper New York State that I found a copy of his book while browsing at a secondhand book stall in a local village market. I was curious to read what he had to say about his wild asparagus and was not surprised to learn that it too was the garden asparagus gone wild. The book is a treasure.

Neil Cleminson, director (front row, far left) and the crew of Channel 4's *In Search of the Wild Asparagus* at Highgate Cemetery in 1982. I am sitting in the centre with the stick.

·····

Great plant collections of Britain and Ireland

Having got the bit between his teeth, Arthur, whom I came to admire for his thoughtfulness and integrity, was back with another idea. This time, recognizing my interests in plant exploration, he proposed a series to be titled *The Great Plant Collections*, featuring six of the many gardens in Britain and Ireland which are particularly notable for their outstanding plant collections. Subsequently, we were asked to film a further three. The collections we finally selected were those at Caerhays Castle (Cornwall), Bodnant Garden (North Wales), Birr Castle (Ireland), Wakehurst Place (Sussex), Inverewe (Scotland), Bressingham Gardens (Norfolk), Westonbirt Arboretum (Gloucestershire), Mount Stewart (Northern Ireland) and the The Savill and Valley Gardens (Berkshire). We filmed them in that order, beginning in spring and ending in autumn 1984.

As with the previous series, the ebullient and fun-loving Neil Cleminson was the director with a crew most of whom were already familiar to me. It proved to be one of the most enjoyable television experiences of my life, principally because of its focus on plants, people and places. Each garden had its own special features and history and all had connections with famous plant explorers. Most importantly, each had a strong cast of plants to film and discuss. It gave us the perfect opportunity to highlight the foresight and passion of those who introduced and established them as well as the skills and dedication of those who cared for them.

There were, for me certainly, many special moments, one of which was at Caerhays in March 1984 where not only did we meet the owner Julian Williams and his head gardener Philip Tregguna, both of whom knew the garden and its plants intimately, we also had as a bonus the privilege of interviewing Frank Knight, former director of the RHS Garden at Wisley, where he served from 1955 up to his retirement in 1969. He had started his career as a garden boy at another famous Cornish garden, Werrington Park near Launceston, and had known Caerhays well. Frank, now aged 85 and long retired, had agreed to be interviewed in a walk down 'memory lane' where we admired and discussed the Asiatic tree magnolias and their hybrids as well as the

.....

Former Wisley director Frank Knight, aged 85, revisiting Caerhays Castle in Cornwall in March 1984 for the Channel 4 series *The Great Plant Collections*. Head gardener Philip Tregunna is on his right.

Tree magnolias including *M. sargentiana* var. *robusta* (far right) at Caerhays Castle, Cornwall.

camellias and rhododendrons in full bloom. He then sat on a bench with Philip and me and reminisced about his time at Werrington Park and his experiences with E.H. Wilson and George Forrest collections then being grown for the first time in British gardens. He also talked about his time as a young probationer at the Royal Botanic Garden Edinburgh from 1919 to 1923 where he and his friend and fellow propagator Harry Bryce helped to unpack, sow and grow seeds collected by Forrest in China. 'When Forrest returned home from his expeditions he could hardly wait to visit the nursery to see how his seedlings were

.....

getting on,' Frank recalled. I could well believe that meeting the great man himself and hearing at first hand his comments and stories about his exploits is something the young staff would never forget. Much to our regret, Frank did not live to see the programme, dying in March the following year, only a month before it was transmitted.

Other than a most enjoyable one-hour, one-off programme *A Count of Flowers*, filmed in the famous garden La Mortola on the French Riviera on New Year's Day 1986, my association with Granada TV came to an end, though it was not the end of my contact with Arthur and Neil and we remain friends to this day. Nor was it the end of my association with Channel 4. The year following my departure from BBC's *Gardeners' World* in 1989, I received a call from Derek Clark, Director of Programmes at HTV West in Bristol. They had been commissioned by Channel 4 to make a new 12-part series of gardening programmes and were looking for someone to front it – would I be interested? I was indeed interested and agreed to him visiting me at my home, by now in Chandler's Ford, in August to see my garden and to have further discussions. He had no difficulty convincing me I should be involved, especially when he casually mentioned that the series had been commissioned by Sue Shephard, who had commissioned my two series with Granada and *A Count of Flowers*. He invited me to Bath to meet Adrian Brenard and Jo Readman, director and researcher for the new series, whose enthusiasm for the project further convinced me I had made the right decision.

Gifted amateur gardeners

In some respects the brief was not dissimilar to that for *Gardeners' World*, minus Barnsdale. We would be travelling countrywide throughout Britain and Northern Ireland meeting gifted amateurs in their gardens and allotments, discussing their specialities and celebrating their achievements while sharing tips and new ideas. Derek was well aware of my strengths as well as my weaknesses in terms of gardening expertise so I was encouraged and relieved when informed that our team would include two other presenters, one of whom, Rebecca Pow, was the environmental reporter with HTV West and presenter of the popular

.....

The presenters and crew of Channel 4's Garden Club at the Bath Botanical Gardens in the early 1990s.

Derrick Cook and his sister Rowlatt in their garden at Red Gables, near Evesham, Worcestershire in September 1993.

All Muck and Magic series for Channel 4. The third presenter, Matthew Biggs, had been recommended to Derek by the Royal Botanic Gardens, Kew where he had recently completed his training. He had no previous experience of presenting but he was a quick learner, full of energy and curiosity. He was, like me, a plantsman at heart but unlike me equally comfortable and competent with other garden matters including fruit and vegetables and whatever else came his way.

In the event, *Garden Club*, as the series was titled, ran for five years until the retirement of Sue Shephard and the arrival of a 'new broom' at Channel 4 brought it to a close. It was also the beginning of a new phenomenon in gardening television, the make-over. Looking back on those five years of filming, I believe I can speak for all of those who were

.....

involved as presenters and in production when I say they were the happiest of times. We had our challenges and triumphs too, for example our filming at Red Gables, the garden of Derrick Cook near Evesham in Worcestershire. He shared the house with his sister Rowlatt, herself a keen gardener and professional florist who treated us to delicious home-made ice cream and strawberry tarts. Our researcher had reported that Derrick was passionate about his plants and his garden was 'right up my street'. He was also deaf, having been so since contracting scarlet fever as a child. He could, however, lip read. 'He is looking forward to meeting you,' she added. I was already hooked and Adrian and I arranged to visit him the afternoon before filming so that we could get to know him without the presence and pressure of a film crew.

On our meeting it was immediately clear to us that here was a passionate gardener and plantsman. He couldn't wait to get started so off we went, the two of us with Adrian following in our wake. For starters, he showed me a handsome ginger lily (*Cautleya cathcartii*) he had collected which he believed to be from the same colony as the one described in my book *Plant Hunting in Nepal*. It turned out that he and Rowlatt were quite adventurous travellers. On we went with Derrick pointing out first one and then another special plant, here a viburnum, there a honeysuckle, over there an *Arisaema* species as yet unnamed. As he talked or gesticulated I watched his face and it was like that of a schoolboy in a toy shop, a beaming smile for the plants which flourished, an exasperated frown and hunching of his shoulders for the few which hadn't and all the while his love for them bubbling over like a mountain spring. Very soon it mattered not whether I understood his pronunciations because his face and gestures said it all. When Adrian and I returned to our hotel that evening we were in no doubt that this could and would be a success.

Next morning, with cameramen at the ready and sound engineer in position, Derrick and I set out once more on our adventure. It went like a dream, with Derrick leading the way as he had the previous day. He even threw in a few practical tips, as when he demonstrated how he kept his shrubs from becoming over-large or spindly simply by pinching out their growing tips. 'Pinching now saves pruning later' was his

.....

motto. At the end of the filming, when Adrian called it a wrap, I wasn't the only one with tears in my eyes. It was the same, apparently, when the programme was transmitted. According to Rowlatt, 'there wasn't a dry eye in Evesham'.

April Fool's Day

Another programme I shall always remember, though for a very different reason, was filmed at Cambridge in March 1984. Someone pointed out that the transmission date would be 1 April, in other words April Fools' Day. It seemed to us the perfect excuse to play a prank of some kind on camera. I can't be sure now who came up with the idea but it was agreed that I should record a piece in the University Botanic Garden, my alma mater, announcing an amazing new breakthrough in the breeding of the first black-flowered daffodil. To this end the camera crew were given the task of producing the necessary evidence which they achieved, following several experiments in isolating and carefully spraying the flowers with a black dye. To make the story more plausible, I selected a miniature daffodil, 'Tête-á-Tête' and a large-trumpeted garden hybrid. Satisfied with the results, I was then filmed on the rock garden announcing the breakthrough with a cock and bull story of how some years ago a keen bulb enthusiast had found this one-off wild *Narcissus* while hiking in the mountains of north-west Spain. He brought it home and in the utmost secrecy crossed it with several large-flowered garden daffodils, eventually producing a truly black daffodil. At this point I revealed the evidence from off camera. The programme was transmitted as usual in the evening, long after the April Fool midday deadline, and HTV subsequently received plenty of calls and letters, most of them from viewers who immediaely realized it was a hoax while just a few admitted to having been fooled. A few days later, while

An April Fools' Day programme for Channel 4's *Garden Club* in 1994 featured a black daffodil.

.....

227

attending a daffodil show and competition in the RHS Halls in London, I was stopped by a man accompanied by his wife and daughter. He was clearly excited and told me that he was a daffodil grower and had won several awards in the competition classes that very morning. He then got to the point, telling me in a conspiratorial manner how he had seen the programme and was very anxious to be put in touch with the man who had bred the black daffodil. I thought he was pulling my leg, but it became obvious that he believed my story. I gently explained that it had been screened on April Fools' Day and was a prank. His wife realized the truth and led her slightly confused-looking husband away. It was meant to be just a bit of fun, but I was left with a guilty feeling following this chance encounter. Naturally, the true nature of the story was revealed when we filmed the next programme.

Gardener's Question Time

During the five years of *Garden Club*, we presenters and our production team and film crew had become like a family and a happy one at that, so it was natural that its unexpected demise came something of a shock, though we were experienced enough to know that these things happen and that life goes on. And so it did for us all. As for my own media activities, I was invited in 1998 to become a panellist on that much-loved national treasure *Gardeners' Question Time* on which two

Panel members of BBC Radio 4's *Gardeners' Question Time* in 2000. From left, Pippa Greenwood, Eric Robson (chairman), Bunny Guinness, Roy Lancaster, Anne Swithinbank, Bob Flowerdew, Nigel Colborne, John Cushnie.

.....

of my favourite gardeners, Geoffrey Smith and Clay Jones, had served. Indeed, Geoffrey had just recently left the panel when I took part in my first recording at the Pewsey Vale Gardening Club, Wiltshire, in September that year. Produced for BBC Radio 4 by Taylor-Made Productions, its producer Trevor Taylor and his production assistant, now his wife, Jo King were thorough professionals, especially in their dealings with what was essentially a team of individuals each with his or

The GQT team visit my garden in Chandler's Ford in June 2002. I am at the rear with Pippa Greenwood, Jo King centre, plus Matthew Biggs (left) and Trevor Taylor.

her strengths and idiosyncrasies. At the end of the day, it was clear to me that what mattered to Trevor was a well-balanced programme containing reliable information and advice, personal experience and anecdotes, a sense of humour and a good rapport with the audience both at the recordings and with listeners at home.

Making the programmes for GQT involved a lot of travelling countrywide, visiting an unending variety of venues where we would enjoy light refreshments in the Green Room before facing our audiences to record two programmes per session. Written questions were placed in a box in the vestibule by members of the audience as they arrived and these were collected, reviewed and selected by the producer and the question master, usually the inimitable Eric Robson, to ensure a balanced selection for each show, bearing in mind the expertise and special interests of the panel members. There was no point in revealing yet another question on slugs or honey fungus if these or other regular topics had been dealt with in the previous programme. Panellists had no prior knowledge of the questions as that would affect the spontaneity of their answers and spoil the fun. And entertainment is an essential ingredient of GQT's success for both audiences and panel, as anyone who has attended or listened to a recording will know.

.....

I remained a member of the panel until January 2005 and of all the programmes I was involved with the quirkiest and most memorable was one we recorded in September 2000 at the headquarters of the British Naturist Foundation near Orpington in Kent. The venue was in a large gardened estate and my first inkling of the nature of its activities as I drove through the entrance was the sight of two people pruning roses, naked except for a belt with a holster for their secateurs. For this special programme Bob Flowerdew, Ann Swithinbank and I, with Eric as question master, had assembled with Trevor and Jo in a private room in the main building. It happened to be a warm summer's day and it was agreed that we men would wear casual, open-necked shirts in deference to our audience, who we observed taking their places in chairs set out on the lawn. As we nonchalantly approached our places on a raised dais above the audience I jauntily asked one rather large lady, totally naked like her companions, whether she had a question for us. Her instant retort left me speechless: 'Yes mate, I've got one for you – when are you going to get your kit off, then?' We settled in our seats and surveyed our audience, of all shapes and sizes. We found it momentarily disconcerting but once the questions started we got on with it and it was just like any other recording – well, almost.

Meetings with notable gardeners

Having retired from the regular panel appearances I continued to be involved in several one-off recordings at venues which included Buckingham Palace, the Chelsea Flower Show, the Courson Flower Show in France and a special Belgian edition featuring brussel sprouts, chicory and chocolate. The most challenging project that Trevor invited me to do was a series of ten interviews with well-known people about their gardening lives. Some of these were individuals for whom gardening was a favourite pastime, such as Lord Heseltine whose garden, especially his arboretum, in Oxfordshire continues to bring him great pleasure and satisfaction. He had purchased a large selection of rare and unusual trees and shrubs from the Hillier Nurseries in the 1980s and that was just the beginning. For several years I visited the arboretum in an advisory capacity and I was impressed with his knowledge and his enthusiasm

.....

LEFT Lord Heseltine, an avid dendrologist, here in his arboretum at Thenford in Oxfordshire.

ABOVE *Tilia endochrysea*, a rare Chinese species showing its striking red emerging leaves in the Thenford Arboretum.

for all woody plants. He was meticulous with his records and prepared his own labels with an engraving machine he kept in his study. Among the most notable of his trees were (still are) a rare evergreen Himalayan oak (*Quercus semecarpifolia*), a little-known spruce (*Picea farreri*) from Myanmar (Burma) and adjacent Yunnan and a newly introduced Chinese linden (*Tilia endochrysea*) with beautifully red-tinted young foliage.

Another tree-loving interviewee was the physicist and astronomer Professor Sir Bernard Lovell, whom I had first met many years previously at the Hillier Arboretum and in 1982 when lecturing at the home of the Jodrell Bank Radio Telescope. He took me on a detailed tour of the arboretum he had planted around his home in Cheshire, testing me at one point on the identity of a rare Chinese tree of special interest to him. Fortunately, it happened to be one of my favourites – *Poliothyrsis sinensis*, of which the leaves emerge pink and downy followed in July and August by panicles of creamy-yellow flowers which have a sweet smell of popcorn. When I asked him why he had become so interested in trees, he replied, with a twinkle in his eye, 'Well, I needed something to bring me back to earth.'

.....

LEFT A discussion with Professor Sir Bernard Lovell in his arboretum in Cheshire about the rare *Poliothyrsis sinensis*.

BELOW Alan Bloom relaxes in the Dell Garden at his home at Bressingham Hall in Norfolk in August 1986.

In late October 2004 I interviewed nurseryman, plantsman and lifelong 'son of the soil' Alan Bloom, whose nursery at Bressingham near Diss in Norfolk and Dell Gardens at Bressingham Hall are famous wherever hardy perennials are grown, particularly in Europe and North America. His garden and that of his son Adrian at Foggy Bottom had previously featured in my *Great Plant Collections* series for Channel 4 and I was pleased to have the chance to talk with him again. He had kindly invited me to stay for the night before the interview and I arrived by car in the early evening. The door was opened by a carer who showed me into a downstairs room, Alan's study, where he also slept on a bed in the corner. Now of a great age, he rose from a chair to welcome me, inviting me to sit within reach of a fireplace filled with sticks and faggots which he asked me to light, pointing to a box of matches on a table. I was told later that Alan had written his many books and articles in this very room. His carer asked me if I would join Alan for supper which she was about to prepare. Alan insisted that I should and so we settled down for a long-awaited chat. He had lots of questions of his own to ask, mainly about my recent travels and the plants I had seen and collected seed of. We were fully engrossed in conversation when his carer returned with our meals on trays for

.....

convenience. I had noted a record player, an old radiogram and a stack of vinyl records on a corner table and on my commenting on this he asked if I enjoyed classical music. 'Yes,' I replied, at which he rose to his feet and, moving to the table, sifted through the records, one of which he selected. 'Do you know Schubert's 'Moments Musical'? he asked. I didn't, or rather, I couldn't be sure so he placed it on the turntable, carefully lowering the stylus, before returning to continue his meal, our trays on our laps and a now crackling log fire ablaze in the hearth. 'We don't have to talk while we're listening,' he suggested and that was fine by me. As I had enjoyed the Schubert he continued with more of the same, which is how I came to hear that composer's Impromptu in G flat minor D899 No. 3 for the first time, played by Alfred Brendel. Ever since, it has remained my favourite among Schubert's work for the piano. I now have my own copy on a CD which I find myself reaching for whenever I need to ease a stressful journey by car.

The following morning there was a chill wind blowing and so with Trevor Taylor recording, we conducted our interview inside the house, Alan in a favourite chair from which he could see through a window the original island beds of hardy perennials which he famously pioneered all those years ago. The interview was broadcast in January the following year. Two months later, now in his ninety-ninth year, Alan passed away. His death was mourned by a great many people, including members of the Hardy Plant Society, which he had co-

Bressingham Hall near Diss, Norfolk, and the original island beds of perennials created by Alan Bloom.

.....

233

founded in 1957, becoming its first chairman and then its president for life. In 2008, I had the honour of being invited to become its new president, which I was delighted and proud to accept.

RHS Chelsea Flower Show

During the late 1990s and into the new millennium I continued as a specialist presenter with both BBC TV and for four years with Channel 4 at the RHS Shows, in particular their flagship Chelsea Flower Show. Having first visited this show in 1962 as a student, my association with it had continued over 50 years, first as an exhibitor and salesman with the Hillier Nurseries then as an RHS judge and finally as a presenter for TV and radio. My recollections and experiences, especially those concerning the plants, the exhibitors and the visitors would fill more than a chapter. One Chelsea Show I particularly recall was that in 1988, celebrating the show's 75th anniversary. For this special occasion I joined with Peter Seabrook and Alan Titchmarsh in what turned out to be a memorable week. I believe it was Peter's idea that we should wear black ties and tuxedos, the first and only occasion this happened. One of my contributions required me to stroll nonchalantly through a rock garden on the embankment site. On a signal, I set off, negotiating the rocks before stopping to say my piece to camera. So far so good. I then moved on, drawing viewers' attention to the candelabra primulas by a stream. All went swimmingly, if you will pardon the pun, until, in attempting to stride across the stream from one rock to another, my leather-soled shoes slipped and the next second I was standing ankle deep in the water. Undeterred, I continued talking about the primulas, emphasizing how these commonly grow in such situations in the wilds of China. I then looked towards the cameraman for his reaction only to find him and the film crew doubled up with laughter. My trial by water continued when asked to introduce the Plant Heritage exhibit staged by the Cambridge Group while lounging with a glass of champagne in a punt. Some years later I was interviewed on the Hillier Nursery exhibit at Chelsea by Alan for my first live presentation, and naturally we talked about plants.

I had so much fun when filming those shows. I was mostly involved in reviewing the nursery exhibits in the Great Pavilion, formerly the

.....

LEFT Black tie
presentation
on the rock garden at
the 75th anniversary of
the Chelsea Flower Show
in 1988.

BELOW Talking plants
with Alan Titchmarsh
on the Hillier exhibit
for my first Chelsea
Live broadcast.

Great Marquee, where I enjoyed interviewing the nurserymen and women, many of whom had become friends over the years. Some of them specialized in particular groups of plants such as Ian Butterfield from Buckinghamshire with his exquisite *Pleione* species and hybrids and Matthew Soper from Hampshire with his immaculate displays of carnivorous plants, including eye-popping plants of *Nepenthes* and *Sarracenia*. In the 1960s I had been lucky enough to see the last of the huge floral exhibits staged by seed companies such as Carters and Suttons and over the years I grew to love the bustle and buzz of last-minute preparations on the Sunday and the Monday with trolleys and barrows full of plants and flowers arriving from all parts of Britain and abroad, accompanied by an equally diverse assortment of people for whom Chelsea was the pinnacle of their endeavours, a realization of their dreams.

Inevitably, all good things come to an end and the end of my contribution to the Chelsea Flower Shows as a television presenter was at least my own decision. I can remember the moment quite clearly. I had arrived at the showground early on the Monday, having been informed that I would be recording, as usual, a review of the specialist nursery exhibits in the Great Pavilion. It was to be used in a special plantsman's edition of the Friday evening transmission. I immediately

.....

Terry and Cath Hunt of Edrom Nurseries, Berwickshire, with their spectacular *Paris japonica*, a Japanese woodland perennial, in May 2003.

began my tour of the exhibits, stopping to talk to the exhibitors involved, which was necessary and for me the best part of the exercise. Eventually I headed off to meet up with a director charged with filming my contribution who to my disappointment turned out to be the same person I had worked with the previous year. She was the only director in my television career with whom I had no rapport. There was nothing I could do to change things and so I described to her the exhibits I had seen and those which I would like to include in my review. Her reply had me speechless: 'First things first, you have exactly six minutes.' 'Six minutes for each exhibit?' I asked, more in hope than certainty. 'Six minutes for the whole piece,' she retorted. We were standing next to one of my favourite plantsman's exhibits staged by Terry and Cath Hunt of Edrom Nurseries from Berwickshire. It was expertly and lovingly arranged and full of woodland treasures including a magnificent clump of *Paris japonica* with beautiful snow-white flowers. 'I could spend six minutes on this exhibit alone and that wouldn't include the exhibitor's name and location,' I told her, to which she replied, matter of factly 'Well, it's up to you, you can spend six minutes on this or else two minutes each on three exhibits.' I was so angry with her uncompromising and to me uncaring and disrespectful attitude that I promised myself it would be for the last time. Meanwhile, there was a job to be done and I did my best to cover three nurseries. Even that was subsequently edited down. I felt I had let the exhibitors down too.

.....

Specialist Nurseries

However, it wasn't the end of my close relationship with the specialist nursery fraternity. For many years I have been contributing articles on an occasional basis to the horticultural magazines and journals on plant subjects close to my heart. *Gardeners' Chronicle, Country Life, Gardeners' World Magazine, Amateur Gardening, Gardens Illustrated, Hortus, The English Garden* and the West Coast American *Pacific Horticulture* are just a few of those where I have enjoyed good relationships. Nor must I forget the RHS *The Plantsman* and the long-running (since 1789) *Curtis's Botanical Magazine*, which are my favourite plantsman's journals. Contributions to the publications of specialist societies, especially *The Hardy Plant*, have been an added source of pleasure. By far my most continuous regular contributions, however, have been made to the RHS *Journal*, now *The Garden*, for which to date I have been contributing for over 40 years under four editors, Elspeth Napier, Suzanne Mitchell, Ian Hodgson and currently Chris Young. During this time I have covered a great number of plant-related topics but none more pleasurable than those featuring Britain's specialist nurseries.

A series which began in February 1995 with Hardy's Cottage Plants in Hampshire has since taken me to over one hundred nurseries countrywide featuring a huge range of plants from alpines, perennials, ferns, bamboos, hardy orchids, eucalypts, bulbous and tender plants to trees, shrubs and climbers. In the early years I provided my own

Enjoying a visit to David Austin's Roses and a magnificent wall display of *Rosa brunonii* 'La Mortola' with photographer Tim Sandall (left) and Deputy Editor of *The Garden* Phil Clayton (right), June 2016.

.....

photographs by way of illustration. Since 2000 these have been taken by Tim Sandall. In 2007 Philip Clayton, then Features Editor now Deputy Editor, started to accompany us. The three of us have enjoyed an excellent relationship, Phil like me, a passionate plantsman and Tim, one of horticulture's leading photographers, always up for a challenge and ready to go the extra mile to obtain the desired images. It helps that we also share a similar sense of humour, which is often needed in some of the circumstances we occasionally find ourselves in. Most important to me, however, are the opportunities this series has provided to keep in touch and develop a rapport with those many plant devotees, young and not so young, who have accepted the challenge of making a living from something close to their hearts if not always to their bank manager's. Their passion, skills and quiet determination in face of public caprice and of the elements and changing fashions deserves the support of all gardeners. I salute them.

CHAPTER NINE

A plantsman's travels

In September 1971 I realized a long-cherished dream when I found myself in the Himalaya as a member of the University of North Wales Bangor Expedition to East Nepal. It was an experience like no other before or since. Over a period of three months it took us on a circular trek from Dharan in East Nepal via the Milke Danda and the Jaljale Himal to the villages of Topke Gola and Thudam close to the Tibetan border, returning down the Arun valley. One of the many memories of this adventure I particularly treasure came at the end of our second day in the mountains, 4 October, at 11,000ft (3474m) on the Milke Danda ridge. We emerged from the dark canopy of the rhododendron and bamboo forest to find a high, wide open sky and the welcoming sight of our night's camp being prepared. On reaching the camp we deposited our rucksacks before continuing up a steep slope towards what promised to be a viewpoint above. There was still enough light left as we reached our objective to be greeted by a breathtaking panorama of distant mountains stretching across the northern horizon. But this wasn't all. The sun, now fast-sinking in the west, had cast a last golden glance over the snow-clad summit of Mount Everest (29,029ft/8848m) while to the east, the summit peaks of the mighty Kangchenjunga (28,169ft/8586m) were bathed in the moon's pale light.

Surprise encounter in Hong Kong
One of the many unknowns of travel, no matter how well planned, are the things you might see and just as importantly, the people you might meet, as instanced by an unexpected encounter I had in September 1981 in Hong Kong's Peninsula Hotel. I had arrived the day before, following a three-week botanical expedition to the mountains of western Sichuan close to the border with Tibet. I was now heading

.....

Kangchengjunga, at 8586m (28169ft) the world's third highest mountain, on the Nepal-Sikkim border seen from the Jaljale Himal, East Nepal, in October 1971.

down to breakfast when I bumped into my co-leader, Theresa Atkins, who told me that she had met a very special person in the lift who was now waiting to meet me in the lobby. She wouldn't say who it was but she was clearly excited. Entering the lobby at speed she led me to a group of people who were apparently checking out. I didn't recognize any of the group, not even the big man who had his back to me until, that is, he turned around and the next moment I found myself shaking the hand of Muhammad Ali. Naturally, I was in awe of this legend of the ring and I was amazed when he said, 'I've been hearing about where you've just been and I admire you. There is no way I could do what you do, no way at all.' I was momentarily confused – surely he wasn't referring to our search for flowers. Before I could reply, he and his party were being ushered out to a waiting car. Discussing this afterwards with those of my group who had met him earlier in the lift, we concluded he most probably thought that we were mountaineers!

As my early experiences proved, you don't have to travel far to seek adventure. I have always believed that plant exploration, like charity, begins at home, on your own familiar doorstep, gradually moving further afield as your knowledge expands and your curiosity leads you. In my case, the knowledge and experiences I gained from my travels in Britain have stood me in good stead when visiting other countries, especially in mainland Europe which shares so many of Britain's native plants. The first European country I visited beyond the British Isles was

.....

Saxifraga longifolia flowering high on a rock face in the Spanish Pyrenees in June 1970.

Switzerland in June 1963, when I saw in the wild many of the alpine plants I had first come to know on the rock garden in Bolton's Moss Bank Park and later at the University of Cambridge Botanic Garden. *Primula auricula*, *Soldanella alpina* and *Gentiana kochiana* were just three of those I found on the Rochers-de-Naye 6699ft (2042m) above Montreux on Lake Geneva. Some years later, in the Spanish Pyrenees, I was overjoyed to find and photograph my first wild edelweiss (*Leontopodium alpinum*) as well as the rock hugging *Ramonda myconi* and the magnificent *Saxifraga longifolia*, the last-named in full flower growing on a cliff-face high above the road. Elated, I continued on down the road to be rewarded with my first sight of an Egyptian vulture, white-backed with black-tipped wings outstretched.

Boskoop and beyond

But a country doesn't have to have mountains to keep me happy. Take Holland, for example – the enterprising Dutch are adept at growing plants commercially and not just bulbs. There are nurseries virtually everywhere, often concentrated in areas known for their special growing conditions such as Boskoop, from where huge numbers of hardy nursery plants are exported annually to Britain and northern Europe. I have visited Boskoop on many occasions, touring the nurseries, and along the way I have made some good friends. Two of the first and dearest were Marinus (Rinus) Zwijnenberg and the late Harry van de Laar.

.....

Rinus Zwijnenburg (left) and Harry van de Laar, my first Dutch horticultural friends in Boskoop in September 1972.

For many years Rinus ran his own nursery, separated from those of his neighbours' by narrow canals. He specialized in a wide range of woody plants, mostly shrubs and climbers, many of them of interest to the connoisseur. His catalogue was like a smaller version of Hillier's and because of the variety he was referred to by his colleagues as the 'Hillier of Boskoop'. On retirement Rinus and his wife Corry moved to the island of Texel where they still live. His house is surrounded by a plantsman's garden and a mini-propagation unit – old habits never die.

Harry van de Laar, when I first met him in the 1960s, was responsible for plant trials at the Boskoop Research Station and for many years until his death was editor of *Dendroflora*, an immaculately produced annual bulletin containing trial reports on woody and herbaceous plants plus more specialist accounts of genera grown in Dutch cultivation. He was also responsible over many years for the *Darthiuzer Vademecum*, an impressive catalogue of hardy woody plants grown and offered by the Darthuizer Nursery. His specialist interests included hostas, heathers and heaths (*Calluna* and *Erica*). He twice joined groups I was leading, first to Nepal in 1973 and then China in 1980, and later visited Japan, from where he introduced plants and seed, some of them new to Dutch cultivation.

On one occasion, I joined Harry, Rinus and a friend of theirs, Hans Janssen, on a plantsman's tour through Belgium, where we were kindly entertained by Robert and Jelena de Belder at their famous Arboretum Kalmthout. We then continued into Germany where we spent a day at the Dortmund Botanic Garden in the company of its retired director, Dr Gerd Krüssmann, and his successor, Dr Otto Bunemann. We then

.....

Jelena de Belder with *Hamamelis × intermedia* 'Jelena' at the Arboretum Kalmthout, Belgium, in January 1992.

Rinus Zwijnenburg and me with Dr Hans Simon (centre) in his nursery at Marktheidenfeld in Germany in August 1976.

headed south to Munich to see the Botanic Garden and from there followed a rough road into the mountains to visit the famous Schachen Alpine Garden. On entering the garden we found a man wearing a long brown jacket. I presumed he was Bavarian and was taken aback when he asked in perfect English, 'Are you Roy Lancaster?' We shook hands and he introduced himself as Sam Weller from Romsey in Hampshire, which is only a few minutes' drive from the Hillier Arboretum. Sam explained that he was spending his summer in the rock garden working as a volunteer having previously worked in a bank.

On our return journey to Holland we made a brief stop at the nursery of Dr Hans Simon at Marktheidenfeld. Having shown us around, Hans invited us to share a meal with his family at a large table. While eating

.....

we became aware of music, Beethoven's 'Moonlight Sonata', emanating from a speaker hidden in the chandelier above. Years later he joined me as a judge at the famous Journées des Plantes de Courson (Courson Flower Show) in France.

North America awaits

For many years I had been corresponding with horticulturists and dendrologists in North America as well as meeting some of them at the Hillier Arboretum, without ever having been to the New World myself. Imagine my surprise and excitement, therefore, when in 1975 I received an invitation from the North American Rock Garden Society to speak at a study weekend they planned on having in January the following year in Boston, Massachusetts. Here at last was my big chance so I replied immediately to say yes. I subsequently had requests for a further four talks on different subjects to various audiences from a wide range of organisations which would help by sharing the costs of getting me out there. This entailed me having to extend my stay to eleven days, which pleased me more.

Come the day, 17 January, I flew into a snow-covered Boston to be met by George Pride, associate horticulturist at the Arnold Arboretum of Harvard University, who drove me to his home on the Arboretum's Case Estates. Our journey, for George certainly, was made more hazardous by my frequent shouts and questions on the identities of trees seen by the roadside. I have always found it particularly exciting when visiting a country for the first time to spot and try to identify those plants seen on leaving the airport. It didn't help me or George that all the trees were leafless and dusted with snow. Following a meal and a long discussion I retired for the night, waking early the next morning, raring to explore the wild outdoors. George warned me that the temperature was down to 0°F (−18°C) and advised me to wear my warmest clothes, offering me a hat and a scarf to protect my head. Once outside I headed quickly downhill to a wooded swamp area where I attempted to identify the leafless trees including oaks and maples, collecting twig samples for further study. I don't know how long I was out there wandering from tree to tree but I gradually felt myself getting

.....

Stephen Spongberg with *Pinus engelmannii* on a visit to the Sir Harold Hillier Gardens in October 1995.

E.H. Wilson at the entrance to the administrative building housing the library and herbarium at the Arnold Arboretum.

seriously cold, at which point I headed back to George's home and my first American breakfast. I opened the back door and entered the kitchen, bursting to tell George what I had seen or rather, what I thought I had seen. But my lips were sealed, they would not move nor would any other part of my face, which was frozen. I had never experienced this before, nor have I since. It wasn't long, however, before the warmth of the kitchen, helped by a mug of hot coffee followed by ham and eggs and hash browns, began to work their magic and then I couldn't stop talking. The rest of the day we spent touring the Case Estates, followed in the evening by a meeting and meal with the NARGS committee and invited friends.

.....

Arnold Arboretum

The next day George took me to the Arnold Arboretum at Jamaica Plain, where he introduced me to the horticultural taxonomist Stephen Spongberg and other members of the staff. Steve first showed me round the herbarium followed by the library and archives, where among other historical items I was privileged to see and examine the field notes, journals and full plate black and white photographs prepared by my hero E.H. Wilson in China on his two expeditions for the Arboretum in 1906-09 and 1910. I spent the afternoon with Steve touring the Arboretum collections, which despite the wintry conditions I found fascinating. I even got to see the old Wilson house where the great plant explorer and his family lived during his years as a staff member and then Keeper of the Arboretum.

It had been arranged for me to spend my next three nights with Steve and his wife, Happy, at their home in Waltham and I can still see in my mind's eye the big shagbark hickory (*Carya ovata*) right outside their property. Two days later, they drove me to Cape Cod to see native woody plants at the White Cedar Swamp, the 'cedar' being *Chamaecyparis thyoides*, standing in water and viewed from a boardwalk. Here too grew the shrubby evergreen black-fruited inkberry (*Ilex glabra*) while the red-fruited holly we saw in a nearby reservation was the American holly (*Ilex opaca*) whose leaves lack the dark green gloss of an English holly. It is rarely seen in British cultivation but is represented by numerous cultivars in American cultivation. Later, a brief walk along a sandy shoreline elsewhere revealed several small deciduous shrubs among which Steve pointed out beach plum (*Prunus maritima*) and sweet fern (*Comptonia peregrina*).

The NARGS Weekend began on the 23rd but it was the following evening after the banquet that I gave my main talk, on the 1971 University of North Wales (Bangor) Expedition to East Nepal. My final day was spent first touring the Honeywell Arboretum before heading once more to the Arnold Arboretum where I was taken to the propagation unit to meet Chief Propagator Alfred (Al) Fordham, a legendary figure in his profession who was regarded by his peers as the 'Propagators' Propagator'. Al, who was a founder member of the

.....

International Plant Propagators' Society, gave me an unforgettable tour of his favourite 'habitat', introducing me to a huge range of woody plants then being raised from seed or cuttings or by grafting, including dwarf conifer cultivars, one of his specialities. He then invited me to have lunch with him in a local restaurant, where he introduced me to Boston clam chowder in a bowl of generous size. I have since tried many chowders but none to compare with this one.

During our meal, Al reminisced about his career, starting with his joining the propagation team at the Arnold Arboretum as a student trainee aged 18 in 1929, the year before Wilson's tragic death in a road accident. He had been encouraged to do so by his father who was then superintendent of the R.T. Farquhar Company, a leading nursery and importer of rare plants, especially those collected by Wilson. He had never received a formal degree in horticulture but had been a fast learner and quickly embraced the world of plants, especially woodies and their propagation. Starting under the then chief propagator William H. Judd, he rose through the ranks eventually to become chief propagator himself in 1958. One of the many highlights of his career had been the day in 1948 when the first big seed introduction (1kg/2¼lb) of the dawn redwood (*Metasequoia glyptostroboides*) arrived from China. It was a case of all hands on deck to get it sorted and repackaged into smaller lots for distributing to botanical institutions and individuals worldwide. The Arboretum administrator, Dr Drew Merrill, who had arranged funding to have the Chinese collect the seed the previous year, also carried seed samples with him when attending the International Botanical Congress at Utrecht in the Netherlands in June 1948, sharing it with delegates there. Seed was also sown at the Arboretum and the first sign of germination was a cause for celebration. Thinking about it, on my flight home that evening, I realised that Al Fordham was probably the last member of the Arboretum staff who could claim to have known E.H. Wilson and other luminaries such as Alfred Rehder. Perhaps he had also met the first director, Charles Sargent, who had died just two years before Al joined the Arboretum.

For all kinds of reasons, this visit to Boston, my first to the North American continent, will always remain a high point in my career, if

.....

not my life. It was the start of my own special relationship with North American gardens and gardeners and with its wild places too. In the years since, I have returned many times, on several occasions with my wife and twice with our children. In doing so, I have visited 27 states including Hawaii and four provinces of Canada. Most of these trips have involved lecture engagements and all of them, thanks to the garden world's legendary camaraderie and generosity, have provided me with opportunities galore to explore and enjoy the native flora and fauna in some of the world's most impressive and bountiful landscapes.

White Mountains, New Hampshire

As with China, to deal with all the adventures I have enjoyed in North America is clearly impossible here, so I hope the following brief selection of special days will capture something of the flavour. Staying in the eastern states, a memorable visit in October 1997 to the White Mountains in New Hampshire brought me what still remains my best experience of New England's legendary fall colour. As before, I was hosted in Boston by Steve and Happy Spongberg and it was Steve, together with Peter del Tredici, a colleague from the Arnold Arboretum, who had organized our trip to see the fall colour. We were also joined by another friend of mine, Hugh Angus, from the National Arboretum Westonbirt in Gloucestershire, who happened to be in Boston on his own tour. We visited two main locations the first of which, The Flume, was a stream rushing down a narrow, rocky defile accessed by a boardwalk. Impressive as it was and justifiably a popular tourist attraction, I was more taken by its woodland setting which was well supplied with hiking trails and viewpoints. Here grew a rich selection of native woody plants, especially trees. It was for me like walking through the pages of the Hillier Manual as American basswood (*Tilia americana*), American ash (*Fraxinus americana*), paperbark birch (*Betula papyrifera*) and grey birch (*B. populifolia*), red maple (*Acer rubrum*), American aspen (*Populus tremuloides*) and big-toothed aspen (*P. grandidentata*) contributed their yellow or red tints to the canopy above while the dark presence of the conifers red spruce (*Picea rubens*), balsam fir (*Abies balsamea*) and eastern hemlock (*Tsuga canadensis*) provided dramatic contrast. There was

.....

another, rather special conifer in the understorey, the Canadian yew (*Taxus canadensis*), both male and fruiting female plants which in some places formed large, low colonies. One gnarled veteran had developed a 2ft (60cm) high carpet, entirely enveloping a large boulder.

Elsewhere we found carpeting colonies of bunchberry (*Cornus canadensis*) together with partridge berry (*Mitchella repens*). The shrub which most caught my eye, though, was the hobble bush (*Viburnum lantanoides*) which formed dense, suckering thickets no higher than 3ft (90cm) with spreading branches sporting large, rounded, boldly veined leaves which were in the process of changing from green through orange to a deep claret. We stayed the night at a motel below Mount Washington, which at 6288ft (1916m) is the highest mountain in the north-eastern USA and the most prominent, though not the highest, mountain east of the Mississippi River. Our plan was to rise early the next morning and ascend the

Stephen Spongberg in woodland in the White Mountains of New Hampshire, with *Viburnum lantanoides*, a common understorey shrub, in the foreground.

mountain via the cog railway built in 1869, which was the first of its kind in the world. Our hopes, however, were dashed on awakening to

Sugar maples (*Acer saccharum*) ablaze in the White Mountains of New Hampshire in October 1997.

.....

find the mountain shrouded by a chill mist. It was also raining and both railway and road access were closed. 'No problem,' declared Steve brightly, 'it gives us more time to enjoy the woods,' and his optimism was well rewarded.

Legendary fall colour

We headed for the Swift River, passing at intervals villages with white clapboard houses whose idyllic appearance was enhanced by the fiery blaze of sugar maples (*Acer saccharum*). Having seen the brilliance of their display, those of the few trees I have subsequently seen in British cultivation have invariably proved disappointing. On reaching the river, we lost no time in exploring. The woods here boasted most of the trees we had seen the previous day plus some we had not, chief among which were red oak (*Quercus rubra*), yellow birch (*Betula alleghaniensis*) and two pines, the two-needled red pine *Pinus resinosa* and the five-needled Weymouth pine (*P. strobus*), some of the last named being sizeable trees.

Peter del Tredici and *Betula alleghaniensis*, the yellow birch, in the woods near the Swift River in New Hampshire.

Best of all, for me, was the American beech (*Fagus grandifolia*) which dominated in places, its golden-yellow foliage visible from afar. It is a pity that this tree does not flourish in British cultivation, where it is rare, as well as our native European beech (*Fagus sylvatica*) does in the USA. At one point we followed a trail through beech woodland emerging above the river where a host of red and sugar maples combined with yellow and paper-bark birch to create a breathtaking tapestry which had me spellbound. To think that only three days earlier, I had been admiring such displays from above in a plane preparing to land in Boston. That too, was an impressive sight but as nothing compared with being feet on the ground beneath the forest canopy.

The White Mountains are a part of the northern Appalachian chain; my next memory is of a visit to the southern Appalachians. I remember once

.....

asking an American friend, Paul Meyer, if there was anywhere in the USA to compare with the cool temperate forests of western China in their variety of trees and other woody plants. He thought for a moment and then said, 'The southern Appalachians, especially the Great Smoky Mountains.' Paul and I were in western Sichuan at the time, in September 1981, and it was another 15 years before I was presented with an opportunity of testing Paul's claim in September 1996. I had been invited to give the keynote address at a Global Garden Symposium in Raleigh, North Carolina, organized by J.C. Raulston, then director of the

Ken Moore, assistant director of the North Carolina Botanic Garden at Chapel Hill, with a handsome native wood fern, *Dryopteris kunthii* (now *Thelypteris kunthii*) in September 1996.

University of North Carolina Arboretum, who had visited me at my home the previous year. 'J.C.', as he was known to his friends and colleagues, met me at the airport and drove me to his home, a former film studio in Raleigh. It was several days before the symposium began, days filled with plants and plant people, sadly too many to do justice to them here. I made several new friends including Tony Avent, whose nursery Plant Delights and private garden too were full of plants completely new to me. Ken Moore, assistant director of the North Carolina Botanic Garden at nearby Chapel Hill was another. Ken had a particular interest in native plants, in which the Botanic Garden specialized, and a few days later he took me on an amazing tour of the coastal areas of North Carolina to introduce me to many of

My first meeting with *Sarracenia flava* in the Green Swamp Preserve near Wilmington in North Carolina, September 1996.

The Venus fly trap, *Dionaea muscipula*, was common in the Green Swamp Preserve.

their special native plants including three different pitcher plants, *Sarracenia flava*, *S. purpurea* and *S. rubra*, together with the Venus fly-trap (*Dionaea muscipula*) and several other carnivorous plants in the Green Swamp Preserve near Wilmington.

Southern Appalachian forests

I still had two special days before the symposium to look forward to. Cliff Parks, botanist, *Camellia* grower and international authority on the genus, had offered to be my guide on a trip to the southern Appalachian forests beyond Asheville in the north west of the state. It would be a long drive and a long day before we reached our overnight accommodation in the small town of Highlands, but a day to remember for the rest of my life. An early start from Cliff's home saw us heading west along Interstate 40 to reach Asheville around midday. Just beyond and above the town we joined the Blue Ridge Parkway and that's when the flora began to get really interesting. The Parkway is an impressive scenic highway that follows a winding course 469 miles (755km) along the southern Appalachian mountains through Virginia and North Carolina. Its construction began in the 1930s during the Great Depression, ordered by the then US President Franklin D. Roosevelt to help stimulate the economy and provide work for the unemployed. For budding dendrologists this has to be one of the best places to begin

.....

your journey of exploration, while for the more experienced tree enthusiast it is a place to visit before you die. In fact, you hardly need to get out of the car for the display in places comes right up to the roadside, though the regular pull-offs and car parks with their associated trails allow enthusiasts to make a closer contact with the native flora and that's just what Cliff and I did, many times.

The wealth of tree species we encountered over the next few hours left me breathless and my notebook was on fire as I tried to keep up with the plants Cliff was pointing out almost non-stop. First to catch my eye was an American rowan (*Sorbus americana*), its branches heavy with bunches of gleaming red berries, then followed sorrel trees (*Oxydendrum arboreum*), compact and conical to broadly columnar trees richly clothed with foliage already turning a dark red, competing in places with black tupelo (*Nyssa sylvatica*), its foliage aflame. Elsewhere, silver and red maples (*Acer saccharinum* and *A. rubrum*) with yellow and crimson foliage respectively fought for space with tulip trees (*Liriodendron tulipifera*) and *Sassafras albidum*, while flowering dogwood (*Cornus florida*) and no fewer than four deciduous oaks, *Quercus rubra*, *Q. coccinea*, *Q. velutina* and *Q. prinus*, the basket oak, all showing at least some fall colour, vied for our attention.

In places, where viewing stops allowed, we observed line upon line of forested mountains marching across the border into Tennessee towards a late afternoon sun. We were now at an altitude of around 2900ft (884m) and the air was cool while the mountains were ablaze. Providing a dark

Sorbus americana in fruit was plentiful along the Blue Ridge Parkway and in the Great Smoky Mountains National Park.

Oxydendrum arboreum, the sorrel tree, flowering along the Blue Ridge Parkway. It was common in woodland and even ditches.

.....

evergreen contrast to the main players in the fall colour fraternity were Weymouth pine (*Pinus strobus*) and red spruce (*Picea rubens*). In ravines and on forest margins both cherry birch (*Betula lenta*) and rum cherry (*Prunus serotina*) flourished; just as interesting to me was the shrubby understorey which included *Rhododendron maximum* thriving in shade, while the equally abundant *R. catawbiense* appeared to prefer exposure, or be more tolerant of it. I was pleased also to find *Kalmia latifolia*, the mountain laurel or calico bush, forming its own dense thickets, while in some sheltered places we found small trees of it up to 30ft (9m), their stems moss-covered. 'Centuries old,' remarked Cliff. Another evergreen ground cover in shade was *Leucothoe fontanesiana*, with waves of arching stems reaching 5ft (1.5m) or more, especially above rivers. There is of course a rich ground flora of herbaceous and bulbous perennials in these mountains, which at the time of our visit was mostly past flowering.

Eventually we arrived at our accommodation, a hostel at the University of North Carolina Biological Station in the town of Highlands, which lies on a pleasant green plateau just over 4000ft (1219m) in the mountains not that far from the state borders with South Carolina and Georgia. That night I lay on my bed wide awake, listening to the sounds of crickets and cicadas out there in the dark.

Veteran trees

If the previous day had been an introduction to paradise then the following day was paradise itself. Most of the woody plants we had seen already appeared again and if anything were bigger and older. After breakfast at 7am, Cliff drove me through mist to Horseshoe Cove in a steep, sheltered, wooded valley, eventually parking the car on a quiet dirt road at approximately 3200ft (975m). The ditches on either side were filled with strong saplings of tulip tree, which we waded through to climb up the slope in the mist. At one point Cliff told me to continue more slowly while keeping my eyes straight ahead, which I did. I could see only mist but sensed that I was in the presence of something special and big. Then we remained stationary for ten minutes or more and as the mist lifted and the sun's rays penetrated the forest canopy I saw a

.....

shape emerging which grew bigger and taller until, my God! I was standing before the largest tulip tree I had seen in my life. It was truly awesome, a giant of approximately 150ft (45m) with a single clean, jaw-dropping, furrowed stem 6ft (1.8m) in diameter. Cliff reckoned it was around 150 years old, while another fine specimen higher up the slope he thought might be around 200 years plus. He said that these would have been normal in the years before loggers plied their devastating trade – bigger ones too, he believed.

A brief wander through the forest around revealed other large trees including *Magnolia fraseri*, known as the fishtail magnolia for the conspicuous ear-like auricles of the leaf base. One specimen with two stems reached approximately 70ft (21m) and so it continued, with basswood (*Tilia americana*), eastern hemlock (*Tsuga canadensis*), *Quercus rubra*, *Fraxinus americana* and much more. Understorey shrubs included witch hazel (*Hamamelis virginiana*), *Calycanthus floridus*, *Hydrangea arborescens* and *Clethra acuminata*. Later that day we visited other locations, each of which produced newcomers in *Quercus alba*, *Fothergilla major* and *Xanthorhiza simplicissima*, the yellow-root, a curious shrubby and suckering member of the buttercup family Ranunculaceae, though anything more unlike a buttercup it would be hard to imagine.

Cliff had one more surprise for me when he drove us back to the Blue Ridge Parkway and the town of Cherokee. From here we took the Newfound Gap Road, which snakes its way up into the Great Smoky Mountains to cross the state line into Tennessee via the Newfound Gap, which at 5046ft (1538m) is the highest driveable pass in the National Park. After a brief viewing stop at the pass Cliff drove across the state line and down the other side for an all-too-brief look at old-growth forest which was dominated here by several *Robinia pseudoacacia* around 70ft (21m) tall, with fiery-foliaged Virginia creepers (*Parthenocissus quinquefolia*) scrambling into their crowns. Nearby, a grove of large veteran yellow buckeyes (*Aesculus flava*) stood toe-deep in a sea of yellow-flowered *Impatiens pallida* and to cap it all, a massive flaky-barked mountain silverbell (*Halesia monticola*) of around 70ft (21m) and a tall twin-stemmed yellow-wood (*Cladrastis kentukea*), one of my favourite hardy ornamental trees for its all-round qualities of bark,

.....

The cones on *Abies fraseri* trees on Mount Mitchell were conspicuous, sometimes on small stunted specimens; September 2006.

Mountains in the southern Appalachians, viewed early one morning from the Snowbird Mountain Lodge, September 2006.

flowers (in June) and yellow fall colour. I would have loved to have stayed, but with a major journey ahead we recrossed the pass into North Carolina and Cliff put his foot down. It proved a long and tiring drive, which we shared. On Cliff's watch we observed a lunar eclipse which began at 11.10pm and lasted three hours.

There is a sad postscript to this trip. I so much enjoyed the experience that ten years later, in September 2006, I returned with Sue. Once again, I had been invited to speak at a symposium – one which this time had been organized by friends and colleagues to remember and celebrate the life of J.C. Raulston, who had died tragically aged 56 in a road accident in December 1996. Following the symposium we spent the best part of a week travelling on the Blue Ridge Parkway exploring

.....

areas of the mountains I had not visited earlier including Mount Mitchell (6684ft/2037m), where we saw well-coned trees of the Fraser fir (*Abies fraseri*) and a flock of cedar waxwings. Another memorable experience was the Joyce Kilmer Memorial Forest, 3800 acres (1537 hectares) of virgin forest dedicated to the soldier and poet who wrote what many regard as America's most famous poem, 'Trees' – 'I think that I shall never see/A poem lovely as a tree.' It was later set to music which is how I first came to hear it on the radio. It represents but a fragment of the old pre-logging Appalachian forest and should be visited by all who share Kilmer's thoughts.

In 1984 I was attending a plant symposium at the New York Botanical Garden in the Bronx when I was asked by a fellow speaker if I had ever been to California. I told him I hadn't, to which he replied 'Why not?' He then introduced himself as Wayne Roderick from Walnut Creek, San Francisco, assuring me of a warm welcome and plants galore should I ever make it. Well, I did make it the following year, having persuaded an agent organizing a lecture tour for me to include San Francisco as a final destination. It was October and my tour began in New York at the Brooklyn Botanic Garden where I was hosted by Elizabeth (Betty) Schultz, followed by lectures in Chicago, Ann Arbor, Toronto, Edmonton, Vancouver and finally San Francisco. I was met at the airport by Marshall Olbrich, who with Lester Hawkins founded Western Hills Rare Plant Nursery at Occidental in 1960. He drove me straight to Walnut Creek, where we found Wayne Roderick busy packing a camper van with supplies. There was just time for a tour of Wayne's garden followed by a quick snack and then he was urging me to 'climb aboard for the trip of a lifetime'.

California's conifers

Wayne, who had worked for many years at the University of California Botanical Garden, Berkeley, was an authority on California's native plants. He told me he would try to show me as many of the state's conifers as time would allow and true to his word, he did. I wasn't the first plantsman from England he had played host to and I was fully aware of his legendary hospitality. We headed east across the San

.....

Joaquin Valley, stopping only to buy fresh peaches, plums and pistachio nuts. Towards the end of the day we drove into the foothills of the Sierra Nevada, where Wayne located a camping site in a forest of tall Ponderosa pines (*Pinus ponderosa*). In no time at all he had arranged a ring of rocks to contain a fire and busied himself with the cooking gear. At first, I stood admiring his industry before asking if I might help. 'Help,' he replied, 'this is your first visit to the Ponderosa, so get the hell out of here and look at the plants.' Over the next few days I got used to Wayne's wicked sense of humour and we got along just fine.

We spent a day and a night in the Yosemite National Park before leaving the next morning to visit an impressive grove of the giant redwood (*Sequoiadendron giganteum*) situated on a hot, dry, steep hillside. From here, we continued over a high pass where scattered veterans of the Western juniper (*Juniperus occidentalis* var. *australis*) were conspicuous by their low, heavy crowns and the rich red bark of their short, massive stems. Some appeared to be growing from crevices on bare rock. The road continued towards the Owen's Valley but before the steep descent, a brief stop allowed us a view of a high mountain range across the valley on the California-Nevada border which Wayne told me were the White Mountains, our ultimate destination. We could clearly see the snow-capped White Mountain Peak, the highest in the range at 14,246ft (4342m). Once into the valley we drove south, briefly stopping in the town of Bishop before continuing to Big Pine, where we turned east across Owen's River following a road which at one point passed another road signposted Death Valley. Our road swung to the north and climbed steeply into the mountains.

Owen's Valley bottom is a hot, dry, semi-desert which Wayne told me receives only 6in (15cm) of rain a year, but it supports scattered populations of a range of drought-tolerant plants including low hummocks of *Grayia spinosa*, a greyish-green, spiny shrub of the goosefoot family (Chenopodiaceae) and a grey golden-flowered species of *Chrysothamnus* or rabbit brush. The dry stony slopes we now ascended revealed an interesting shrubby flora including a *Cercocarpus* species, *Purshia tridentata*, blue-grey *Ephedra nevadensis* and grass-green *E. viridis*. Blue-grey needled pinyon pine (*Pinus monophylla*), which I had

.....

Juniperus occidentalis var. *australis* – impressive veteran trees with stout red-barked stems rising from crevices in bare rock; October 1985.

Wayne Roderick collecting cones from *Pinus monophylla* in Owen's Valley.

only previously seen as a lone specimen in the Cambridge University Botanic Garden, was the dominant conifer here, together with the desert or Utah juniper (*Juniperus osteosperma*) with crowded green foliage and masses of small, pale, bloomy fruits.

Eventually, Wayne pulled off the road to locate a suitable campsite for the night, which was now fast approaching. He then suggested we climb further up the slope in order to catch a good view of the sun setting behind the Sierra Nevada we had crossed only that morning. I was happy to do this and we hadn't gone far before I stumbled on my very first wild cactus, *Opuntia erinacea*, the grizzly bear cactus or grizzly bear prickly pear, a low clumping species with white spines in clusters of 4–7. It proved quite common on these dry slopes, along with *Chamaebatiaria millefolium*, the fern bush or desert sweet, a low-growing, ferny-leaved aromatic shrub of the family Rosaceae which I remember first seeing as a pot-grown plant at Hilliers. We finally stopped at around 9000ft (2743m) and sat down on a rock to watch the sun as it gradually sank below the dark, jagged wall of the Sierras which stretched across the western sky. Around 6.25pm, Wayne

.....

Grizzly bear cactus (*Opuntia erinacea*) formed low mounds on the dry stony slopes.

Looking along the ridge trail in the White Mountains, with remnants of winter snow still lingering among the bristlecone pines (*Pinus longaeva*).

returned to our camp to light a fire and prepare our meal, leaving me to spend a while longer enjoying the darkness and the silence. I slept outside that night, tucked snugly in a sleeping bag, staring at the vast blanket of stars above.

Bristlecone pines

The following morning, I was woken early by the calls of scrub jays as they explored our camp site in vain for scraps and before long we were breakfasted and back on the road, driving higher. I noticed at around 10,000ft (3048m) the pinyon pines were joined by limber pines (*Pinus flexilis*) of 18–20ft (5–6m) with stout stems and needles in loose bunches of five. Its cones were conical to cylindrical and up to 6in

.....

(15cm) long. Shortly after, we reached the end of the hard-surfaced road at Schulman's Grove and this is where Wayne pulled off his *pièce de résistance* when he pointed me in the direction of my first Western bristlecone pine (*Pinus longaeva*). We were now just above 10,000ft (3048m) and from where we stood a trail led along the spine of the ridge. The ground was of a thin calcareous nature supporting scattered populations and lone individuals of the bristlecone pine mixed with *Pinus flexilis*, which has longer needles in more open clusters than the much shorter, closely packed needles of *P. longaeva*, which first arrived at the Hillier Arboretum in the 1970s, sent to us I believe by the American botanist Dr D.K. Bailey, who had described and named this pine in 1970. Previous to Bailey's research, this western population had been regarded as belonging to *P. aristata*, which had long been grown at Hilliers and which I eventually had the pleasure of seeing in the wild with Jeffrey Wagner in 1997 in the Rocky Mountains of Colorado, not that far from Denver. *P. longaeva*, however, achieved worldwide fame due to the work of Dr Edmund Schulman in the 1950s in dating the age of selected living trees by counting their growth rings from core samples, a technique known as dendro-chronology. Indeed, it was on the slope which Wayne and I were now climbing that Schulman first dated a bristlecone pine in excess of 4000 years, which he named Pine Alpha. I stood in awe of this tree for some time before continuing our climb.

Pine Alpha was the first of the bristlecone pines (*Pinus longaeva*) to be dated in excess of 4000 years by Edmund Schulman.

We spent a couple of hours on the ridge and though lack of time prevented us from reaching the largest known living bristlecone, the Patriarch (a 12 mile/19km hike) we were able to enjoy and marvel at the huge variety of bristlecones, some individuals of which had magnificent sculptured and coloured stems shaped by the wind and the hostile conditions endured here over thousands of years. Snow lay in depressions and though it was a bright, dry day there was a persistent

.....

ABOVE A striking example of a veteran bristlecone pine, the twisted and reddened stem speaking of the harsh conditions this species has endured over the millennia.

BELOW Another veteran bristlecone pine, one of nature's great survivors.

cold wind. Associated flora included squaw currant (*Ribes cereum*), a low, dense, thorny shrub, and the equally small desert almond (*Prunus fasciculata*), with more thorns. *Opuntia erinacea* was common here and another very different cactus, *Echinocereus triglochidiatus* var. *mojavensis*. Neither of them were in flower. Animal life at this altitude we found thin on the ground though we did see, according to a trail leaflet, a golden-mantled ground squirrel, several noisy pinyon jays and once a red-breasted nuthatch. I have never forgotten this experience, nor a later one in 1992 when accompanied by my wife Sue and our children, Wayne once more treated us to one of his signature Californian adventures.

Space does not allow me to describe here the many other wild places I have visited in North America – not the Siskiyou Mountains, nor the Columbia River Gorges nor even the Cascade Mountains and the old-growth forests of the Pacific North West. However, they will never fade from my memory.

Chile in spring

But what of my other travels? My two visits to Chile in 1997 and 1999, both in November, Chile's springtime, must count as special in terms of the rich variety of plants seen. On the second occasion the group I was leading included several fellow members of the intriguingly named RHS Committee B, now more accurately if prosaically known as the Woody Plant Committee. We started our adventure in the mountains above the capital, Santiago, where we found the slopes sprinkled with small perennials and bulbous

.....

My group of plant enthusiasts beneath a huge though fire-damaged southern beech (*Nothofagus alpina*) east of Chillon in Chile November 1999.

plants including *Placea arzae, Calandrinia grandiflora* and the well named *Horridocactus curvispinus,* a low, swollen dome-shaped cactus with clusters of pale curved spines and a tuft of red, multi-petalled, stemless flowers erupting from its summit like a mini volcano. It was here, while lying prone for a better camera angle, that I almost placed my arm on a Chilean rose – no blushing rose this but a pinky-brown, shaggily hairy tarantula spider (*Grammostola rosea*), whose venom I was later to learn is harmless to humans. It was here too that I saw my first condors, a pair of them circling overhead.

One of the many plant highlights on our subsequent travels was being taken by our guide, a Chilean botanist, to see a yellow-flowered form of the Chilean fire tree (*Embothrium coccineum*), two in fact, both of which had been transplanted by a forester from the wild into his back garden. This had everyone excited and celebrating. The typical red to orange-red flowered form we saw on many occasions in the forests and on blasted heaths and hillsides, while in the lakeside town of Frutillar it had been planted as a street tree, the crowns regularly pruned and shaped. Southern beeches

Placea arzae, a beautiful member of the *Amaryllis* family in the hills above Santiago, Chile.

.....

(*Nothofagus* species) were plentiful, mostly as rainforest trees. *N. dombeyi* we saw on several occasions covering mountain slopes and valleys, the layered crowns of veteran trees reminding me of cedars from a distance, while above them on the ridges the unmistakable outlines of Chile pines or monkey puzzles (*Araucaria araucana*) bore a noble appearance so unlike the often unhappy-looking mop-headed individuals of suburban gardens and parks in Britain.

A big surprise and new to all of us was *Nothofagus nitida*, whose glistening dark green, toothy, evergreen leaves were flushing a striking coppery-red colour. This is a big tree of the rainforest, at least those forests protected from logging, where it commonly occurs with the even larger alerce (*Fitzroya cupressoides*), a giant veteran of which in the Alerce Costero National Park was claimed to be 3850 years old. This struck us as suspiciously precise, though it was undoubtedly an old, old tree with a humbling presence. It reminded me of similar awestruck moments I have spent beneath coastal redwoods (*Sequoia sempervirens*) and other West Coast American conifers as well as giant eucalypts in Tasmania and the kauri pines (*Agathis australis*) in North Island, New Zealand.

It was fun spotting plants familiar to us in European gardens, *Fuchsia magellanica*, *Buddleja globosa*, *Lobelia tupa* and *Berberis darwinii* being just four. More exciting were those quite new to us which we rarely if ever see in British cultivation such as the porcelain orchid (*Chloraea magellanica*), *Blechnum magellanicum*, a spectacular evergreen rainforest

The Chilean rose, a tarantula spider well camouflaged on the dry hillside.

.....

A rare yellow-flowered form of the Chilean fire tree, *Embothrium coccineum*, in a garden in Valdivia, Chile.

The fiery red flowers of *Embothrium coccineum* in the Alerce Andino National Park east of Puerto Montt, Chile.

This massive veteran alerce (*Fitzroya cupressoides*) in the Alerce Costero National Park, Valdivia, Chile is claimed to be 3850 years old.

fern, and the so-called red gorse (*Anarthrophyllum desideratum*) which I saw growing on exposed hills above Lago Gray. There were plenty of striking birds, too – a Magellanic woodpecker in a southern beech wood, flamingos on a blue lagoon and a pair of the rare torrent ducks battling a mountain stream in the Torres del Paine. I make no apologies for mentioning birds in what is essentially an account of plants seen on my travels. There have been days in the field when a special bird has more than made up for the lack of a special plant and if that bird has been blessed with a tuneful song then all the better. Without question, the nightingale has played an important and pleasurable role in my life.

Nightingales

One May evening in France several years ago, I was staying overnight as a guest of Patrice and Hélène Fustier at the Château de Courson, home until quite recently of the famous Les Journées des Plantes de Courson. I have been a member of the Woody Plant Jury of this popular plant show for more than 25 years and on this occasion I was sleeping in a bedroom on the second floor of the château with a window looking out

.....

onto a lake with woods beyond. It was late at night and a storm was approaching from somewhere to the north in the direction of Paris. The air was warm and oppressive and I suddenly became aware of a repetitive sound rising from the lake, becoming louder as I glimpsed through the curtains the first flashes of lightning, which were followed by thunder. The sound increased and I left my bed to peer through the open window, hoping to pinpoint its exact origin. It was, I soon realized, an almighty chorus of frogs. Soon the storm was overhead and the thunder momentarily silenced the frogs, only for them to resume their performance with renewed intensity. And then, it happened. Like a soprano taking to the stage, the rich, full sound of a nightingale sounded loud and clear, rising above the frogs' chorus, filling the night as the storm abated. I returned to my bed and lay there enjoying the performance, eventually drifting into sleep.

Several times on my travels a nightingale's song has enriched a moment of triumph or inspiration. Wandering through a woodland in the mountains of Japan in April 2013 with my friends Mikinori Ogisu and John Massey, we heard a nightingale sing as we were admiring and photographing the carpets of *Hepatica pubescens*, blue of flower, downy of leaf. They were accompanied by other woodlanders which kept us happily occupied for a good hour or so before retiring to the nearby Wildflower Café to enjoy a delicious meal of steamed noodles, watched

The astonishing peaks and ridges of the Torres del Paine, seen across the iceberg-strewn Lago Grey in Chile.

.....

Helleborus thibetanus, photographed in March 2010, possibly growing in the same location as when it was originally discovered by the French missionary and botanist Father Armand David in 1869.

Helleborus thibetanus with its exquisite pink-flushed blooms in the mountains of China's Sichuan province, March 2010.

over by our elderly beaming hosts. The following week, now in China's Sichuan province, we were sitting on a wooded mountainside quietly enjoying the sight of a huge drift of Chinese hellebores (*Helleborus thibetanus*) in full nodding flower when, on cue, a nightingale began singing from the depths of a nearby thicket.

First trip to Japan

I have made four visits to Japan, the first occasion in October 1990 as the guest of the Irish nurseryman and garden designer John Joe Costin. Over three weeks we toured several nurseries and explored many wild places, guided by our Japanese friend Mikinori Ogisu, whom I first met

.....

in 1974 when he was visiting the Hillier Arboretum with a party of Wisley students. We began our tour in Hokkaido, Japan's most northerly large island, working our way south through the main island of Honshu to Osaka in the south. Everywhere, especially in the mountains, the autumn colours were exceptional, especially those of the maples. In the three weeks of our visit we saw 20 different species. Of these, I found *Acer micranthum* and *A. pycnanthum* particularly interesting, the former

Mikinori Ogisu with his former tutor and mentor Mr Kasua Inami, aged 79, who was reputed to have seen every Japanese native plant: April 1996.

distinct in its relatively small, neatly five-lobed, slender pointed leaves which had turned a rich red. It is, in my opinion, one of the best ornamental maples for the smaller garden, while *A. pycnanthum* is one for the larger garden. This is a Japanese version of the better known North American red maple (*A. rubrum*), differing in its relatively smaller, blunter leaves which colour just as brightly as those of its American and Canadian cousin. In a swampy woodland in Gifu Prefecture we were shown a grove of these maples, all multi-stemmed up to 70ft (21m) or more. Their leaves were red above with a contrasting pale or whitish underside.

Another memorable occasion, accompanied once more by Mikinori Ogisu, was a visit in April 1996 to woodland on one of the coastal hills above the Sea of Japan near Niigata in north-west Honshu. There we found a colourful ground cover of *Erythronium japonicum*, *Hepatica japonica* f. *magna*, *Anemone flaccida* and the diminutive pale-flowered, purple-speckled *Fritillaria koidzumiana*. Associated shrubs included *Hamamelis japonica*, the dwarf yellow-flowered *Daphne jezoensis* and evergreen low-growing *Aucuba japonica* var. *borealis*, the females with showy red fruits. Members of the tree canopy included *Styrax japonicus*, *Magnolia kobus*, *Quercus acutissima* and the Japanese hill cherry (*Prunus jamasakura*).

On that same visit, in the city of Nagoya, Mikinori introduced me to his friend and former tutor, Mr Kazua Inami, whom he described as a

.....

great all-round field botanist and one of the first people to establish that *Magnolia stellata*, which we had seen earlier on the Atsumi Peninsula on Japan's east coast, was truly wild in Japan. Said Mikinori, 'He is a walking dictionary and is reputed to have seen every Japanese native plant – and there are 5500 recorded species.' Other than his time spent botanizing as a soldier in China's Heilongjiang Province before the Second World War, Mr Inami had concentrated all his efforts on locating Japan's native flora, from the island of Okinawa in the south to Hokkaido in the north. We met over tea in a hotel. Then aged 79, he was a small man of slight build, with an active face and mind. Following tea we accompanied him back to his home, where the entrance archway was wreathed with *Clematis armandii* in full bloom. He died in 2005 aged 89.

Katsuras and more

Ever since I first saw the katsura trees (*Cercidiphyllum japonicum*) attracting the plaudits at the annual autumn extravaganzas held by Westonbirt, the National Arboretum in Gloucestershire, I have been an avid fan of this tree. It is a common member of the temperate forest community in Japan as well as those in western China. It was however, another katsura I was looking forward to seeing in October 1998 when, accompanied by my wife Sue and guided again by Mikinori Ogisu, I set off to climb the steep trail that leads to the summit of Mount Shirouma (also known as Mount Hakuba), a height of 9619ft (2932m) in the Japanese Alps of central Honshu. We had left our car at the end of the surfaced road close to a large marshy area where the now fading foliage of *Lysichiton camtschatcensis* and the Asiatic form of the true skunk cabbage, *Symplocarpus foetidus* var. *latissimus*, reminded us of the spectacular feature these two perennials must provide when flowering in spring. The deciduous broad-leaved forest in the lower regions of the mountain put me in mind of that which I had encountered in the southern Appalachians of the USA – not that they were of the same species, but both forests share many of the same genera including *Acer*, *Betula*, *Juglans*, *Fagus*, *Aesculus*, *Magnolia* and *Lindera*.

The first trees to catch our attention as we ascended the mountain were the Japanese horse chestnut (*Aesculus turbinata*) and *Cercidiphyllum*

.....

269

japonicum, both large trees with evergreen *Daphniphyllum macropodum* var. *humile* and *Cephalotaxus harringtonia* var. *nana* as low understorey shrubs. Moving higher, we saw the big-leaved *Magnolia obovata* before passing beneath stands of Japanese beech (*Fagus crenata*). Elsewhere, a walnut (*Juglans ailantifolia*) occurred as scattered trees with heavy limbs and bold divided leaves turning yellow, while in moist areas a close relative, the Japanese wingnut (*Pterocarya rhoifolia*), flourished – big trees with impressive crowns and foliage. A snake-bark maple (*Acer rufinerve*) was plentiful, as was the larger-growing *A. pictum*. Another magnolia (*M. salicifolia*) appeared, shrubby in habit here but free-fruiting, while the rich shrub layer included *Hydrangea paniculata* and *H. macrophylla* var. *megacarpa*, together with the flaky-barked *Clethra barbinervis*, *Lindera obtusiloba*, one of my favourites for its reliable yellow autumn colour, and another garden favourite of mine, *Viburnum furcatum*, with deep wine-red, boldly veined leaves and clusters of glistening red berries.

Many trees supported climbing plants and both self-clinging *Hydrangea anomala* subsp. *petiolaris* and the related *Schizophragma hydrangeoides* were plentiful. The crowns of several larger trees were filled with *Vitis coignetiae*, a powerful vine whose long stems sporting bold red and purple-tinted leaves provided spectacular curtains as they tumbled from on high. Elsewhere, it was the unmistakable cream and pink-splashed leaves of *Actinidia kolomikta* which caught the eye. A small ash tree, *Fraxinus sieboldiana*, one of the best of the so-called 'flowering' ashes for smaller gardens, put in an appearance; no fewer than three different birches were present in *Betula maximowicziana*, the well-named monarch birch with its large leaves, *B. grossa*, a Japanese version of the east North American cherry birch (*B. lenta*) with similarly aromatic bark, and the rare *B. corylifolia* which here occurred as a large shrub or small multi-stemmed tree up to 15ft (4.5m) with its characteristic hairy, hazel-like leaves.

Given the number and variety of woody plants (and I have hardly mentioned the perennial flora, which was equally rich), it was well into the afternoon when at around 5000ft (1524m) we decided to take a refreshment break at a small tea house. By this time a pale mist was

.....

gathering and the increasingly cold and damp conditions threatened rain. We considered the wisdom of continuing higher, but Mikinori had yet to reveal to us his special surprise which he promised was but half an hour's climb away. On we went and I for one was thankful that we did, for growing on both sides of the track we came upon one of Japan's rarest maples in *Acer nipponicum* with its bold 3–5 lobed and attractively veined leaves. At that time I knew of only one relatively large tree of 42ft (13m) in British cultivation, growing in the garden at Dawyck in Scotland, now run by the Royal Botanic Garden Edinburgh.

Exciting though it was, the maple was not the main reason Mikinori had brought us to Mount Shirouma. Growing with the maple as well as occupying the tops of large moss-covered boulders further up the track was a second katsura, *Cercidiphyllum magnificum*, which is restricted in the wild to sub-alpine regions of Honshu. It was plentiful here and on the valley slopes below. All were multi-stemmed trees of no great height but widespreading, especially where the snow had lain heavily on them over winter. It differs from *C. japonicum* in several characteristics, including the normally larger, more rounded leaves and in its bark, which is relatively smooth in young trees. There are other less obvious differences, among which the seed wings are important – two in *C. magnificum* and only one in *C. japonicum*. Looking into the valley we could see some impressive individuals and groves of this tree, their leaves turning a striking pale or lemon yellow, contrasting in places with the more fiery colours of *Acer japonicum*.

It was only then that we turned for home, retracing our steps to the car with the rain at our heels. That evening, after supper and a relaxing soak in a hot open air pool, Mikinori handed me five sheets of lined paper on which he had listed all the plants he reckoned we had seen on the mountain. I sometimes revisit this list when I am feeling depressed by winter weather or by the state of world events. Every name conjures up in my mind a special plant in a special place on a very special day.

It had been my intention to write about some of the other wild places of the world I have visited such as Bhutan, South Africa (especially the Drakensberg Mountains), Tasmania and New Zealand but sadly space does not allow in this volume. As for China, my last visit to the

.....

A happy group of friends enjoying our moment with *Daphne ogisui* in Sichuan's Valley of the Daphnes in April 2012.

'Mother of Gardens' in 2013 was my eleventh, six of which were described in my book *A Plantsman's Paradise – Travels in China*. It would take another book to do justice to those other visits, but I cannot resist relating the story of just one rather special plant seen during my visit to Sichuan province in April 2012. I had been invited by Mikinori Ogisu to join him and a few close friends on a week's tour to see some of the plants he had enjoyed seeing over the last 30 years. Two of my fellow travellers, John Massey and Carla Teune, were old friends and John and I enjoyed the same sense of humour and a predilection to burst into song whenever an excuse presented itself.

We did a lot of singing on the day we spent in a remote valley in Sichuan's Ebian County. Mikinori had brought us here to see a new species of *Daphne*, since named *D. ogisui*, which he had discovered quite by accident in 2005. On first entering the valley we could not believe that such an arid-looking location could support anything of interest, but how wrong we were. On closer inspection we found many woody and perennial plants, though none of obvious ornamental merit. Mikinori then pointed to areas of the hillside on the valley's flanks where specks of yellow were apparent. We set off down the valley,

.....

272

crossing a river to reach the nearest slopes and a chance to inspect what proved to be the new *Daphne*. It was a curious species indeed, possibly unique in its dark, erect, typically single leafless stem to 3¼ft (1m) high, crowned with a bold ruff of long, narrow (oblanceolate) evergreen leaves from the centre of which sprang a dense domed head of yellow flowers. We had seen nothing like it, and neither had Mikinori when he first spotted it from a moving car at dusk. Yes, the hills then echoed with the sound of music when we recovered from our initial surprise. It was an experience which this traveller for sure will never forget.

.....

CHAPTER TEN
The world in my garden

In October 1982, Sue and I with our young son Edward and daughter Holly (born in July) left our Winchester home and moved to a property in Chandler's Ford a few miles to the south. Our new home, a late Victorian red-brick house built in 1896 with four bedrooms, offered more space for my collection of books which, together with our business and correspondence files and my slide collection, was steadily increasing. As for the garden, the total size of the plot measured a third of an acre (1335sq m), with a north-facing front garden and a larger, longer, south-facing garden at the rear. A great bonus, I discovered, was the two soil types, an acidic sand (pH5.8) over gravel at the front and a heavier clay soil at the rear. Our first view of the house and garden had left us unsure. Both had been neglected and there was an air of sadness about them as a consequence. We stood at the entrance gate and discussed it for a time before agreeing to grasp the nettle and take up the challenge of making the house a happy family home and the garden a place of pleasure and enjoyment which, with the initial help and advice of our friend David Hutchinson, is what we did.

TOP The front of our present house with its bare walls and grass patch in October 1982.

ABOVE The boringly blank south wall of our house as first seen in October 1982.

Fences and neighbours
Both flanks of our property were occupied by our neighbours' hedges, a mixture of

.....

cherry laurel (*Prunus laurocerasus*) and Japanese privet (*Ligustrum ovalifolium*). Only the Portugal laurel hedge (*Prunus lusitanicus*) along our front, roadside boundary belonged to us. Our gate was flanked by two large, loose-crowned Lawson's cypress, one of which was on our neighbour's property. As for the planting, the only plants of any merit were a large laurustinus (*Viburnum tinus*) and three shrubby specimens of one of my favourite magnolias, *M. liliiflora* 'Nigra', two in the front garden which I subsequently relocated and one in the rear. All three continue to give us great pleasure in spring and again in late summer with their erect, tulip-shaped, vinous purple blooms opening to show their white interior. The rear garden had little else other than two or three small, crooked and struggling apple trees, which I disposed of, and a dilapidated and hazardous wooden-framed greenhouse, which I dismantled.

Other than that, both gardens, most especially that at the rear, supported a wide variety of perennial weeds including the usual suspects: creeping buttercup, couch grass, hedge bindweed, ground elder, Spanish bluebells and their hybrids and, in one corner, the dreaded Japanese knotweed. Almost a third of the front garden was occupied by an overgrown cherry laurel and a large, widespreading *Rhododendron × superponticum* which was the first plant I removed, followed by a length of privet hedge in an advanced state of decline due to honey fungus. I remember well the day I began ripping out the privet and the horrified expression on my neighbour's face when he came out of his house to ask what was going on. I discovered he was a fellow northerner and like me he didn't beat around the bush. An elderly, retired man, he was worried about the threat to his privacy from the gaps I was making in the hedges. I explained that I quite understood and respected his concerns but the diseased and dying privet would be to no one's advantage and my intention was to replace it with a new waist-high fence allowing him and his wife to enjoy the exciting new border of shrubs and perennials I was planning to make. Considering this for a while, he reported back to his wife, who suggested they should wait and see.

Well, I planted the border, describing to my neighbours each plant and the contribution it would make, and I'm pleased to say it did the

.....

The tree den I constructed for our children, Edward and Holly, in a huge cherry laurel. Let the adventures begin!

In October 1982 I transported two truckloads of plants from our Winchester garden to the new one.

trick. For ever after, up to their death, they took pleasure in watching our garden grow and flourish. They even allowed me to construct a tree den for our children in a huge cherry laurel on our joint boundary and encouraged them to access their large rear garden, mostly lawn, through a gap in their hedge to play ball games. For several years, we even enjoyed our family bonfires and fireworks there on 5 November while our neighbours watched from their window.

Plant diversity

In addition to the contents of our previous home, we had brought with us two small truckloads of plants from our previous garden, most of which I had containerized the winter before for just such an occasion. Naturally, I was anxious to get their roots into the ground as soon as possible and if I made a mistake it was this. Ideally, I should have spent a year clearing and preparing the site before planting as I began with no detailed design plan or planting in mind other than to make use of the two distinct soil types and the two aspects, sun and shade. I did, however, know what I wanted from the garden, most important of

.....

which was a place to grow as wide a variety of plants as practical including trees and shrubs, climbers, perennials, annuals and bulbs, plus a few alpines or rock plants in troughs.

Having recently left the Hillier Arboretum with its many acres and huge plant collections I felt I needed my own reference collection under my nose, so to speak, readily accessible for me to study and photograph when preparing articles, books and lectures as well as in my advisory role. I wasn't to know that some years down the line, long after Sir Harold Hillier's death in 1985 aged 80, just two years after he was knighted, I would be invited to join the Gardens' Advisory Committee and eventually to become in 2007 a patron of what is now known as the Sir Harold Hillier Gardens, a privilege and a pleasure I enjoy and respect to this day.

Climbers and shrubs

When I first set eyes on the house I was struck by its nakedness. Not a single leaf, let alone flower, adorned its exterior and I decided to change that by planting a selection of climbers and shrubs. I had four walls and four aspects to address and started with the sunless north-facing wall which had at its base a narrow border, a little under 3ft (90cm) deep. One of the first climbers I planted here was *Schizophragma integrifolium*, a powerful self-clinging relative of hydrangea with bold deciduous leaves and broad flattened heads (corymbs) of tiny, cream, fertile flowers sporting conspicuous creamy-white leaf-like marginal bracts. This I had grown from seed collected in October 1980 from a plant covering a tall tree stump on the forested slopes of Emei Shan, a mountain in west Sichuan, China. It flowers in July and so large are the heads that I have given it the cultivar name 'Emei Shan'. Also flourishing in this border is the large-leaved, boldly toothed male form of *Aucuba omeiensis*, again from Emei Shan

Schizophragma integrifolium 'Emei Shan' a self-clinging deciduous climber on the north wall flowering in July.

.....

TOP *Cobaea pringlei*, a vigorous Mexican scrambler whose flowers are produced from midsummer to the first frosts of autumn.

ABOVE *Lonicera calcarata*, a powerful high-climbing hardy honeysuckle from China, thrives on the south wall of the house. Its flowers are fragrant.

which I introduced at the same time. It has reached 15ft (4.5m) here but is capable of small tree size in its native Sichuan.

Around the corner on the west-facing wall above a large, surprisingly hardy, salmon-red flowered *Grevillea victoriae* from south-east Australia grows *Holboellia brachyandra*, introduced from the forests of North Vietnam in 2003 by Dan Hinkley and Bleddyn Wynn-Jones, two of the most well-travelled and successful plant explorers of the modern era. A tall, vigorous evergreen twiner, it produces drooping racemes of fragrant white male and female flowers in April and May, the females larger than the males. I have yet to see the edible sausage-shaped, purple fruits. White flowers are also a feature of the Mexican herbaceous perennial *Cobaea pringlei*, whose luxurious growth for several years clothed this wall for up to 20ft (6m) before a particularly severe winter put paid to the tubers. Its twining leaf tendrils cling to any support while the beautiful, long-stalked, white, bell-shaped blooms are produced continuously from midsummer until the first frosts of late autumn or early winter cripple all growth above ground. Its tubers need protecting from the winter cold. It is named for Cyrus Guernsey Pringle (1838–1911) an American botanist, plant explorer and plant breeder who spent 35 years travelling in Canada, the USA and Mexico discovering many new species. It is said to be pollinated in the wild by bats, but in my garden, as far as I am aware, the plant only seemed to attract flies.

Against the wall by our front door grows a 10ft (3m) bush of *Camellia* 'Spring Festival' which I love for its upright, compact habit, its relatively small, coppery young foliage in spring and its miniature, neatly double pink flowers which are freely produced

.....

in mid to late spring. It is one of the best for the smaller garden on an acidic soil or else in a large container of lime-free compost.

The relatively shaded east-facing wall is mainly clothed by the large yellow-splashed leaves of a Persian ivy (*Hedera colchica* 'Sulphur Heart') which requires an annual pruning to prevent it from invading our attic space. I tolerate this as much for its attraction to nesting and roosting birds as for its boldly variegated tapestry. Nearby on another wall grows *H. pastuchovii* 'Ann Ala', whose ovate to elongated leaves have created a striking two-toned green tapestry. When it comes to the warmer south-facing wall the choice of climber is enormous and I have experimented with a host of candidates, among which the most successful are two high-twining honeysuckles, one of which, *Lonicera calcarata* (the name referring to the spurred flowers), can attain dizzying heights in tall forest trees in its native Sichuan. It is much too powerful for its present location but I content myself with an annual hard pruning rather than removing it altogether. From late May through to July it produces paired, two-lipped flowers in the leaf axils all along the arching branches. These change colour as they mature from creamy-white to peach-pink and finally a burnt orange, all three colours showing at the same time with a sweet fragrance as a bonus. It was introduced to British cultivation as seed by Mikinori Ogisu in 1997. For a time this plant resisted all attempts at propagation before its successful layering by Alan Postill, Hillier's master propagator, who has since rooted it from cuttings.

Dramatically different is the Mexican *Lonicera pilosa*, a slender-stemmed, fragile-looking twiner with small sea-green leaves and pendant terminal clusters of tubular flowers of a brilliant orange-red with a yellow-tinted mouth in May and June. It came as no surprise to learn that these flowers are pollinated by humming birds in the wild, as are those of another Mexican native, *Abelia floribunda*, a slender-stemmed shrub which is best trained on

A Mexican honeysuckle, *Lonicera pilosa*, enjoys a sunny position on the south wall of the house, flowering in May and June.

.....

FAR LEFT *Rosa chinensis* var. *spontanea*, the wild China rose, first flowered on the south wall of the house from May through June in 1996.

LEFT *Clematis courtoisii*, a beautiful and rare Chinese species which requires winter protection here. It flowers in May.

supporting wires against a warm, sunny wall where it is capable, given time and space, of reaching 10ft (3m) in both height and spread. My plant has trespassed into a neighbouring evergreen *Ceanothus* 'Skylark', whose deep blue flower clusters from late spring through summer provide a pleasing contrast with the pendant, tubular, cerise-red flowers of the *Abelia*. How I wish their charms would attract humming birds all the way to my garden. However, in cultivation here both are visited by bees which craftily source the nectar by simply cutting a hole in the base of the flower tube.

Two of the most vigorous woody plants on this wall are roses. In 1990 Mikinori Ogisu introduced to British cultivation, probably for the first time, the wild China rose (*Rosa chinensis* var. *spontanea*), which he had rediscovered growing in the Yangtze Valley area of Sichuan's Leibo County in May 1983. From seed collected on a second visit four years later he brought seedlings to England, distributing them among friends including Graham Thomas, who had long urged him and others to try to relocate this 'lost' wild rose, one of the main parents of the well-known China roses of gardens. I received a few seedlings which I in turn distributed, keeping one for my own garden which flourished

.....

against the south-facing wall beneath our son's bedroom, growing rapidly to reach the roof overhang at around 20ft (6m). Five years later, in 1996, it flowered for the first time over a period of five weeks from May into June, attracting regular visits from plantsmen friends with cameras. Our son Edward, then swotting for his exams, threatened to charge them 10p a time for the use of his bedroom window, which provided the best close-ups of the single, pale pink maturing to deep red blooms, curiously with no discernible fragrance, at least not to my nose. Eventually, I lost this plant in an attempt to transplant it, though I have recently planted another elsewhere.

The other rose on this wall which flourishes still is 'Constance Spry', the first of the English rose series produced by talented rosarian and rose breeder David Austin. Introduced in 1961, it is still to my eyes and nose one of his best, though it has its drawbacks. Its large, globular, fully double blooms are a soft blush pink and according to Graham Thomas, whose acute olfactory powers were legendary, are scented of myrrh. It blooms freely over a relatively limited period in early summer and here combines most effectively with the flowers of *Lonicera calcarata* and the light blue of free-flowering *Clematis* 'Perle d'Azur'. I am a fan of clematis of all kinds and have grown several over the years, including the pure white, bell-flowered, winter-flowering evergreen *C. urophylla* and the rarely seen *C. courtoisii*, a relative of the wild *C. florida* var. *normalis*. Both are Chinese and less than hardy in my garden, so they are grown in containers under glass.

Ericaceous favourites

Having previously gardened for several years on a chalk soil I had been longing to grow some of my favourite ericaceous and lime-hating shrubs such as rhododendrons, along with camellias and trees such as *Embothrium coccineum* and many of the magnolias. Now was the chance and I lost no time in planting a selection. First to go in was *Rhododendron yakushimanum* 'Koichiro Wada', named for the Japanese nurseryman who first introduced this species to Exbury Gardens on the Solent in 1934. It hails from the windswept, rain-drenched mountain tops of Yakushima, an island off the southern tip of Japan,

.....

Our son Edward, aged three in 1983, planting *Rhododendron yakushimanum* 'Koichiro Wada' assisted by his godfather, David Hutchinson.

and is ideally suited to the British climate. It has subsequently been used as a parent of countless hybrids, some of quality, some not, and I chose to plant the wild selection that now bears Mr Wada's name for its low, compact, mounded habit, its 'candles' of white-felted emerging leaves in spring together with its rose-pink opening to apple-blossom pink and finally white bell-shaped flowers in dense rounded trusses. It was planted in a new island bed by our son, aged three, with help from our friend and his godfather David Hutchinson. It provided an annual highlight for almost 25 years before finally succumbing to an attack by honey fungus. We miss it still.

Other rhododendrons were planted, including Japanese evergreen azaleas, though the azalea we most treasured was a deciduous Knaphill hybrid named 'Homebush', whose perfectly globular heads of semi-double, rose-madder blooms with paler shading in May was one of the high points of our garden in spring.

We also planted a selection of camellias, most of them in the borders along our boundary in the front garden. They are still here and have grown to around 10ft (3m), providing us with a touch of the exotic just when we most welcome it in late winter and spring. The free-flowering, rose-red, semi-double 'Freedom Bell' is usually the first off the starting blocks in February or earlier, followed by 'Inspiration', with large semi-double blooms of a deep pink, 'Brigadoon', 20ft (6m) tall with large semi-double, rose-pink blooms, and 'Anticipation', with large blooms of

. . . . .

Deutzia pulchra, a prince among deutzias. This plant was introduced as seed from Taiwan by Tony Kirkham and Mark Flanagan in 1992.

peony form and a deep rose. The last two are selections of the hybrid *C. japonica* × *C. saluenensis* known as *C.* × *williamsii*. All four have the RHS Award of Garden Merit and their blooms, when they mature and before they fade, are shed to form pools of colour on the drive.

Notable shrubs

Over 30 years, plants including some trees and shrubs have come and gone but of those shrubs that continue to perform well I should mention the following, beginning with *Deutzia pulchra*, one of several species I grow and in my eyes a prince of the genus. My specimen, which has now reached 10ft (3m) though controlled by an annual pruning of the old flowering shoots when they are spent, was grown from seed collected in the mountains of Taiwan in 1992 by Tony Kirkham and his bosom pal, the late Mark Flanagan, whose unexpected death aged 56 in December 2015 stunned family and friends alike. Among the many fine plants this talented and successful duo introduced or reintroduced to cultivation, this is one of the class acts of the shrub world and a great garden all-rounder with its bold deciduous willow-like leaves and its striking racemes

Mark Flanagan and Tony Kirkham in the mountains of Taiwan in 1992 where seed of their *Deutzia pulchra* was collected.

.....

of white, bell-shaped flowers draping the arching branches in June and July. As a bonus its pale bark exfoliates to reveal a rich cinnamon-coloured interior, particularly eye-catching in winter.

In 1983 I received from the Shanghai Botanic Garden a small packet of seeds labelled *Sinocalycanthus chinensis*, a shrub and a genus from east China quite new to me. Having germinated it I planted one seedling in my rear garden and the rest I gave away. In June 1989 my plant, now 6 x 6ft (1.8 x 1.8m), produced its first flowers, which reminded me of those of a small, white-petalled magnolia with an inner ring of smaller yellow petals beautifully set off by the large, glossy green deciduous foliage which turns yellow before falling in autumn. In the 1990s a hybrid between this species and a species of the related American genus *Calycanthus* (*C. floridus*) was raised under the name *Sinocalycalycanthus* × *raulstonii* 'Hartlage Wine'. Mercifully, for gardeners at least, it was subsequently decided to merge the Chinese species with the genus *Calycanthus*, a triumph for the 'lumpers' over the 'splitters', so my plant became *Calycanthus chinensis* and the hybrid, *Calycanthus* × *raulstonii* 'Hartlage Wine'. I now have the latter growing close by the former and the freely produced maroon to wine-red flowers with creamy-white tipped inner petals are a joy to behold in early summer. One more thing: the so called 'petals' in this genus are regarded by purists as 'tepals' (as they are in *Magnolia*) but I am not a purist.

The beautiful flowers of *Calycanthus chinensis* from east China. My plant first flowered in June 1989 and was awarded a First Class Certificate by the RHS in 1996.

I have never considered myself as being an avid collector to the extent that I will try to obtain every species, variety and cultivar of a particular genus to grow in my garden. Unlike Galanthophiles (snowdrop collectors), some of whom go to what seem like extraordinary lengths in adding to their collection of a single genus, I have never felt that urge. I can quite understand their particular passion but I neither could nor would go to the financial extremes that some collectors do. I have a modest collection of snowdrops as the genus is one of my favourite

.....

flowers, but that's as far as it goes. Nevertheless, it is curious how, without consciously meaning to, I have found myself gradually assembling collections partly by means of gifts from gardening friends. I never set out to collect Asiatic shrubby hypericums nor mahonias and yet I now find myself with a reasonable collection of both, though neither comes close to being a passion. My collection of *Hypericum* species stems from my association with Dr Norman Robson, a world if not the world authority on the genus, who encouraged me to collect seed and herbarium specimens for him on my visits to the Himalaya and China. As a result I ended up growing a selection of shrubby species, some new to cultivation if not to science, in my garden. He was kind enough to name a species from Yunnan in 1980 as *H. lancasteri*. It is a relatively small mounded shrub with conspicuous red-tinted, spreading sepals beneath typical golden yellow petals.

When it comes to *Mahonia*, I am currently growing 39, a paltry number compared to those I could plant had I the space, the funds and the desire to do so. The majority of these, the species at least, have been given to me, most of them by Mikinori Ogisu from his own collections, including the Chinese *M. shenii*, *M. leptodonta*, *M. subimbricata* and *M. ogisui*. One of several Mexican species I treasure is *M. russellii*, named for the late Jim Russell who had collected its berries in the pocket of his khaki shorts where they lodged, forgotten, until a spell in his sister's washing machine revealed a tell-tale purple stain. The seed was sown, it germinated and seedlings were distributed to other sources including the Royal Botanic Gardens, Kew, where it eventually flowered and was adjudged to be a previously undescribed species. It has reached 10ft (3m) below our north-facing wall and is the only species I am aware of which regularly produces its large, lax, panicles of pink-tinted creamy-white flowers twice a year, in spring or early summer and again in autumn.

Two other species, *Mahonia eurybracteata* and *M. gracilipes*, both autumn flowering, are my own introductions from the forests of Emei Shan in 1980. I entrusted these on my return to the late John Bond, then keeper of the Savill and Valley Gardens in Windsor Great Park. Both flourished and are now not uncommon in the gardens of enthusiasts, as are the increasing hybrids between the two, known as *M. × savilliana*.

.....

Her Majesty The Queen, invited by John Bond to examine the leaves of *Mahonia gracilipes* when officially opening the new Queen Elizabeth Temperate House at the Savill Garden in 1995.

M. gracilipes is unusual if not unique in its combination of a low suckering habit, drooping airy sprays of tiny red and white flowers and the chalk white undersurface to the large blue-green leaflets. It was the latter characteristic which John drew to the attention of Her Majesty the Queen when, in 1995, she officially opened the newly completed Queen Elizabeth Temperate House in the Savill Garden. A plant grown from a cutting of the original has formed a low, suckering colony in a shady corner of our rear garden.

By far the most spectacular species I grow, in flower and foliage, is *M. huiliensis*, another autumn-flowering Ogisu introduction from China's Sichuan province. This is a strong-growing shrub to 10ft (3m) or so with bold terminal clusters of long, spike-like racemes of yellow flowers above a handsome assemblage of sharply toothed, much-divided leaves. I also treasure a beautiful form of *M. nitens* from the Arboretum Kalmthout in Belgium in which the neatly pinnate and spine-toothed, polished green leaves in winter develop a blood-red stain at the base of the leaflets which largely fades as temperatures rise.

One of my favourite foliage shrubs, particularly for its reliable autumn colour, is *Lindera obtusiloba*. It is native to the Far East and I have seen it in China and Japan; here a multi-stemmed specimen flourishing in the acidic soil in my front garden never fails to perform come late September or October, when the large, often three-lobed leaves gradually turn from green to yellow with orange or purple tints. The small clusters of mustard-yellow flowers in late winter I find more interesting than eye-catching.

Sharing the joy

For winter interest I grow *Daphne bholua* in several selections, including 'Darjeeling', which begins flowering in autumn, 'Peter Smithers' and 'Jacqueline Postill'. For many years, a large specimen of the last named

.....

grew in a border close to our front door and when in flower and scenting the air around it was a regular source of conversation. Early one morning I was woken by a knocking on our front door which on opening revealed our milkman standing in the dark, milk bottles in hand, asking me if I could 'spare me a slip from this shrub'. Anxious to return to my warm bed I fetched my secateurs and a polythene bag and a few minutes later, clutching his booty, he headed for the gate, whistling cheerfully as he went.

We have had several garden-loving postmen over the years whom I have supplied with seedlings, offsets and cuttings and so too Dot, our neighbour to whom I have passed spare plants through a hole in the hedge. Many shrubs and trees grown from seed are scattered across our neighbourhood in a local school ground, a churchyard and sundry private gardens. One of these, the rare *Docynia delavayi*, a relative of the quince (*Cydonia oblonga*) collected as seed in Yunnan, China

Mahonia huiliensis, a spectacular autumn-flowering Chinese species introduced by Mikinori Ogisu in 1996, here seen in September 2014.

by Chris Brickell and Alan Leslie in 1999, I planted in the churchyard, where it produced a large crop of fruits one year which I carried around in my car to share with gardening friends. Two of my favourite trees, the Chinese dove tree (*Davidia involucrata*) and the Carolina snowbell (*Halesia carolina*), I gave as saplings in 1984 to Dot, suggesting that she plant them where I and passersby might see and admire them as they matured. She planted both by her hedge flanking the road. They are now around 25ft (8m) tall with well-shaped crowns and flower prodigiously in spring. The dove tree I grew from seed gathered from a tree, a Wilson introduction in Hillier's West Hill Nursery in 1980. It took all of 20 years before its first flowering, when we joined Dot beneath the tree to drink its good health with a glass of champagne. Now it flowers regularly and freely and I can see its pendant white handkerchief-like flowers from where I sit writing in my study. I had not the space to accommodate the ultimate size of this tree but I have since planted a selection of it in the lawn in our rear garden. Known as 'Sonoma' and raised in California, it

.....

Davidia involucrata 'Sonoma' flowering in June 2013. Nurserymen John Hillier (right) and Peter Catt share my pleasure.

was presented to me by my good friend Robert Vernon, an ex-student at the Hillier Nurseries. For 20 years I had been visiting Robert's excellent Bluebell Nursery near Ashby-de-la-Zouch in Leicestershire to give an annual lecture in the village hall at Blackfordby and latterly to lead tours of his then new arboretum at nearby Smisby. The *Davidia* was a gift of thanks and was a mere 4ft (1.2m) yet sporting 11 flowers when planted in June 2004. Twelve years later, in May 2016, it measured just 7½ft (2.3m) tall and survived a late frost to produce 100 flowers with bracts a third to half as long again as those of the typical tree.

First of many trees
The first tree I planted here, at the end of the rear garden in 1983, was *Cornus* 'Porlock' which at 30ft (9m) still produces a spectacular display of creamy-white flowers in June maturing to a deep pink in July, followed in autumn by a heavy crop of pendulous, stalked strawberry-red fruits. Despite the many fine flowering dogwoods available today, this and its sister seedling 'Norman Hadden' remain two of the best. Norman Hadden, the man in whose garden these two arose – Underway in the Somerset village of West Porlock – must have been thrilled on their first flowering. I visited his garden with my friend Michael Hickson many years ago and enjoyed a tour given by the man himself, whose love of plants as well as birds, butterflies and Shetland sheepdogs was a joy.

.....

From 1984 I began planting a wide variety of trees, many of which are still flourishing, though a magnificent snow gum (*Eucalyptus pauciflora* subsp. *debeuzevillei*) which had reached approximately 50ft (15m) had to be felled in 2014 as a result of an attack by honey fungus. In the rear garden too is an *Acer cappadocicum* var. *sinicum* of similar size, whose young leaves in spring are a fine coppery red. This was grown from seed I collected close to Sichuan's border with Tibet in September 1981. Nearby is a specimen of *Magnolia* 'Heaven Scent', whose pink-flushed white blooms provide an impressive and reliable display from late April through May, normally escaping the frosts which can destroy those of earlier bloomers.

By far the most spectacular flowering tree in the rear garden, dominating it when in flower, is *Magnolia cylindrica*. The erect white blooms, stained purple at base, flood the naked branches in April before eventually falling to create a sumptuous white carpet on the ground beneath. They are replaced in late summer or early autumn by conspicuous cylindrical, lumpy, rosy-pink fruiting spikes whose orange-red seeds emerge through apertures to dangle individually on a slender thread. This tree, planted in 1984, was grown from seed of wild origin growing in Zhejiang province in east China, sent to me by the Shanghai Botanic garden. According to TROBI, mine, along with my 'Heaven Scent', are the current Champions in size, now in excess of 30ft (9m).

I grow several maples, including the Chinese paper-bark maple (*Acer griseum*) and *Acer triflorum*, the latter grown from seed collected in South Korea by my American friend and ex-Hillier student Paul Meyer and his colleagues in 1984. Early in spring this tree breaks its downy, thrice-divided leaves accompanied by small, demure, yellow-green flowers in clusters of three. Its autumn tints can vary from an old gold in a normal year to a brilliant red and gold in an exceptional one. It was another American friend, Tim Brotzman from Madison, Ohio, who in 1994 gave me the snake-bark maple which dominates the front garden. *Acer* 'White Tigress' is said to be a hybrid between *A. tegmentosum* from north-east Asia and an unnamed Japanese species, but to my eye it belongs to the former species which, ten years earlier in 1984, I had seen in the forests of the Changbaishan National Nature Reserve on the

.....

Sino-Korean border. No matter its true origin, this is one of the best of the so-called snake-bark maples with its thin green bark striated white, less dramatically on older stems. It is an excellent ornamental tree with a vase-shaped crown especially attractive in winter, while the big, bold, five-lobed leaves turn a bright yellow often with orange tints in early autumn. My tree is currently around 20ft (6m) tall.

Another tree producing excellent and reliable autumn tints, also in the front garden, is *Parrotia subaequalis*, a rare Chinese species which since it was planted in 2001 has now (2016) achieved a height of 12ft (3.6m) with an ascending crown of slender branches. It looks to become a smaller, less robust tree than its better-known cousin *P. persica* with smaller leaves which slowly develop a brilliant range of purple, red and crimson tints before falling.

Acer 'White Tigress', an excellent snake-bark maple with butter-yellow autumn foliage.

From a 1991 seed introduction made in Leibo County in south Sichuan by Mikinori Ogisu I am the proud owner of a *Carpinus fangiana*, named for its discoverer the Chinese Professor Fang Wen-Pei. I admit to being a fan of these oft-neglected hornbeams. I have also grown *C. pubescens* from my own introduction, *C. viminea* and *C. rankanensis* but *C. fangiana* is by far the most exciting in its long, beautifully veined leaves and its long, drooping, tail-like, green fruiting catkins, which like the leaves, are the largest in the genus. To see the rounded, richly leafy crown of my specimen, now 18ft (5.5m) high, draped summer-long with catkins like the exposed tails of hidden green monkeys thrills even the most knowledgeable of visitors when seen for the first time. In June 1993, while exploring with Ogisu the primitive mountain forests of Leibo County, I saw veteran trees of Fang's hornbeam up to 60ft (18m), plus one with a girth of 7ft 4in (2.23m) at 5ft (1.5m). Companion trees included *Davidia involucrata*, *Cercidiphyllum japonicum*, *Tetracentron sinense*, *Fagus longipetiolata* and *Castanopsis platyacantha* with an understorey of *Rehderodendron macrocarpum*, *Acer oliverianum* and

.....

vast thickets of the Qiongzhu cane (*Chimonobambusa tumidissinoda*) with its characteristic swollen plate-like nodes.

Keeping my hornbeam company in the rear garden are *Nothaphoebe cavaleriei* and *Carrierea calycina*, both of Chinese origin. The former, an evergreen tree of the bay family Lauraceae, is exceptionally fast-growing – mine is a TROBI Champion now in excess of 30ft (9m). The insignificant greenish flowers are compensated for by the large, handsome, aromatic leaves which are a lustrous deep green above and glaucous beneath. I love to point them out at night with a flashlight for those visitors interested enough to join me. This tree was planted in 1996 as a small seedling, a gift from J.C. Raulston at the University of North Carolina Arboretum (now the J.C. Raulston Arboretum), whose own specimen subsequently perished in its first winter outside. Surprisingly, it has proved remarkably hardy here with no frost damage despite a temperature of 14°F (−10°C) on several occasions, though it suffered minor damage one winter when the weight of snow caused a few broken branches. It is a continuing reminder of a remarkable and generous friend.

Carpinus fangiana, a large-leaved Chinese hornbeam with extraordinary long fruiting catkins like the tails of green monkeys.

Carrierea calycina, known in the wild as the goat-horn tree (yang-jiao-shu in Mandarin) for its spindle-shaped seed capsules, was first introduced to Western cultivation from west Sichuan by E.H. Wilson in 1908. It remained a rare tree and by the close of the century had been reduced to just two examples, the best of which, planted at Birr Castle in 1916, had achieved 50ft (15m) in 2015. In 1994, it was reintroduced as seed from China's Guizhou Province by British-born Peter Wharton, curator of the David C. Lam Asian Garden, which he had a major role in developing at the University of British Columbia Botanic Garden in Vancouver. He lost no time in distributing the seed to botanical institutions around the temperate world and to individuals, one of whom was me. It was just one of many seed lots of woody plants he sent me with instructions to 'spread

.....

it around'. The tree in my garden was from this batch and it began flowering for the first time on Sunday 30 June 2004. The curious cup-shaped flowers of a pale greenish-cream are borne in terminal candelabra-like panicles. Equally ornamental are the slightly pendulous, shining, dark green, glossy leaves which possess a distinctive drip-tip and a long reddish petiole. My tree has also produced the characteristic seed capsules. That this species is now firmly established in many gardens in Britain and North America is a just tribute to the diligence and determination of this experienced and knowledgeable plant explorer and conservationist who tragically died before his time in June 2008, aged just 54.

Exotics

When it comes to a touch of the exotic I have planted a good selection of smaller trees over the years which contribute interesting foliage and in some cases attractive flowers as well. Two such are *Hoheria sexstylosa* 'Stardust', a dense columnar evergreen, broadening in maturity with narrow, glossy leaves which are joined in summer by masses of small white flowers. It is fast-growing and free-seeding in sunny sheltered sites. In recent years I have also had great success with several of the *Schefflera* species with their long-stalked, evergreen leaves divided into long, finger-like leaflets. *S. taiwaniana*, a Bleddyn and Sue Wynn-Jones introduction from Taiwan (though it was first introduced by the late Joseph Needham to his garden Tregye in Cornwall) is proving the most satisfactory and I love its sheaves of emerging new leaves each spring which rise like a silvery, downy fountain from the summits of the stems. Another Wynn-Jones introduction from Taiwan is *Fatsia polycarpa*, like *Schefflera* a member of the ivy family, Araliaceae. This is more of a large shrub, at least initially, with large, long-stalked, deeply lobed, matt-green leaves in sharp contrast to the more commonly grown glossy-leaved *F. japonica*.

Ever since my first experiences with tropical plants in Malaysia, in particular the Singapore Botanic Gardens, I have been an admirer of palms. The Botanic Gardens even have a Palm Valley planted with the most exciting examples of these exotics I have ever seen. Naturally, I longed to grow palms in a garden of my own and though the choice for

.....

British gardens is limited due to our climate, I have succeeded with two. One of these, a fan palm (*Trachycarpus wagnerianus*), planted from a pot in 1996, now has a shaggy brown fibre-swaddled stem to 10ft (3m) with a bold crown of long-stalked, rounded leaves up to 2ft (61cm) across which are divided to the base into numerous rigid, leathery, finger-like lobes. In May, from the summit of the stem appear decurved, branched heads densely packed with tiny male yellow flowers with abundant pollen. This is a slower-growing and ultimately smaller version of the more commonly planted Chusan palm (*T. fortunei*). This, together with its smaller firmer leaves, makes it more suitable for exposed sites and smaller gardens.

Trachycarpus wagnerianus, the perfect hardy palm for the smaller garden, with bold leaves and conspicuous male flower heads in May.

Living around the corner from us when we moved into Chandler's Ford lived an elderly lady by the name of Mrs Amy Doncaster, whom I had first met in the 1960s on her occasional visits to the Hillier Arboretum. She had a good eye for a plant and her garden of 1 acre (0.4 hectare) was filled with a lifetime's gatherings, from rhododendrons and camellias to miniature daffodils, day lilies and epimediums. In places, erythroniums carpeted the ground in shade and then there were her snowdrops, on which she was an authority.

It was while viewing the snowdrops one day that I asked her if she had a favourite. She immediately pointed out a robust clump with her stick, saying "S. Arnott' is one.' 'Oh yes,' I replied, 'I have heard of 'Sam Arnott". At this she began stabbing the ground (and my foot) with her stick, at the same time shouting, 'No, no, no.' I had obviously upset her. 'Did you know him?' she asked. 'No,' I replied fearfully. 'Well, l can tell you that S. Arnott was a respected Victorian Scottish Provost. I cannot imagine he would have allowed even his own family to be so

.....

Mrs Amy Doncaster, a well-known local gardener who had a special interest in snowdrops, rhododendrons, epimediums and woodland perennials.

familiar.' I gulped and was duly chastened but she hadn't finished. 'I would be grateful if you would tell your colleagues of the press at the RHS Shows that the name is 'S. Arnott'.' I promised to do so and ever after, I recall this ticking-off when I discuss this plant. Fortunately, my blunder did not prevent her from having her helper Doris dig me up a clump for my own garden where it flourishes today, scenting the February air around.

I responded to Mrs Doncaster's kindness with plants of my own, one of which was a seedling I had introduced of *Epimedium acuminatum* from Emei Shan in Sichuan, China, from my visit there in 1980. She was delighted – after all, she had once been addressed in Latin by no less an authority than Professor William Stearn: '*Ave! Epimedorum Regina carissima*' ('Hail! Most dear Queen of Epimedium'). On 11 April 1994 I attended her hundredth birthday party in a nearby nursing home, when I presented her with a plant of *Epimedium stellulatum* 'Wudang Star', another of my own collections from the Wudang Shan in China's Hubei province. In December the following year she passed away.

I grow several of the newer Chinese introductions of *Epimedium*, most from Mikinori Ogisu collections, though none romp like the plant of *E. pinnatum* subsp. *colchicum* that I introduced from woodland in Abkhazia. I have a number of hardy cranesbills, too, including the pink-flowered woodlander *Geranium gracile* which with *G. ibericum* and *G. psilostemon* I collected in north-east Turkey in 1997. I was accompanied on the trip by that excellent gardener the late Bill Baker, a dentist by profession whose garden at the Old Rectory Cottage in Tidmarsh, Berkshire, was an Aladdin's cave of both woody and herbaceous plants, including bulbs. Bill was the perfect gentleman, softly spoken, considerate, hugely knowledgeable on plants and generous in sharing them. When inviting me to his garden he always urged me to bring a

.....

FAR LEFT Bill Baker, a modest yet hugely knowledgeable and generous amateur gardener and plantsman who gave me numerous plants for my garden.

LEFT Richard Duke and his late wife Pam with *Cornus controversa* 'Variegata'. He is a green-fingered, kind-hearted gardener who keeps an eye on our garden when we are away from home.

friend and a car with an empty boot. Examples of his generosity are everywhere in my garden and also in that of my friend Richard Duke, who until his retirement was our local butcher. He is a successful and avid grower of a wide variety of plants which he propagates and shares among his friends, even giving away his last one if it causes pleasure. It is Richard I rely on to keep an eye on my garden when Sue and I are away. So keen a gardener is he that for several years he propagated plants to sell in his butcher's shop and he always sold out. On one occasion a regular customer asked him for a pound of pork sausages, a leg of lamb, two *Corydalis flexuosa* and five *Eucomis zambesiaca*. If a plant was in short supply it was requested before the sausages.

Among the many hardy ferns I have grown, *Polystichum munitum*, the Western sword fern, is a particular favourite. Its big bold clumps of laddered fronds can be seen as an understorey in the coniferous and broad-leaved forests of north-west America from Alaska south to California and in places beyond. I have several clumps in my garden and I would not be without them, especially at Christmas when the wintergreen fronds provide a brilliant competitive game for children and adults alike, just as they once did, apparently, in Native American communities. It is a test of lung capacity and entails competitors taking

.....

The perfect guest! Our friend John Massey arriving with a gift of yellow-flowered hellebores and a bottle of wine to celebrate our first grandchildren.

Cordyline indivisa, the mountain cabbage tree of New Zealand, makes a bold statement in our rear garden.

one deep breath before counting out loud, the numerous segments of a single frond, beginning at the base. Whoever gets nearest to the frond tip before running out of breath is the winner.

I grow as many perennials in my garden as space and tree roots will allow: sun-loving perennials such as eryngiums, euphorbias, pulsatillas, tulip species, *Triteleia laxa* and many other bulbs in the front garden and on the patio; roscoeas, arisaemas, anemones, hellebores and a host of other woodlanders in the rear garden. A recent beautiful hellebore selection with primrose-yellow flowers arrived one wintry day in a box with a bottle of wine in the arms of our friend John Massey of Ashwood Nurseries, the perfect guest. Among other welcome gifts, many from Mikinori Ogisu, are the hardy *Lysimachia paridiformis* var. *stenophylla*, *Paeonia decomposita* and a number of less hardy but curious *Aspidistra* species including white-flowered *A. dolichanthera*, yellow-flowered *A. longipedunculata* and amusingly named *A. fungilliformis*. I grow them in pots and while none compare in vigour with that Victorian parlour favourite *A. elatior*, their unusual flowers would undoubtedly have left Gracie Fields, singer of 'The Biggest Aspidistra in the World', quite speechless.

. . . . .

296

Bringing plants home

A bold clump of the summer-flowering *Gladiolus cardinalis* with its white-blotched, glowing scarlet flowers was a gift, one of many, from the ever-generous Gary Dunlop who gardens on a hilltop above Belfast. Given its habitat by waterfalls in South Africa, I am amazed that it does so well with me but then *Fascicularia bicolor* and *Ochagavia carnea*, both members of the pineapple family Bromeliaceae, have made huge clumps on the top of a dry stone wall in our rear garden, a far cry from their native habitat as epiphytes in trees and on cliffs in Chile. Equally impressive to visitors is a strong-growing specimen of the mountain cabbage tree (*Cordyline indivisa*), whose massive head of glaucous green, strap-shaped, evergreen leaves sits atop a 6ft (1.8m) stem. I have fond memories of seeing this species in the wild in the North Island of New Zealand where a scattered population, some of them large individuals with branched crowns, grew in a ravine in the shadow of Mount Ruapehu (9176ft/2797m), an active volcano in the Tongariro National Park, the fictional Mount Doom and Mordor in the film adaptation of Tolkien's *Lord of the Rings*.

Veronica umbrosa 'Georgia Blue', meanwhile, whose carpeting, evergreen growth makes an effective ground cover beneath shrubs or on a wall top, reminds me of a snow-covered forest margin in the Western Caucasus where I found it covering large areas. A single rooted fragment was enough to establish it in my garden. Its purple-tinted leaves and white-eyed blue flowers in spring are a welcome sight following a dreary winter. This seems to me an appropriate place to bring this particular garden tour to a close, though I have by no means mentioned all.

Our garden today is totally unlike that which first greeted us in 1982. It has played many roles and served many purposes over the years. A playground and an adventure park for our children when young; a trial ground for new plants; a place to sit and dream; a place to be alone or with family and friends. It has been, too, a space to share with wildlife: hedgehogs and field mice; moths and butterflies, especially holly blues; birds (40 species to date); bumble, mining, mason and leaf-cutter bees; hoverflies; dragonflies from our neighbour Dot's pond; frogs and toads; slugs, snails, the occasional slow-worm and countless

.....

The front of our house in July 2016 with its ferns, mahonias and, foreground, *Acer* 'White Tigress'

A view from the rear garden in July 2016 with *Magnolia cylindrica* (right) well-stocked borders and a wealth of climbers and shrubs on the south wall of the house.

bugs and beetles including the stag's-horn beetles breeding in the decaying stumps in the hedges. Finally and most importantly, our garden has been a place to share with those of a like mind, in particular botanists, gardeners and horticultural students from home and abroad.

For the past 20 years or so, Sue and I have been regularly hosting student groups from horticultural colleges and other places of learning, most especially those from the RHS Garden Wisley and the Royal Botanic Gardens, Kew. On one of these occasions, in July 1998, we entertained a group of 24 Wisley students representing several countries worldwide including, for the first time, a student from Bhutan and one from Sikkim. We usually rendezvous at the Sir Harold Hillier Gardens in the morning for a tour which can last anything from two to three hours before heading for my home, where Sue has prepared a good old-fashioned English afternoon tea of sponge cakes, flapjacks, chocolate

.....

Where are they now? A group of Wisley students visiting our garden in July 1998, among whom several countries were represented including Bhutan and Sikkim.

brownies and strawberry scones which, weather permitting, we eat outside in the garden. First, however, is another tour, or rather a general wandering about which enables me to pin-point plants of special interest and tell yet more stories. Questions are asked, opinions voiced and personal experiences shared as we enjoy being among plants. We end the day, on dry days certainly, sitting in the sun listening to the students as they discuss their future plans and their dreams.

Sue says this keeps me young. It certainly keeps my mind active and ultimately, takes me via fond memories back to the days when I too was a student, when everything was new and exciting which is where this story began.

Appendices

Select Bibliography

Bean, W. J. (edited by Desmond Clarke and Sir George Taylor) *Trees and Shrubs Hardy in the British Isles*. Volumes I, II, III and IV (8th edition). London: John Murray, 1970-1980 with a supplement (Volume V) by Desmond Clarke published London: John Murray, 1988

Clancey, Philip Alexander. *A Preliminary List of the Birds of Natal and Zululand*, Durban: Durban Museum, 1953

Clement, E. J., M. C. Foster and D. H. Kent. *Alien Plants of the British Isles: A Provisional Catalogue of Vascular Plants (excluding Grasses)*. Botanical Society of the British Isles, 1994

Dandy, J. E. *List of British Vascular Plants*. London: British Museum, 1958

Gibbons, Euell. *Stalking the Wild Asparagus*. Putney, Vermont: A. C. Hood, 1962

Greenless T. and T. K. Holden. *Flora of Bolton*, (Lancashire and Cheshire Naturalist, 1920-1)

Hillier, John G. and Roy Lancaster (Consultant Editors), James Armitage, Dawn Edwards, Neil Lancaster (RHS Editors) and Richard Sanford (Compiler). *The Hillier Manual of Trees and Shrubs*. London: Royal Horticultural Society, 2014

Hubbard, C. E. *Grasses*, London: Penguin Books, 1968

Johns, Reverend. *Flowers of the Field*, London: Routledge & Kegan Paul, 1949

Johnson, A. T. and H. A. Smith. *Plant Names Simplified*. London: W.H. & L. Collingridge, 1958

Krüssmann, Gerd (edited by Hans-Dieter Warda, translated by Michael E. Epp, technical editor Gilbert S. Daniels). *Manual of Cultivated Broad-leaved Trees & Shrubs*). Portland, OR: Timber Press, 1984

Krüssmann, Gerd (edited by Hans-Dieter Warda, translated by Michael E. Epp, technical editor Gilbert S. Daniels). *Manual of Cultivated Conifers*). Portland, OR: Timber Press, 1985

Lancaster, Roy. *Plant Hunting in Nepal*. London: Croom Helm, 1981; revised edition published as *A Plantsman in Nepal*, Woodbridge: Antique Collector's Club, 1985

Lancaster, Roy. *A Plantsman's Paradise Travels in China*, Woodbridge: Antique Collector's Club 1989. Second edition published under Garden Art Press for Antique Collector's Club, Woodbridge, 2008.

Lawrence, D. H. *Lady Chatterley's Lover*. London: Heinemann, 1956

Lousley, J. E. *Wild Flowers of Chalk & Limestone*. The New Naturalist. London: Collins, 1950

Maund, Benjamin. *The Botanic Garden*, London 1826-1832

McAllister, H. A. *The Genus Sorbus*. Botanical Magazine Monograph. London: Kew Publishing, 2005

.....

Recommended Reading

Royal Horticultural Society, Anthony Huxley (editor), Mark Griffiths (editor), Margot Levy (editor) *The New Dictionary of Gardening* (4 volumes), London: Macmillan, 1999

Stearn, William T. *Botanical Latin*. London: Thomas Nelson & Sons, 1966

Stearn, William T. *Stearn's Dictionary of Plant Names for Gardeners*, Portland, OR: Timber Press, 2002

Stokoe, W. J. *The Observer's Book of Wild Flowers*, London: Frederick Warne, 1951

Brewis, Lady Anne, Paul Bowman, Francis Rose and Richard Mabey *The Flora of Hampshire*, Harley Books in association with The Hampshire and IOW Wildlife Trust, 1996

Tolkien, J. R. *Lord of the Rings*, London: George Allen & Unwin, 1968

Warner, F. I. *List of Flowering Plants and Ferns*. Winchester: Warren & Son, 1872

Wilson, E. H. (edited by Charles Sprague Sargent) *Plantae Wilsonianae*. Cambridge: The University press, 1913-17

Yeo, Peter. *Hardy Geraniums*. London: Croom Helm 1985

Cox, Peter and Peter Hutchinson. *Seeds of Adventure*. Woodbridge: Garden Art Press, 2008

Flanagan, Mark and Tony Kirkham. *Plants from the Edge of the World*. Portland, OR: Timber Press, 2005

Flanagan, Mark and Tony Kirkham. *Wilson's China – A Century On*. London: Kew Publishing, 2009

Gardner, Christopher and Basak. *Flora of the Silk Road – The Complete Illustrated Guide*. London: I.B. Tauris, 2014

Grimshaw, John and Ross Bayton. *New Trees*. London: Kew Publishing, 2009

Hillier, Jean. *Hillier: The Plants, The People, The Passion*. Hillier Nurseries, 2014

Hinkley, Dan. *The Explorer's Garden: Rare and Unusual Perennials*. Portland, OR: Timber Press, 1999

Hinkley, Dan. *The Explorer's Garden: Shrubs and Vines*. Portland, OR: Timber Press, 2009

Hudson, Frederick W. *Loyal to the End*. Blackburn: Cremer Press, 2006

Macfarlane, Robert. *The Wild Places*. London: Granta Books, 2008

O'Brien, Seamus. *In the Footsteps of Augustine Henry*. Woodbridge: Garden Art Press, 2011

Smith, M.D. *Leverhulme's Rivington*. Adlington: Wyre Publishing,1984

Tudge, Colin. *The Secret Life of Trees – How they Live and Why they Matter*. London: Allen Lane, 2005

.....

Index

Page numbers in *italic* type
refer to pictures.

.....

· · · · ·

Roy in his front garden October 2016
standing by *Lindera obtusiloba* with the fiery
red of *Parrotia subaequalis* beyond.

.....

About the Author

Born in Bolton, Lancashire in 1937, Roy Lancaster's earliest recollection of garden plants were the dahlias, chrysanthemums and roses grown by his father in his childhood garden. His own interest in plants began by chance in his mid-teens: he was a keen birdwatcher and then developed an eye for native flora, which soon became a passion.

Roy began his gardening career close to home with Bolton Parks Department aged 15. Then a two-year stint as a national serviceman with HM Forces in Malaya enriched his experience of tropical plants and this, along with a 3-month plant collecting expedition to Nepal in 1971, strengthened his love for the world's high places and their plants.

Two years as a gardening student at the Cambridge Botanic Garden, followed by 18 years with the Hillier Nurseries in Hampshire, gave him the perfect platform from which to launch a successful freelance career which included memorable broadcasts on TV and radio, award-winning journalism, two classic books on plant-hunting and consultancy work at home and abroad.

Roy Lancaster has received numerous awards for his contribution to horticulture including the Veitch Memorial Medal in 1972 and the prestigious Victoria Medal of Honour in 1989. These were followed by an OBE for services to horticulture in 1999 and a CBE in 2014. He was made an Honorary Doctor of Science by the University of Bolton in 2010 and by the University of Winchester in 2016. He holds many positions of authority in the plant world including President of the Maple Society, President of the Hardy Plant Society and Vice President of the Royal Horticultural Society.

His fathomless plant knowledge, popular plant introductions and continuing curiosity about the natural world make him an inspiring figure for gardeners and young horticulturists.

.....

Picture acknowledgements

This is an appropriate place to put on record my thanks to Jennifer Harmer, archivist of the Hardy Plant Society, who with great patience over a period of weeks gave time to scanning many colour slides for use in this book. I would also like to thank the following organizations and individuals for use of their photographs:

BBC Radio 4/Trevor Taylor 228
Bolton Libraries and Museum Service 22, 25
Cambridge University Botanic Garden 113 (left), 127
Clifford Heyes 41, 109, 123 (left)
Crown Estate Commissioners 286
Guido Braem/Mr Helman 82 (top)
Harry van de Laar 243
Hillier Nurseries/Hatton Gardener 126
John Massey 267, 272
Ken Moore, 251
Kevin Hobbs, photo of RL on back cover
Mary Comber-Miles 165
Matthew Soper 71 (top), 82 (bottom), 87,
Michael Warren 185, 186, 201 (top)
Mrs Marion Greenhalgh 27 (left)
Peter O'Byrne 76
Phillip Cribb 83 (right)
President and Members of Harvard University. Arnold Arboretum Archives 33, 245 (right)
Rev. C.E. Shaw 34 (left)
RHS/Neil Hepworth 2, 290, 296 (right)
RHS/Tim Sandall 237
Sue Lancaster 229, 288, 310
The Loyal Regiment (North Lancashire) 79
Tony Kirkham 283 (bottom)

Every effort has been made to credit copyright holders. The author and publisher would be glad to amend in future editions any errors or omissions brought to their attention.

.....